Cooking for Kids

:·Contents·:

Breakfast

Butterfly Pancakes

~Taste of Home Test Kitchen

1 cup all-purpose flour

1 teaspoon sugar

3/4 teaspoon baking powder

1/2 teaspoon salt

1 egg

1 cup buttermilk

1 tablespoon butter, melted

Assorted fresh fruit

1. In a bowl, combine the flour, sugar, baking powder and salt. In another bowl, beat the egg, buttermilk and butter. Stir into the dry ingredients just until moistened.

2. To form each butterfly wing, pour 2 tablespoonfuls of batter onto a lightly greased hot griddle. Pour 1 tablespoon of batter below and touching the larger one. Turn when bubbles form on top of pancakes; cook until second side is golden brown.

3. To assemble, place two wings on a serving plate, forming a butterfly. Top with fruit. **Yield:** 5 butterfly pancakes.

Cinnamon Syrup

~Janice Nightingale, Cedar Rapids, Iowa

1/2 cup butter

1/4 cup maple pancake syrup

3/4 to 1 teaspoon ground cinnamon

In a saucepan over low heat, heat butter, syrup and cinnamon until butter is melted. Stir until smooth. Serve warm over pancakes, French toast or waffles. **Yield:** about 3/4 cup.

Breakfast Pizza

~Rae Truax, Mattawa, Washington

1 tube (8 ounces) refrigerated crescent rolls

1 pound bulk pork sausage

1 cup frozen shredded hash brown potatoes, thawed

1 cup (4 ounces) shredded cheddar cheese

3 eggs

1/4 cup milk

1/4 teaspoon pepper

1/4 cup grated Parmesan cheese

1. Unroll crescent dough and place on a greased 12-in. pizza pan; press seams together and press up sides of pan to form a crust.

2. In a skillet, brown sausage over medium heat; drain and cool slightly. Sprinkle sausage, hash browns and cheddar cheese over crust.

3. In a bowl, beat eggs, milk and pepper; pour over pizza. Sprinkle with Parmesan cheese. Bake at 375° for 28-30 minutes or until golden brown. Let stand for 10 minutes before cutting. **Yield:** 6-8 servings.

Cherry Berry Smoothies

~Shonna Thibodeau, Fort Huachuca, Arizona

1 cup cherry juice

1 carton (8 ounces) vanilla yogurt

1 cup frozen unsweetened raspberries

1/2 cup seedless red grapes

3 to 4 teaspoons sugar

In a blender, combine all ingredients. Cover and process until well blended. Pour into glasses; serve immediately. **Yield:** 3 servings.

Ham 'n' Cheese Brunch Strips

~Taste of Home Test Kitchen

2 tablespoons Dijon mustard
8 slices white bread, crusts removed
8 slices Swiss cheese
4 thin slices deli ham
2 tablespoons butter, softened

1. Spread mustard over four slices of bread. Top each with a slice of cheese, ham and another cheese slice. Top with remaining bread. Butter the outside of the sandwiches.

2. Cook on a griddle or in a large skillet over medium heat until golden brown on both sides. Remove to a cutting board; cut each sandwich lengthwise into thirds. **Yield:** 4 servings.

French Toast Fingers

~Mavis Diment, Marcus, Iowa

✓ Uses less fat, sugar or salt. Includes Nutritional Analysis and Diabetic Exchanges.

2 eggs
1/4 cup milk
1/4 teaspoon salt
1/2 cup strawberry preserves
8 slices day-old white bread
Confectioners' sugar, optional

1. In a small bowl, beat eggs, milk and salt; set aside. Spread preserves on four slices of bread; top with the remaining bread. Trim crusts; cut each sandwich into three strips. Dip both sides in egg mixture.

2. Cook on a lightly greased hot griddle for 2 minutes on each side or until golden brown. Dust with confectioners' sugar if desired. **Yield:** 4 servings.

Nutritional Analysis: One serving of three strips (prepared with egg substitute, fat-free milk and sugar-free preserves and without confectioners' sugar) equals 235 calories, 500 mg sodium, 2 mg cholesterol, 42 g carbohydrate, 10 g protein, 4 g fat. **Diabetic Exchanges:** 2 starch, 1 meat, 1/2 fruit.

Berry Cream Pancakes

~Taste of Home Test Kitchen

1 cup all-purpose flour

1 teaspoon sugar

3/4 teaspoon baking powder

1/2 teaspoon salt

1 egg

1 cup buttermilk

1 tablespoon butter, melted

CREAM FILLING:

1 package (8 ounces) cream cheese, softened

3/4 cup confectioners' sugar

1/2 teaspoon vanilla extract

3 cups sliced fresh strawberries

1. In a bowl, combine the flour, sugar, baking powder and salt. In another bowl, beat the egg, buttermilk and butter. Stir into the dry ingredients just until moistened.

2. Pour batter by 1/3 cupfuls onto a greased hot griddle. Turn when bubbles form on top of pancakes; cook until second side is golden brown.

3. Meanwhile, in a small mixing bowl, beat the cream cheese, confectioners' sugar and vanilla until smooth. Spread down the center of each pancake; top with strawberries. Fold pancake over filling. **Yield:** 8-10 filled pancakes.

Bacon Cheese Strips

~Linn Morrison, Mesilla Park, New Mexico

1/3 cup mayonnaise

1 egg, beaten

1/2 teaspoon Worcestershire sauce

1/8 teaspoon ground mustard

5 to 6 drops hot pepper sauce

Dash pepper

1 cup (4 ounces) shredded cheddar cheese

8 bacon strips, cooked and crumbled

8 bread slices, crusts removed and toasted

Paprika, optional

In a bowl, combine the first seven ingredients; mix well. Stir in bacon. Spread over toast. Sprinkle with paprika if desired. Cut each slice of toast into three strips. Place on a baking sheet. Bake at 350° for 12-14 minutes or until cheese is melted. **Yield:** 2 dozen.

Pull-Apart Cinnamon Sticks

~Elvera Dallman, Franklin, Nebraska

1 tube (11 ounces) refrigerated
breadsticks

3 tablespoons butter, melted

1/3 cup sugar

1/2 teaspoon ground cinnamon

1. Unroll breadsticks and cut in half widthwise. Place butter in a shallow bowl. In another shallow bowl, combine sugar and cinnamon. Dip one side of each breadstick in butter, then in cinnamon-sugar.

2. Place sugared side up in a greased 9-in. pie plate, overlapping layers. Bake at 375° for 20-25 minutes or until golden brown. Serve warm. **Yield:** 6 servings.

Editor's Note: This recipe was tested with Pillsbury refrigerated breadsticks.

Bacon and Egg Bundles

~Edith Landinger, Longview, Texas

1 teaspoon butter

12 to 18 bacon strips

6 eggs

Fresh parsley sprigs

1. Lightly grease six muffin cups with the butter. In a large skillet, cook the bacon over medium heat until cooked but not crisp. Drain on paper towels.

2. Cut six bacon strips in half width-wise; line the bottom of each muffin cup with two bacon pieces. Line the sides of each muffin cup with one or two bacon strips. Break an egg into each cup.

3. Bake, uncovered, at 325° for 12-18 minutes or until whites are completely set and yolks begin to thicken but are not firm. Transfer to a serving plate; surround with parsley. **Yield:** 6 servings.

Honey Bear French Toast

~Priscilla Weaver, Hagerstown, Maryland

18 slices Texas toast bread *or* 1-inch-thick slices Italian bread

1/4 cup all-purpose flour

1 tablespoon sugar

1/8 teaspoon salt

1 cup milk

3 eggs, beaten

3 tablespoons butter

36 miniature chocolate chips

Warm honey

1. Using a 3-1/2-in. bear-shaped cookie cutter, cut bread into bear shapes. In a bowl, combine flour, sugar, salt, milk and eggs until smooth. Dip both sides of bread into egg mixture.

2. In a skillet, melt butter. Fry French toast for 2-3 minutes on each side or until golden brown. Transfer to serving plates; insert chocolate chips for eyes. Drizzle with honey. **Yield:** 18 slices.

Apple Syrup

~Barbara Hill, Oil Springs, Ontario

 Uses less fat, sugar or salt. Includes Nutritional Analysis and Diabetic Exchanges.

1 tablespoon cornstarch

1/4 teaspoon ground cinnamon

1/4 teaspoon ground nutmeg

1-1/4 cups unsweetened apple juice

Sugar substitute equivalent to 4 teaspoons sugar

In a small saucepan, combine the cornstarch, cinnamon, nutmeg and apple juice until smooth. Bring to a boil; cook and stir for 2 minutes or until thickened. Remove from the heat; stir in sugar substitute. **Yield:** 1-1/4 cups.

Nutritional Analysis: One serving (2 tablespoons) equals 20 calories, trace fat (trace saturated fat), 0 cholesterol, 1 mg sodium, 5 g carbohydrate, trace fiber, trace protein. **Diabetic Exchange:** Free food.

Banana Chip Muffins

~Coleen Johnson, Elbridge, New York

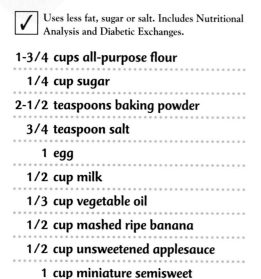

☑ Uses less fat, sugar or salt. Includes Nutritional Analysis and Diabetic Exchanges.

1-3/4 cups all-purpose flour

1/4 cup sugar

2-1/2 teaspoons baking powder

3/4 teaspoon salt

1 egg

1/2 cup milk

1/3 cup vegetable oil

1/2 cup mashed ripe banana

1/2 cup unsweetened applesauce

1 cup miniature semisweet chocolate chips

1. In a large bowl, combine the flour, sugar, baking powder and salt. Combine the egg, milk, oil, banana and applesauce; stir into dry ingredients just until moistened. Fold in the chocolate chips.

2. Fill greased muffin cups two-thirds full. Bake at 400° for 20 minutes or until a toothpick comes out clean. Cool for 5 minutes before removing from pan to a wire rack. **Yield:** 1 dozen.

Nutritional Analysis: One muffin (prepared with fat-free milk) equals 232 calories, 11 g fat (3 g saturated fat), 18 mg cholesterol, 206 mg sodium, 32 g carbohydrate, 1 g fiber, 3 g protein. **Diabetic Exchanges:** 2 fat, 1 starch, 1 fruit.

Banana Split Muffins

~Elaine Anderson, Aliquippa, Pennsylvania

1-1/2 cups all-purpose flour

1 cup sugar

1/2 cup miniature semisweet
    chocolate chips

1/2 cup chopped walnuts

1 teaspoon baking soda

1 teaspoon salt

3 medium ripe bananas, mashed

1/2 cup mayonnaise

6 maraschino cherries, halved

1. In a bowl, combine flour, sugar, chocolate chips, walnuts, baking soda and salt. In another bowl, combine bananas and mayonnaise. Stir into the dry ingredients just until moistened.

2. Fill greased or paper-lined muffin cups three-fourths full. Bake at 375° for 20-25 minutes or until a toothpick comes out clean.

3. Press a cherry half, cut side down, into the top of each muffin. Cool for 5 minutes before removing from pan to a wire rack. **Yield:** 1 dozen.

Editor's Note: Reduced-fat or fat-free mayonnaise may not be substituted for regular mayonnaise in this recipe.

Pizza Omelet

~Sandy Cook, Melvin, Michigan

2 eggs

2 tablespoons milk

1 tablespoon butter

1/4 cup pizza sauce

10 slices pepperoni

1/4 cup shredded mozzarella cheese

1 tablespoon shredded Parmesan
    cheese

1. In a bowl, beat eggs and milk. In a skillet over medium heat, melt butter. Add egg mixture. As eggs set, lift edges, letting uncooked portion flow underneath. When eggs are completely set, remove from the heat.

2. Spread pizza sauce over half of the eggs; top with the pepperoni and mozzarella cheese. Fold in half; sprinkle with Parmesan cheese. Serve immediately. **Yield:** 1 serving.

Sausage Breakfast Loaf

~Luella Drake, Auburn, Indiana

1 pound smoked kielbasa *or* Polish sausage, julienned

1-1/2 cups (6 ounces) shredded mozzarella cheese

2 eggs

1-1/2 teaspoons minced fresh parsley

1/2 teaspoon onion salt

1/2 teaspoon garlic salt

1 tube (13.8 ounces) refrigerated pizza crust

1. In a large skillet, saute the sausage; cool. In a bowl, combine the sausage, cheese, 1 egg, parsley, onion salt and garlic salt.

2. Unroll pizza crust; roll into a 12-in. x 8-in. rectangle. Spread sausage mixture down the center of dough. Bring dough over filling; pinch seams to seal. Place seam side down on a greased baking sheet; tuck ends under.

3. Beat remaining egg; brush over top. Bake at 350° for 25-30 minutes or until golden brown. Let stand for 5 minutes before slicing. **Yield:** 6 servings.

Peachy Fruit Smoothies

~Taste of Home Test Kitchen

1-1/4 cups milk

1 cup (8 ounces) lemon yogurt

1 cup orange juice

3 tablespoons sugar

1/2 teaspoon vanilla extract

1 package (16 ounces) frozen unsweetened peach slices

In a blender or food processor, combine all the ingredients; cover and process until blended and smooth. Serve immediately. **Yield:** 6 servings.

Ham and Egg Pizza

~Carol Smith, Wichita, Kansas

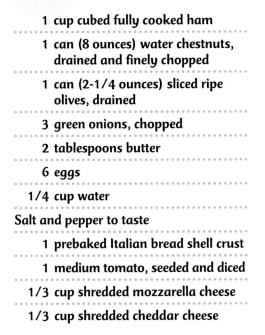

1 cup cubed fully cooked ham

1 can (8 ounces) water chestnuts, drained and finely chopped

1 can (2-1/4 ounces) sliced ripe olives, drained

3 green onions, chopped

2 tablespoons butter

6 eggs

1/4 cup water

Salt and pepper to taste

1 prebaked Italian bread shell crust

1 medium tomato, seeded and diced

1/3 cup shredded mozzarella cheese

1/3 cup shredded cheddar cheese

1. In a large skillet, saute the ham, water chestnuts, olives and onions in butter until heated through. In a bowl, beat the eggs, water, salt and pepper; add to skillet. Cook over medium heat until eggs begin to set, stirring occasionally.

2. Place crust on a pizza pan or baking sheet; top with egg mixture. Sprinkle with tomato and cheeses. Bake at 425° for 7-10 minutes or until cheese is melted. **Yield:** 6-8 servings.

Oatmeal Breakfast Bars

~Barbara Nowakowski, North Tonawanda, New York

4 cups quick-cooking oats

1 cup packed brown sugar

1 teaspoon salt

1-1/2 cups chopped walnuts

1 cup flaked coconut

3/4 cup butter, melted

3/4 cup orange marmalade

In a mixing bowl, combine the oats, brown sugar and salt. Stir in remaining ingredients and mix well. Press into a greased 15-in. x 10-in. x 1-in. baking pan. Bake at 425° for 15-17 minutes or until golden brown. Cool on a wire rack. **Yield:** about 2-1/2 dozen.

Strawberry Yogurt Shakes

~Laurel Adams, Dryden, Ontario

1 carton (16 ounces) plain yogurt

1 cup milk

1/2 cup honey

1-1/2 cups frozen unsweetened
    strawberries

1/4 cup toasted wheat germ

1/4 teaspoon almond extract

Dash salt

In two batches, process all ingredients in a blender until smooth. Pour into chilled glasses; serve immediately. **Yield:** 6 servings.

Crispy French Toast

~Flo Burtnett, Gage, Oklahoma

✓ Uses less fat, sugar or salt. Includes Nutritional
Analysis and Diabetic Exchanges.

1/2 cup egg substitute

1/2 cup fat-free milk

1/4 cup orange juice

1 teaspoon vanilla extract

Dash ground nutmeg

12 slices day-old French bread
    (3/4 inch thick)

1-1/2 cups crushed cornflakes

1. In a shallow dish, combine the egg substitute, milk, orange juice, vanilla and nutmeg. Add bread; soak for 5 minutes, turning once. Coat both sides of each slice with cornflake crumbs.

2. Place in a 15-in. x 10-in. x 1-in. baking pan coated with nonstick cooking spray. Bake at 425° for 10 minutes; turn. Bake 5-8 minutes longer or until golden brown. **Yield:** 12 slices.

Nutritional Analysis: 1 slice equals 147 calories, 1 g fat (trace saturated fat), trace cholesterol, 359 mg sodium, 28 g carbohydrate, 1 g fiber, 5 g protein. **Diabetic Exchange:** 2 starch.

Amy's Green Eggs and Ham

~Amy Church, Camby, Indiana

1 package (10 ounces) frozen chopped broccoli, cooked and drained

6 hard-cooked eggs, halved

1/4 cup mayonnaise

2 tablespoons Dijon mustard

1/4 cup chopped fully cooked ham

1 tablespoon sliced green onions

CHEESE SAUCE:

2 tablespoons butter

2 tablespoons all-purpose flour

1-1/4 cups milk

Dash *each* salt and paprika

1 cup (4 ounces) shredded cheddar cheese

2 tablespoons grated Parmesan cheese

1. In a greased 11-in. x 7-in. x 2-in. baking dish, layer broccoli and eggs. Combine the mayonnaise, mustard, ham and onions; spread over eggs.

2. In a saucepan, melt butter; add flour. Cook and stir until bubbly. Gradually add milk, salt and paprika; cook and stir until boiling. Cook and stir 2 minutes more. Remove from the heat; stir in cheddar cheese until melted.

3. Pour over casserole. Sprinkle with Parmesan cheese. Bake, uncovered, at 400° for 10-12 minutes or until heated through. **Yield:** 6 servings.

Peanut Butter 'n' Jelly Mini Muffins

~Vickie Barrow, Edenton, North Carolina

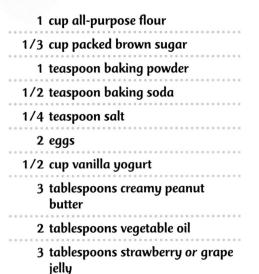

1 cup all-purpose flour

1/3 cup packed brown sugar

1 teaspoon baking powder

1/2 teaspoon baking soda

1/4 teaspoon salt

2 eggs

1/2 cup vanilla yogurt

3 tablespoons creamy peanut butter

2 tablespoons vegetable oil

3 tablespoons strawberry *or* grape jelly

1. In a large bowl, combine the flour, brown sugar, baking powder, baking soda and salt. In a small mixing bowl, beat the eggs, yogurt, peanut butter and oil on low speed until smooth; stir into the dry ingredients just until moistened.

2. Fill greased or paper-lined miniature muffin cups half full. Top each with 1/4 teaspoon jelly and remaining batter. Bake at 400° for 10-12 minutes or until golden brown. Cool for 5 minutes before removing from pans to wire racks. **Yield:** 2-1/2 dozen.

Editor's Note: Muffins may be baked in regular-size muffin cups for 16-18 minutes; use 3/4 teaspoon jelly for each instead of 1/4 teaspoon. Recipe makes 10 muffins.

Cinnamon Bread Rolls

~Cathy Stanfield, Bernie, Missouri

24 slices soft white sandwich bread, crust removed

2 packages (8 ounces *each*) cream cheese, softened

1-1/2 cups sugar, *divided*

2 egg yolks

2 teaspoons ground cinnamon

1 cup butter, melted

Flatten bread with a rolling pin. In a mixing bowl, beat cream cheese, 1/2 cup sugar and yolks. Spread on bread; roll up jelly-roll style. Combine cinnamon and remaining sugar. Lightly dip rolls in butter, then in cinnamon-sugar. Place on ungreased baking sheets. Bake at 350° for 20 minutes. **Yield:** 2 dozen.

Fluffy Scrambled Eggs

~Chris Pfleghaar, Elk River, Minnesota

6 eggs

1/4 cup evaporated milk *or* half-and-half cream

1/4 teaspoon salt

1/8 teaspoon pepper

1 tablespoon vegetable oil

2 tablespoons process cheese sauce

In a bowl, beat eggs, cream, salt and pepper. In a skillet, heat oil; add egg mixture. Stir in cheese sauce. Cook and stir gently over medium heat until eggs are completely set. **Yield:** 3 servings.

Ham and Cheese Bagels

~Kristin Dallum, Vancouver, Washington

1 package (3 ounces) cream cheese, softened

6 miniature bagels, split

3 ounces thinly sliced fully cooked ham

4 ounces cheddar cheese, thinly sliced

6 thin slices tomato

1 tablespoon chopped red onion

1/4 cup pineapple tidbits

1/4 teaspoon dried parsley flakes

1. Spread cream cheese over cut sides of bagels. Place on an ungreased baking sheet with cream cheese side up. Cut the ham and cheddar cheese into 2-in. squares; place over cream cheese.

2. Top half of the bagels with tomato and onion and half with pineapple and parsley. Bake at 350° for 10 minutes or until cheese is melted. **Yield:** 1 dozen.

Puppy Dog Pancakes

~Taste of Home Test Kitchen

1 cup all-purpose flour

1 teaspoon sugar

3/4 teaspoon baking powder

1/2 teaspoon salt

1 egg

1 cup buttermilk

1 tablespoon butter, melted

1 tablespoon chocolate syrup

2 drops strawberry syrup

8 semisweet chocolate chips

1. In a bowl, combine the flour, sugar, baking powder and salt. In another bowl, beat the egg, buttermilk and butter. Stir into the dry ingredients just until moistened. Place 2/3 cup of batter in a small bowl; stir in chocolate syrup. Place 1 teaspoon of batter in another bowl; stir in strawberry syrup.

2. For puppy ears, pour eight 1 tablespoonfuls of chocolate batter onto a lightly greased large hot griddle. For muzzle and eyes, spoon eight 1 teaspoonfuls and eight 1/4 teaspoonfuls of chocolate batter onto the griddle. For tongues, spoon four 1/8 teaspoonfuls of pink batter onto the griddle. For heads, pour four 1/3 cupfuls of plain batter onto the griddle. Turn when bubbles form on top of pancakes; cook until the second side is golden brown.

3. To assemble, arrange ears, eyes, muzzle and tongue on plain pancakes; top eyes with chocolate chips. **Yield:** 4 puppy dog pancakes.

Fruity Oatmeal

~Sarah Hunt, Everett, Washington

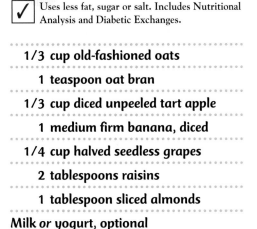

☑ Uses less fat, sugar or salt. Includes Nutritional Analysis and Diabetic Exchanges.

1/3 cup old-fashioned oats

1 teaspoon oat bran

1/3 cup diced unpeeled tart apple

1 medium firm banana, diced

1/4 cup halved seedless grapes

2 tablespoons raisins

1 tablespoon sliced almonds

Milk *or* yogurt, optional

Toss the first seven ingredients; divide between two bowls. Top with milk or yogurt if desired. Serve immediately. **Yield:** 2 servings.

Nutritional Analysis: One 1/2-cup serving (calculated without milk or yogurt) equals 182 calories, 5 mg sodium, 0 cholesterol, 37 g carbohydrate, 4 g protein, 4 g fat. Diabetic Exchanges: 1-1/2 fruit, 1 starch, 1/2 fat.

Brunch Punch

~Rosa Griffith, Christiansburg, Virginia

2 cans (46 ounces *each*) tropical punch-flavored soft drink

1 cup pineapple juice

3/4 cup lemonade concentrate

1 can (12 ounces) ginger ale, chilled

In a punch bowl or large container, combine the first three ingredients. Cover and refrigerate. Stir in ginger ale just before serving. **Yield:** about 3 quarts.

Peanut Butter Syrup

~Janice Nightingale, Cedar Rapids, Iowa

1/2 cup maple syrup

1/4 cup peanut butter

Waffles, pancakes *or* French toast

In a saucepan over low heat, heat syrup and peanut butter until the peanut butter is melted. Stir until smooth. Serve warm over waffles, pancakes or French toast. **Yield:** about 2/3 cup.

Triple Berry Muffins

~*Michelle Turnis, Hopkinton, Iowa*

3 cups all-purpose flour

1-1/2 cups sugar

4-1/2 teaspoons ground cinnamon

3 teaspoons baking powder

1/2 teaspoon salt

1/2 teaspoon baking soda

2 eggs

1-1/4 cups milk

1 cup butter, melted

1 cup fresh blueberries

1/2 cup fresh raspberries

1/2 cup chopped fresh strawberries

1. In a large bowl, combine the first six ingredients. In another bowl, beat the eggs, milk and butter; stir into dry ingredients just until moistened. Fold in berries. Fill greased or paper-lined muffin cups three-fourths full.

2. Bake at 375° for 18-20 minutes or until a toothpick comes out clean. Cool for 5 minutes before removing from pans to wire racks. **Yield:** about 1-1/2 dozen.

Cinnamon Monkey Bread

~*Lisa Combs, Greenville, Ohio*

4 tubes (7-1/2 ounces *each*) refrigerated buttermilk biscuits

1/2 cup sugar

2 teaspoons ground cinnamon

1/2 cup butter, melted

1/2 cup packed brown sugar

1. Cut each biscuit into four pieces; shape into balls. In a small bowl, combine sugar and cinnamon. Roll each ball in cinnamon-sugar. Arrange evenly in a greased 10-in. fluted tube pan. Sprinkle with the remaining cinnamon-sugar.

2. Combine butter and brown sugar; pour over the top. Bake at 350° for 35-40 minutes or until golden brown. Cool for 5 minutes before inverting bread onto a serving platter. **Yield:** 1 loaf.

Honey Fruit Cups

~Taste of Home Test Kitchen

4 cups cut-up fresh fruit (pears, apples, bananas, grapes, etc.)

1 carton (6 ounces) mandarin orange, vanilla or lemon yogurt

1 tablespoon honey

1/2 teaspoon grated orange peel

1/4 teaspoon almond extract

Divide fruit among individual serving bowls. Combine yogurt, honey, orange peel and extract; spoon over the fruit. **Yield:** 4 servings.

Granola Chip Shakes

~Elaine Anderson, Aliquippa, Pennsylvania

3/4 to 1 cup milk

4 tablespoons butterscotch ice cream topping, *divided*

2 cups vanilla ice cream, softened

1/2 cup granola cereal

2 tablespoons miniature semisweet chocolate chips

1. In a blender, combine milk, 2 tablespoons butterscotch topping and ice cream; cover and process until smooth. Pour into chilled glasses.

2. Drizzle with remaining topping; sprinkle with half of the granola and chocolate chips. Use a knife to swirl topping into shake. Top with remaining granola and chips. **Yield:** 2-1/2 cups.

Smiley Face Pancakes

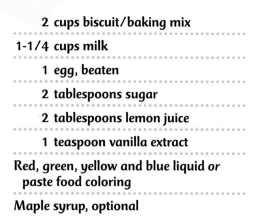

~Janette Garner, Carmel, Indiana

2 cups biscuit/baking mix

1-1/4 cups milk

1 egg, beaten

2 tablespoons sugar

2 tablespoons lemon juice

1 teaspoon vanilla extract

Red, green, yellow and blue liquid *or* paste food coloring

Maple syrup, optional

1. In a bowl, combine the biscuit mix, milk, egg, sugar, lemon juice and vanilla; mix until smooth. Place 1 tablespoon of batter each in four bowls. Color one red, one green, one yellow and one blue. Drop remaining batter by 1/4 cupfuls onto a lightly greased hot griddle.

2. To create faces, paint colored batter on pancakes with a new small paintbrush. Cook until bubbles form on the top. Turn and cook until second side is golden. Serve with syrup if desired. **Yield:** about 1 dozen.

Breakfast Bread Pudding

~Alma Andrews, Live Oak, Florida

12 slices white bread

1 package (8 ounces) cream cheese, cubed

12 eggs

2 cups milk

1/3 cup maple syrup

1/4 teaspoon salt

1. Remove and discard crusts from bread; cut bread into cubes. Toss lightly with cream cheese cubes; place in a greased 13-in. x 9-in. x 2-in. baking pan. In a large mixing bowl, beat eggs. Add milk, syrup and salt; mix well. Pour over bread mixture. Cover and refrigerate 8 hours or overnight.

2. Remove from refrigerator 30 minutes before baking. Bake, uncovered, at 375° for 40-45 minutes or until a knife inserted near the center comes out clean. Let stand for 5 minutes before cutting. **Yield:** 6-8 servings.

Double Chocolate Banana Muffins

~Donna Brockett, Kingfisher, Oklahoma

1-1/2 cups all-purpose flour

1 cup sugar

1/4 cup baking cocoa

1 teaspoon baking soda

1/2 teaspoon salt

1/4 teaspoon baking powder

1-1/3 cups mashed ripe bananas

1/3 cup vegetable oil

1 egg

1 cup (6 ounces) miniature
   semisweet chocolate chips

1. In a large bowl, combine the first six ingredients. In a small bowl, combine bananas, oil and egg; stir into dry ingredients just until moistened. Fold in chocolate chips.

2. Fill greased or paper-lined muffin cups three-fourths full. Bake at 350° for 20-25 minutes or until a toothpick comes out clean. Cool for 5 minutes before removing from pan to a wire rack. **Yield:** about 1 dozen.

Glazed Apples and Sausage

~Jennie Wible, Hamilton Square, New Jersey

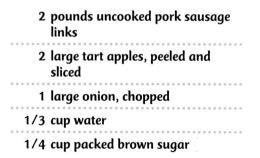

2 pounds uncooked pork sausage
   links

2 large tart apples, peeled and
   sliced

1 large onion, chopped

1/3 cup water

1/4 cup packed brown sugar

Cook the sausage according to package directions. Meanwhile, in a large saucepan, combine the apples, onion, water and brown sugar. Cook over medium heat for 5-8 minutes, stirring occasionally. Add the sausage; heat through. **Yield:** 8 servings.

Berry-Stuffed French Toast

~Monica and Lisa Hannahan, Dayton, Ohio

RASPBERRY SYRUP:

2 cups unsweetened raspberries

3/4 cup packed brown sugar

3 tablespoons butter

1 teaspoon ground cinnamon

1-1/2 teaspoons vanilla extract

FRENCH TOAST:

1 package (8 ounces) cream cheese, softened

1/2 cup sour cream

18 slices sourdough bread

1/2 cup raspberry preserves

1 teaspoon vanilla extract

6 eggs

1/4 cup half-and-half cream

1-1/2 teaspoons ground cinnamon

Confectioners' sugar and additional raspberries, optional

1. For syrup, combine raspberries, brown sugar, butter and cinnamon in a saucepan. Bring to a boil. Reduce heat; simmer, uncovered, for 5-7 minutes or until syrup is desired consistency. Remove from the heat and stir in vanilla; set aside.

2. In a mixing bowl, beat cream cheese and sour cream. Spread about 3 tablespoons on each slice of bread. Combine preserves and vanilla; spread over cream cheese mixture on nine slices. Top with remaining bread, cream cheese side down, to make a sandwich.

3. In a shallow bowl, combine the eggs, cream and cinnamon. Dip both sides of bread into egg mixture. Cook on a hot greased griddle for 3-4 minutes on each side or until golden brown. Cut in half diagonally. If desired, sprinkle with confectioners' sugar and garnish with raspberries. Serve with raspberry syrup. **Yield:** 9 servings.

·•Lunch·•·

Sandwich Bear

~Sue Schuller, Brainerd, Minnesota

1 package (8 ounces) cream cheese, softened

1 cup mayonnaise

1 tablespoon prepared mustard

1/4 cup chopped green onions

1 unsliced round loaf of bread (1 to 1-1/2 pounds and 10 inches)

6 unsliced rolls (one 5 inches and five 3-1/2 inches)

3/4 pound thinly sliced deli ham

1 cup (4 ounces) shredded cheddar cheese, *divided*

3/4 pound thinly sliced deli turkey

Leaf lettuce, optional

2 large pitted ripe olives

1. In a mixing bowl, beat cream cheese until light and fluffy. Stir in mayonnaise, mustard and onions.

2. Slice bread and rolls one-third from the bottom of each. Carefully hollow out tops of bread and rolls, leaving a 1/2-in. shell.

3. Spread cream cheese mixture on cut sides. Fill loaf with ham and half of the cheddar cheese. Fill the rolls with turkey and remaining cheese. Replace all tops.

4. To assemble bear, place loaf on lettuce if desired on a large board. Place 5-in. roll on top for head and four small rolls for paws. Cut the remaining small roll in half for ears. Use one olive for nose. Cut remaining olive in half; secure with a toothpick for eyes. Cover and refrigerate up to 2 hours. **Yield:** 16 servings.

Lasagna Sandwiches

~Gail Rotheiser, Highland Park, Illinois

1/4 cup sour cream

2 tablespoons chopped onion

1/2 teaspoon dried oregano

1/4 teaspoon seasoned salt

8 slices Italian *or* other white bread

8 bacon strips, halved and cooked

8 slices tomato

4 slices mozzarella cheese

2 to 3 tablespoons butter

1. Combine the first four ingredients; spread on four slices of bread. Top each with four bacon pieces, two tomato slices and a slice of cheese; top with remaining bread.

2. In a skillet over medium heat, melt 2 tablespoons butter. Cook sandwiches on both sides until bread is lightly browned and cheese is melted, adding more butter if necessary. **Yield:** 4 servings.

Italian Chicken Rice Soup

~Wendy Sorensen, Logan, Utah

1 can (49-1/2 ounces) chicken broth

1 jar (26 ounces) meatless spaghetti sauce

1-1/2 cups cubed cooked chicken

2 tablespoons minced fresh parsley

1/2 to 1 teaspoon dried thyme

3 cups cooked rice

1 teaspoon sugar

In a soup kettle or Dutch oven, combine the broth, spaghetti sauce, chicken, parsley and thyme. Bring to a boil. Reduce heat; simmer, uncovered, for 10 minutes. Stir in rice and sugar. Simmer, uncovered, for 10 minutes or until heated through. **Yield:** 10 servings (2-1/2 quarts).

Chili Bread

~Marian Dinwiddie, Roy, Washington

1 loaf (1 pound) French bread

1 can (16 ounces) kidney beans, rinsed and drained

1 can (15 ounces) chili without beans

3/4 to 1 cup spaghetti sauce

1 garlic clove, minced

1 medium tomato, chopped

2 green onions, thinly sliced

1 cup (4 ounces) shredded mozzarella cheese

2 tablespoons grated Parmesan cheese

Cut bread in half lengthwise; place with cut side up on a foil-lined baking sheet. Combine beans, chili, spaghetti sauce and garlic; spread over the bread. Top with tomato and onions. Sprinkle with cheeses. Bake at 350° for 10-12 minutes or until the cheese is melted. **Yield:** 8 servings.

Easy Cheesy Nachos

~Laura Jirasek, White Lake, Michigan

1 package (14-1/2 ounces) tortilla chips

2 cans (15 ounces *each*) chili without beans

1 pound process American cheese, cubed

4 green onions, sliced

1 medium tomato, chopped

Divide tortilla chips between six plates and set aside. In a saucepan, warm chili until heated through. Meanwhile, in another saucepan, heat cheese over medium-low heat until melted, stirring frequently. Spoon chili over the chips; drizzle with cheese. Sprinkle with onions and tomato. **Yield:** 6 servings.

Sticks 'n' Stones Salad

~Nancy Zicker, Port Orange, Florida

✓ Uses less fat, sugar or salt. Includes Nutritional Analysis and Diabetic Exchanges.

5 celery ribs, julienned

2 large carrots, julienned

1 can (8 ounces) sliced water chestnuts, drained

2 tablespoons olive oil

2 tablespoons cider vinegar

1 teaspoon sugar

1 teaspoon Dijon mustard

1/2 teaspoon salt

1/4 teaspoon dill weed

1. Place celery and carrots in a saucepan; cover with water. Bring to a boil. Cook, uncovered, for 3-4 minutes; drain and rinse with cold water. Drain thoroughly. Transfer to a large bowl; add the water chestnuts.

2. In a small bowl, whisk the oil, vinegar, sugar, mustard, salt and dill. Pour over vegetables and toss to coat. Serve immediately. **Yield:** 4 servings.

Nutritional Analysis: One serving (3/4 cup) equals 121 calories, 7 g fat (1 g saturated fat), 0 cholesterol, 396 mg sodium, 14 g carbohydrate, 5 g fiber, 1 g protein. **Diabetic Exchanges:** 3 vegetable, 1 fat.

Lunch-Box Handwiches

~Callie Myers, Rockport, Texas

1 loaf (1 pound) frozen bread dough, thawed

2-1/2 cups finely chopped fully cooked ham

1 cup (4 ounces) shredded Swiss cheese

1 egg yolk

1 tablespoon water

1. Allow dough to rise according to package directions. Punch down; divide into 10 equal pieces. Roll each piece into a 5-in. circle. Place about 1/4 cup ham and 2 tablespoons cheese on each circle; press filling to flatten. Mix egg yolk and water; brush on edges of circles. Fold into semi-circles and pinch edges to seal. Brush tops with egg yolk mixture.

2. Place on a greased baking sheet. Bake at 375° for 15-20 minutes or until golden brown. Serve warm or cold. **Yield:** 10 sandwiches.

Top-Dog Hot Dogs

~Kathy Burggraaf, Plainfield Township, Michigan

8 hot dogs

8 hot dog buns, sliced

1 jar (10 ounces) hot dog relish *or* chili sauce

1 small green pepper, chopped

1 small onion, chopped

1 small tomato, chopped and seeded

Shredded mozzarella cheese

Cook hot dogs according to package directions. Place in buns; top with relish or chili sauce, green pepper, onion and tomato. Sprinkle with mozzarella cheese. **Yield:** 8 servings.

Bacon Biscuit Wreath

~Kathy Kirkland, Denham Springs, Louisiana

1 jar (5 ounces) sharp American cheese spread

3 tablespoons butter-flavored shortening

1 tube (12 ounces) flaky biscuits

4 bacon strips, cooked and crumbled

2 tablespoons minced fresh parsley

1. In a small saucepan, melt the cheese spread and shortening; stir until blended. Pour into a well-greased 6-cup ovenproof ring mold or 9-in. fluted tube pan. Cut each biscuit into quarters and place over the cheese mixture.

2. Bake at 400° for 12-14 minutes or until golden brown. Immediately invert pan onto a serving platter and remove. Sprinkle with bacon and parsley. Serve warm. **Yield:** 10 servings.

Tuna Schooners

~Judy Archuleta, Escalon, California

1 can (6 ounces) tuna, drained and
   flaked

1/2 cup chopped apple

1/4 cup mayonnaise

1/4 teaspoon salt

4 lettuce leaves

2 English muffins, split and toasted

8 tortilla chips

In a bowl, combine the tuna, apple, mayonnaise and salt; mix well. Place lettuce on muffin halves; top with the tuna mixture. Place tortilla chips in tuna mixture to resemble sails. **Yield:** 2-4 servings.

School Day Chowder

~Karen Ann Bland, Gove, Kansas

1/2 pound hot dogs, halved
   lengthwise and sliced

1 cup sliced celery

1/2 cup sliced carrot

1/2 cup chopped green pepper

1/4 cup chopped onion

1/4 cup butter

1/4 cup all-purpose flour

1/8 teaspoon pepper

2-1/2 to 3 cups milk

2 cups (8 ounces) shredded cheddar
   cheese

In a large saucepan, combine hot dogs, celery, carrot, green pepper, onion and butter. Cook and stir over medium heat until vegetables are tender. Stir in flour and pepper until blended. Gradually add milk. Bring to a boil; cook and stir for 2 minutes or until thickened. Add cheese; stir until melted. **Yield:** 5 servings.

Mousy Pear Salad

~Marie Hoyer, Hodgenville, Kentucky

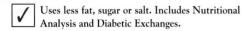

✓ Uses less fat, sugar or salt. Includes Nutritional Analysis and Diabetic Exchanges.

2 **cups shredded lettuce *or* lettuce leaves**

1 **can (15 ounces) pear halves, drained**

24 **raisins**

1 **slice process American cheese**

Black shoestring licorice—cut into four 3-inch pieces and sixteen 1-inch pieces

1 **red maraschino cherry, quartered**

1. On four salad plates, place lettuce and a pear half, cut side down. Insert two raisins at narrow end of pear for eyes. Tuck four raisins under pear for feet.

2. For ears, cut small teardrop-shaped pieces from cheese; place just above the eyes. Insert one 3-in. licorice piece into wide end of each pear for a tail. Insert four 1-in. pieces into each face for whiskers. Place a cherry piece under whiskers for nose. **Yield:** 4 servings.

Nutritional Analysis: One serving (prepared with reduced-fat process American cheese) equals 150 calories, 126 mg sodium, 3 mg cholesterol, 36 g carbohydrate, 2 g protein, 1 g fat. **Diabetic Exchanges:** 2 fruit, 1/2 starch.

Grilled 'PBJ' Sandwiches

~Barb Trautmann, Ham Lake, Minnesota

4 **tablespoons peanut butter**

2 **tablespoons strawberry jam**

4 **slices English muffin *or* white toasting bread**

2 **tablespoons butter, softened**

Confectioners' sugar, optional

Spread peanut butter and jam on two slices of bread; top with remaining bread. Butter the outsides of sandwiches; cook in a large skillet over medium heat until golden brown on each side. Dust with confectioners' sugar if desired. **Yield:** 2 servings.

Lunch Box Pizzas

~Rhonda Cliett, Belton, Texas

1 tube (7-1/2 ounces) refrigerated buttermilk biscuits, separated into 10 biscuits

1/4 cup tomato sauce

1 teaspoon Italian seasoning

10 slices pepperoni

3/4 cup shredded Monterey Jack cheese

1. Flatten each biscuit into a 3-in. circle and press into a greased muffin cup. Combine the tomato sauce and Italian seasoning; spoon 1 teaspoonful into each cup. Top each with a slice of pepperoni and about 1 tablespoon of cheese.

2. Bake at 425° for 10-15 minutes or until golden brown. Serve immediately or store in the refrigerator. **Yield:** 10 servings.

Club Quesadillas

~Victoria Hahn, Northampton, Pennsylvania

1/2 cup mayonnaise

8 flour tortillas (8 inches)

4 lettuce leaves

2 medium tomatoes, sliced

8 slices deli turkey

8 slices deli ham

8 slices provolone cheese

8 bacon strips, cooked

Salsa

Spread mayonnaise on each tortilla. On four tortillas, layer lettuce, tomatoes, turkey, ham, cheese and bacon; top with remaining tortillas. Cut into quarters. Serve with salsa. **Yield:** 4 servings.

Butterfly Sandwiches

~Maggie Lanksbury, Seattle, Washington

1 pound boneless skinless chicken breasts

3 green onions, chopped

1/4 cup shredded carrot

1/4 cup shredded cheddar cheese

1 envelope (1 ounce) ranch salad dressing mix

3/4 cup mayonnaise

18 slices white bread

18 fresh baby carrots

36 fresh chive pieces (about 1-1/2 inches long)

36 carrot strips (about 1-1/2 inches long)

Sliced stuffed olives

1. Place chicken in a large skillet; add enough water to cover. Bring to a boil. Reduce heat; cover and simmer for 12-14 minutes or until chicken is tender and juices run clear. Drain and cool.

2. Shred chicken; place in a bowl. Add onions, carrot and cheese. Combine the salad dressing mix and mayonnaise; add to the chicken mixture. Spread over half of the bread slices; top with remaining bread. Diagonally cut each sandwich in half, creating four triangles.

3. To form wings, arrange two triangles with points toward each other and crust facing out. For each butterfly body, place one baby carrot between triangles; insert two chives into filling for antennae. Place one carrot strip in the center of each triangle. Place olive slices on the wings. **Yield:** 9 servings.

Fruit Kabobs with Dip

~Taste of Home Test Kitchen

Assorted fruit–green grapes, watermelon balls, cantaloupe balls and strawberry halves

1 cup (8 ounces) plain yogurt

1/2 medium ripe banana

4 teaspoons honey

1/8 teaspoon ground cinnamon

Thread fruit alternately onto skewers. In a blender, combine remaining ingredients; cover and process until smooth. Serve with kabobs. **Yield:** 1-1/2 cups dip.

Biscuit Tostadas

~Terrie Stampor, Sterling Heights, Michigan

- 1 pound ground beef
- 1 jar (16 ounces) salsa, *divided*
- 1 tube (17.3 ounces) large refrigerated biscuits
- 2 cups (8 ounces) shredded Colby-Monterey Jack cheese
- 2 cups shredded lettuce

1. In a skillet, cook beef over medium heat until no longer pink; drain. Add 1-1/2 cups salsa; heat through. Split each biscuit in half; flatten into 4-in. rounds on ungreased baking sheets.

2. Bake at 350° for 10-12 minutes or until golden brown. Top with meat mixture, cheese, lettuce and remaining salsa. **Yield:** 16 servings.

Pizza English Muffins

~Lea Deluca, St. Paul, Minnesota

- 2 pounds ground beef
- 1-1/2 pounds bulk pork sausage
- 1 medium onion, chopped
- 1 can (6 ounces) tomato paste
- 1 teaspoon garlic salt
- 1 teaspoon dried oregano
- 1/2 teaspoon cayenne pepper
- 3 packages (12 ounces *each*) English muffins, split
- 3 cups (12 ounces) shredded mozzarella cheese
- 2 cups (8 ounces) shredded cheddar cheese
- 2 cups (8 ounces) shredded Swiss cheese

1. In a Dutch oven, cook the beef, sausage and onion over medium heat until meat is no longer pink; drain. Stir in the tomato paste, garlic salt, oregano and cayenne pepper. Spread over the cut side of each English muffin. Place on baking sheets. Combine the cheeses; sprinkle over the meat mixture.

2. Freeze for up to 3 months or bake at 350° for 15-20 minutes or until heated through. **Yield:** 6 dozen.

To use frozen Pizza English Muffins: Bake at 350° for 30 minutes.

Applesauce Sandwiches

~Eunice Bralley, Thornville, Ohio

1 cup applesauce

8 slices bread

1/4 cup butter, softened

1 tablespoon sugar

1/4 teaspoon ground cinnamon

Spread the applesauce on four slices of bread; top with remaining bread. Lightly butter the outsides of sandwiches. Toast on a hot griddle for 3-4 minutes on each side or until golden brown. Combine sugar and cinnamon; sprinkle over hot sandwiches. Serve immediately. **Yield:** 4 servings.

Corn Dogs

~Ruby Williams, Bogalusa, Louisiana

3/4 cup yellow cornmeal

3/4 cup self-rising flour

1 egg, beaten

2/3 cup milk

10 small wooden sticks

10 hot dogs

Oil for deep-fat frying

In a bowl, combine cornmeal, flour and egg; mix well. Stir in milk to make a thick batter; let stand 4 minutes. Insert sticks into hot dogs; dip in batter. Heat oil to 375°. Fry corn dogs until golden brown, about 5-6 minutes. Drain on paper towel. **Yield:** 10 servings.

Editor's Note: As a substitute for self-rising flour, place 1 teaspoon baking powder and 1/4 teaspoon salt in a measuring cup. Add enough all-purpose flour to equal 3/4 cup.

Puppy Dog Salad

~Jenni Miller, Olathe, Kansas

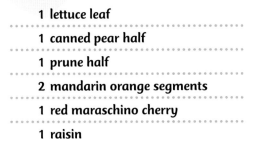

- 1 lettuce leaf
- 1 canned pear half
- 1 prune half
- 2 mandarin orange segments
- 1 red maraschino cherry
- 1 raisin

Place lettuce on a salad plate; place the pear cut side down over lettuce. For ear, place the prune on the wide end of pear. Place orange segments along the bottom for collar. Place cherry at the narrow end of pear for nose. Add raisin for the eye. **Yield:** 1 serving.

Thick Turkey Bean Chili

~Keri Scofield Lawson, Fullerton, California

- 1 pound ground turkey
- 2 cans (16 ounces *each*) baked beans, undrained
- 1 can (16 ounces) kidney beans, rinsed and drained
- 1 can (15-1/2 ounces) sloppy joe sauce
- 1 can (14-1/2 ounces) diced tomatoes, undrained
- 1 tablespoon brown sugar
- 1/4 teaspoon *each* garlic powder, salt and pepper
- Shredded cheddar cheese, sour cream and tortilla chips, optional

In a large saucepan, cook the turkey over medium heat until no longer pink; drain. Stir in beans, sloppy joe sauce, tomatoes, brown sugar and seasonings. Simmer, uncovered, for 30 minutes or until heated through. Serve with cheese, sour cream and tortilla chips if desired. **Yield:** 8-10 servings.

Tropical Fruit Salad

~Nancy Stinson, Texarkana, Texas

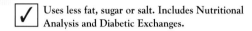

✓ Uses less fat, sugar or salt. Includes Nutritional Analysis and Diabetic Exchanges.

2 cans (8-1/4 ounces *each*) tropical fruit salad

1/2 cup pineapple *or* vanilla yogurt

1 teaspoon honey

1 small apple, chopped

1/2 cup halved fresh strawberries

1/2 cup halved green grapes

Drain fruit salad, reserving 1/4 cup juice (discard remaining juice or save for another use). In a bowl, combine the yogurt, honey and reserved juice. Fold in fruit salad, apple, strawberries and grapes. Serve immediately. **Yield:** 4 servings.

Nutritional Analysis: One 3/4-cup serving (prepared with reduced-fat yogurt) equals 143 calories, trace fat (trace saturated fat), 1 mg cholesterol, 23 mg sodium, 35 g carbohydrate, 2 g fiber, 1 g protein. **Diabetic Exchange:** 2-1/2 fruit.

Cherry Coke Salad

~Judy Nix, Toccoa, Georgia

1 can (20 ounces) crushed pineapple

1/2 cup water

2 packages (3 ounces *each*) cherry gelatin

1 can (21 ounces) cherry pie filling

3/4 cup cola

1. Drain pineapple, reserving juice; set fruit aside. In a saucepan or microwave, bring pineapple juice and water to a boil. Add gelatin; stir until dissolved. Stir in pie filling and cola.

2. Pour into a serving bowl. Refrigerate until slightly thickened. Fold in reserved pineapple. Refrigerate until firm. **Yield:** 10-12 servings.

Turkey Ranch Wraps

~Taste of Home Test Kitchen

8 thin slices cooked turkey

4 flour tortillas (7 inches)

1 large tomato, thinly sliced

1 medium green pepper, cut into thin strips

1 cup shredded lettuce

1 cup (4 ounces) shredded cheddar cheese

1/3 cup ranch salad dressing

Place two slices of turkey on each tortilla. Layer with tomato, green pepper, lettuce and cheese. Drizzle with salad dressing. Roll up tightly and serve immediately. **Yield:** 4 servings.

Hot Dog Roll-Ups

~Lyletta Searle, Morgan, Utah

8 hot dogs

1 block (4 ounces) cheddar cheese, cut into 8 strips

2 bacon strips, cooked and crumbled

1 tube (8 ounces) refrigerated crescent rolls

1. Cut a lengthwise slit in each hot dog; fill with a strip of cheese and about 1/2 teaspoon bacon. Separate crescent dough into eight triangles. Place a hot dog on the wide end of each triangle; roll toward the point.

2. Place cheese side up on an ungreased baking sheet. Bake at 375° for 12 minutes or until golden brown. **Yield:** 8 servings.

Beef 'n' Cheese Wraps

~Sue Sibson, Howard, South Dakota

4 flour tortillas (10 inches)

1 carton (8 ounces) onion and chive cream cheese spread

1 cup shredded carrots

1 cup (4 ounces) shredded Monterey Jack cheese

1 pound thinly sliced cooked roast beef

Leaf lettuce

Spread one side of each tortilla with cream cheese; top with the carrots and Monterey Jack cheese. Layer with beef and lettuce. Roll up tightly and wrap in plastic wrap. Refrigerate for at least 30 minutes. Cut in half or into 1-in. slices. **Yield:** 4 servings.

Hot Diggety Dogs

~Linda Blankenmyer, Conestoga, Pennsylvania

20 saltine crackers

5 slices process American cheese, quartered

Ketchup, mustard and pickle relish

2 hot dogs

Place crackers on a lightly greased baking sheet. Top with cheese, ketchup, mustard and relish. Cut each hot dog into 10 slices; place one slice on each cracker. Bake at 350° for 10-12 minutes or until the cheese is melted. **Yield:** 20 snacks.

Editor's Note: If serving small children, cut hot dog slices in half; double the amount of crackers and cheese.

Raisin Bagel Stackers

~Cynthia DeKett, Lyndonville, Vermont

✓ Uses less fat, sugar or salt. Includes Nutritional Analysis and Diabetic Exchanges.

2 **cinnamon raisin bagels (3-1/2 inches), split**

4 **teaspoons reduced-fat cream cheese**

4 **lettuce leaves**

1/4 **pound shaved deli smoked turkey breast**

2 **fresh dill sprigs**

2 **green onions, sliced**

2 **slices (1/2 ounce *each*) reduced-fat Swiss cheese**

4 **thin tomato slices**

1/8 **teaspoon *each* salt and pepper**

2 **teaspoons reduced-fat mayonnaise**

Lightly toast bagels; spread cream cheese on bottom halves. Layer with lettuce, turkey, dill, onions, cheese and tomato. Sprinkle with salt and pepper. Spread mayonnaise on top halves of bagels; place over tomato. **Yield:** 2 servings.

Nutritional Analysis: One serving equals 321 calories, 5 g fat (2 g saturated fat), 32 mg cholesterol, 1,029 mg sodium, 46 g carbohydrate, 3 g fiber, 22 g protein. **Diabetic Exchanges:** 3 starch, 2 lean meat.

Lunch Box Special

~Bernice Morris, Marshfield, Missouri

1/2 **cup peanut butter**

1/4 **cup orange juice**

1/2 **cup finely chopped apples**

1/2 **cup finely chopped dates**

1/2 **cup chopped walnuts, optional**

8 **slices bread**

In a bowl, mix the peanut butter and orange juice until smooth. Add apples, dates and walnuts if desired. Spread on four slices of bread; top with remaining bread. **Yield:** 4 servings.

Hot Dog Soup

~Kim Holliday, Bellefonte, Pennsylvania

4 medium carrots, cut into thin strips

2 medium potatoes, peeled and cubed

2 medium parsnips, peeled and chopped

1 medium onion, chopped

1/4 cup butter

2 tablespoons all-purpose flour

1 package (1 pound) hot dogs, halved lengthwise and cut into bite-size pieces

1 can (12 ounces) evaporated milk

1 can (10-3/4 ounces) condensed cream of mushroom soup, undiluted

1 cup water

1 teaspoon dried basil

1/2 teaspoon pepper

1. In a soup kettle or large saucepan, saute the carrots, potatoes, parsnips and onion in butter for 5 minutes. Stir in flour until blended. Add the hot dogs, milk, soup, water, basil and pepper; bring to a boil.

2. Reduce heat; cover and simmer for 25-30 minutes or until vegetables are tender, stirring occasionally. **Yield:** 8 servings (2 quarts).

10-Minute Taco Salad

~Cindy Stephan, Owosso, Michigan

2 cans (16 ounces *each*) chili beans, undrained

1 package (10-1/2 ounces) corn chips

2 cups (8 ounces) shredded cheddar cheese

4 cups chopped lettuce

2 small tomatoes, chopped

1 small onion, chopped

1 can (2-1/4 ounces) sliced ripe olives, drained

1-1/4 cups salsa

1/2 cup sour cream

In a saucepan or microwave-safe bowl, heat the beans. Place corn chips on a large platter. Top with beans, cheese, lettuce, tomatoes, onion, olives, salsa and sour cream. Serve immediately. **Yield:** 8 servings.

Pizza Grilled Cheese

~Robin Kettering, Newville, Pennsylvania

1 tablespoon butter, softened

2 slices bread

1 slice provolone *or* mozzarella cheese

6 slices pepperoni

3 tablespoons pizza sauce

Additional pizza sauce, optional

Butter one side of each slice of bread. Place one slice in a skillet, butter side down. Top with the cheese, pepperoni, pizza sauce and second bread slice, butter side up. Cook over medium heat until golden brown, turning once. Serve with additional pizza sauce if desired. **Yield:** 1 serving.

Oodles of Noodles Soup

~*Lorri Reinhardt, Big Bend, Wisconsin*

3/4 **pound boneless skinless chicken breasts, cubed**

2 **medium carrots, sliced**

1 **small onion, chopped**

2 **celery ribs, sliced**

1 **garlic clove, minced**

5 **cups water**

1/4 **teaspoon pepper**

2 **packages (3 ounces *each*) chicken ramen noodles**

1. In a large saucepan coated with nonstick cooking spray, saute the chicken, carrots, onion, celery and garlic until chicken is no longer pink. Add water, pepper and contents of seasoning packets from the noodles. Bring to a boil. Reduce heat; cover and simmer for 15-20 minutes or until carrots are tender.

2. Break noodles into pieces and add to soup; cover and cook for 3 minutes or until tender. **Yield:** 6 servings.

Turkey Divan Pizza

~*Charlotte Smith, Pittsburgh, Pennsylvania*

1 **prebaked Italian bread shell crust (16 ounces)**

2 **teaspoons olive oil**

1/2 to 1 **teaspoon garlic salt**

2 **cups fresh broccoli florets**

1-1/2 **cups cubed cooked turkey**

1 **can (10-3/4 ounces) condensed broccoli cheese soup, undiluted**

1/3 **cup milk**

1/2 **cup shredded cheddar cheese**

2 **tablespoons dry bread crumbs**

1 **tablespoon butter, melted**

1. Place pizza crust on a baking sheet. Brush with oil; sprinkle with garlic salt. Top with broccoli and turkey. Combine soup and milk; spread over broccoli and turkey. Sprinkle with cheddar cheese. Toss bread crumbs and butter; sprinkle over the top.

2. Bake at 400° for 13-15 minutes or until cheese is melted and broccoli is crisp-tender. **Yield:** 6-8 servings.

Baked Deli Sandwich

~Sandra McKenzie, Braham, Minnesota

1 loaf (1 pound) frozen bread dough, thawed

2 tablespoons butter, melted

1/4 teaspoon garlic salt

1/4 teaspoon dried basil

1/4 teaspoon dried oregano

1/4 teaspoon pizza seasoning

1/4 pound sliced deli ham

6 thin slices mozzarella cheese

1/4 pound sliced deli smoked turkey breast

6 thin slices cheddar cheese

Pizza sauce, warmed, optional

1. On a baking sheet coated with nonstick cooking spray, roll dough into a small rectangle. Let rest for 5-10 minutes. In a small bowl, combine the butter and seasonings. Roll out dough into a 14-in. x 10-in. rectangle. Brush with half of the butter mixture.

2. Layer the ham, mozzarella cheese, turkey and cheddar cheese lengthwise over half of the dough to within 1/2 in. of edges. Fold dough over and pinch firmly to seal. Brush with remaining butter mixture.

3. Bake at 400° for 10-12 minutes or until golden brown. Cut into 1-in. slices. Serve immediately with pizza sauce if desired. **Yield:** 4-6 servings.

Honeybee Ham Salad Sandwich

~Sheila Bradshaw, Columbus, Ohio

1/2 pound ground fully cooked ham

1/4 cup mayonnaise

2 hard-cooked eggs, chopped

1/4 cup chopped pecans

1/4 cup crushed pineapple, drained

2 tablespoons honey

1 round loaf (1 pound) Italian bread

1 round Italian roll (6 inches)

2 packages (one 8 ounces, one 3 ounces) cream cheese, softened

1 tablespoon heavy whipping cream

8 to 10 drops yellow food coloring

1/4 cup butter, softened

1 can (6 ounces) pitted large ripe olives, drained

1 pimiento strip

1 celery rib, cut into thirds

1. In a bowl, combine the ham, mayonnaise, eggs, pecans, pineapple and honey until blended. Slice the loaf and roll in half horizontally. Cut a third off one end of the loaf; slice the smaller portion in half.

2. In a mixing bowl, beat cream cheese, cream and food coloring until light and fluffy. Spread over top of all bread sections and roll. Spread butter over the inside of bread sections and roll; fill with ham salad.

3. To assemble, place large loaf piece on a serving platter or covered board for bee's body. Place roll next to body for head. For wings, position two small loaf pieces, rounded edges facing each other, above body.

4. Set aside 12 whole olives. Slice remaining olives in half lengthwise; make stripes on body with halved olives. Cut 11 olives into slices. Position one slice on head for eye; decorate wings with remaining slices. Add pimiento for mouth. Place last whole olive on one piece of celery; insert into top of head for antenna. Insert remaining celery into ham salad for legs. **Yield:** 10-12 servings.

Cheeseburger Mini Muffins

~Teresa Kraus, Cortez, Colorado

1/2 pound ground beef

1 small onion, finely chopped

2-1/2 cups all-purpose flour

1 tablespoon sugar

2 teaspoons baking powder

1 teaspoon salt

3/4 cup ketchup

3/4 cup milk

1/2 cup butter, melted

2 eggs

1 teaspoon prepared mustard

2 cups (8 ounces) shredded cheddar cheese

1. In a skillet, cook beef and onion over medium heat until meat is no longer pink; drain. In a bowl, combine the flour, sugar, baking powder and salt. In another bowl, combine the ketchup, milk, butter, eggs and mustard; stir into the dry ingredients just until moistened. Fold in the beef mixture and cheese. Fill greased miniature muffin cups three-fourths full.

2. Bake at 425° for 15-18 minutes or until a toothpick comes out clean. Cool for 5 minutes before removing from pans to wire racks. Refrigerate leftovers. **Yield:** 5 dozen.

Editor's Note: Muffins may be baked in regular-size muffin cups for 20-25 minutes; recipe makes 2 dozen.

Piggies in Blankies

~Iola Egle, McCook, Nebraska

2 cups biscuit/baking mix

1/2 cup water

1 can (14 ounces) sauerkraut, rinsed and drained, *divided*

1 pound hot dogs

1. In a bowl, combine biscuit mix and water until a soft dough forms. Turn onto a floured surface; knead 5-10 times. Roll dough into a 13-in. circle; cut into 10 wedges. Place 1 tablespoon sauerkraut on each wedge. Place a hot dog at the wide end; roll up each wedge tightly. Place on an ungreased baking sheet.

2. Bake at 450° for 12-15 minutes or until golden brown. Heat remaining sauerkraut; serve with the hot dogs. **Yield:** 10 servings.

Apple Peanut Salad

~Heidi Wilcox, Lapeer, Michigan

4 medium apples, diced

3 cups salted dry roasted peanuts

1 carton (8 ounces) frozen whipped topping, thawed

In a large bowl, combine the apples, peanuts and whipped topping. Cover and refrigerate until serving. **Yield:** 10 servings.

BLT Pizza

~Marilyn Ruggles, Lees Summit, Missouri

1 prebaked Italian bread shell crust (16 ounces)

1/2 cup mayonnaise

2 teaspoons dried basil

1/2 teaspoon garlic powder

1/8 teaspoon onion powder

12 bacon strips, cooked and crumbled

3/4 cup shredded cheddar cheese

3/4 cup shredded mozzarella cheese

1-1/2 cups shredded lettuce

2 medium tomatoes, thinly sliced

1. Place the crust on an ungreased 12-in. pizza pan. In a bowl, combine the mayonnaise, basil, garlic powder and onion powder; spread over crust. Set aside 1/4 cup bacon. Sprinkle cheeses and remaining bacon over crust.

2. Bake at 425° for 8-12 minutes or until cheese is melted. Top with lettuce, tomatoes and reserved bacon. Cut into wedges. Serve immediately. **Yield:** 4-6 servings.

Editor's Note: Reduced-fat or fat-free mayonnaise may not be substituted for regular mayonnaise in this recipe.

·.·Snacks·.·

Peanut Butter Honeybees

~Heather Bazinet, Ingleside, Ontario

1/2 cup creamy peanut butter

2 tablespoons butter, softened

1/2 cup confectioners' sugar

3/4 cup graham cracker crumbs (about 12 squares)

1 square (1 ounce) semisweet chocolate

1/3 cup sliced almonds, toasted

1. In a mixing bowl, cream peanut butter, butter and sugar until smooth. Add crumbs; mix well. Shape teaspoonfuls of dough into 1-1/4-in. ovals; place on a waxed paper-lined baking sheet.

2. Place chocolate in a small microwave-safe bowl; microwave on high for 1 minute or until melted. Transfer melted chocolate to a resealable plastic bag; cut a small hole in corner of bag.

3. Pipe three stripes on each bee. Insert two almonds into each bee for wings. Use a toothpick to poke holes for eyes. Store in the refrigerator. **Yield:** 4 dozen.

Sweet Graham Snacks

~Artimece Schmidt, Farmington, New Mexico

10 to 12 graham crackers, broken into quarters

1 cup butter

1/2 cup sugar

1/3 cup ground nuts

1. Line a 15-in. x 10-in. x 1-in. baking pan with graham crackers. In a saucepan, bring butter and sugar to a boil; boil for 2 minutes. Remove from the heat; stir in nuts. Spoon over the graham crackers.

2. Bake at 325° for 10 minutes. Immediately remove from pan onto foil. Cool. Break apart. **Yield:** 3-4 dozen.

Pepperoni Pizza Dip

~Connie Bryant, Wallingford, Kentucky

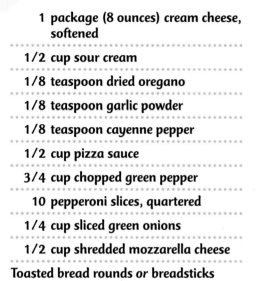

1 package (8 ounces) cream cheese, softened

1/2 cup sour cream

1/8 teaspoon dried oregano

1/8 teaspoon garlic powder

1/8 teaspoon cayenne pepper

1/2 cup pizza sauce

3/4 cup chopped green pepper

10 pepperoni slices, quartered

1/4 cup sliced green onions

1/2 cup shredded mozzarella cheese

Toasted bread rounds *or* breadsticks

1. In a mixing bowl, combine the first five ingredients. Spread into an ungreased 9-in. pie plate or serving plate. Cover with pizza sauce; top with green pepper, pepperoni and onions.

2. Bake at 350° for 10 minutes. Sprinkle with cheese. Bake 5-8 minutes longer or until cheese is melted. Serve with bread rounds or breadsticks. **Yield:** 8-10 servings.

Butterscotch Popcorn Bars

~Carol Stone, Waverly, Tennessee

2 quarts unsalted popped popcorn

1 cup salted peanuts

1 cup raisins

1/2 cup butter

1 package (10-1/2 ounces) miniature marshmallows

1 cup butterscotch chips

1. In a large bowl, combine the popcorn, peanuts and raisins. In a large saucepan over low heat, melt butter. Stir in the marshmallows and chips until melted and smooth.

2. Pour over popcorn mixture and stir until evenly coated. Immediately pour into a greased 13-in. x 9-in. x 2-in. pan and press down evenly. Cool before cutting. **Yield:** 3 dozen.

Treasure-Filled Apples

~Regan Ritter, Arlington, Texas

6 medium tart apples

1/2 cup sugar

1/4 cup red-hot candies

1/4 teaspoon ground cinnamon

1. Cut tops off apples and set tops aside. Core apples to within 1/2 in. of bottom. Place in a greased 8-in. square baking dish.

2. In a bowl, combine sugar, candies and cinnamon; spoon 2 tablespoons into each apple. Replace the tops. Spoon any remaining sugar mixture over the apples.

3. Bake, uncovered, at 350° for 30-35 minutes or until apples are tender, basting occasionally. **Yield:** 6 servings.

Veggie Cheese People

~Taste of Home Test Kitchen

Baby carrots

Celery ribs

Cherry *or* grape tomatoes

Small to medium zucchini and yellow summer squash

Sweet yellow, red *or* green peppers

Miniature dill *or* sweet pickles

Stuffed olives and pitted ripe olives

Hard-cooked eggs

Pimientos

String cheese and bulk cheddar cheese

Wooden skewers and toothpicks

Cut vegetables and cheese into desired shapes. To create people, thread the shapes onto skewers; use toothpicks to attach arms and legs. Insert skewers into a block of cheese if desired.

Ladybug Appetizers

~Taste of Home Test Kitchen

2 ounces cream cheese, softened

2 tablespoons sour cream

1/2 teaspoon snipped chives

1/8 teaspoon minced parsley

1/8 teaspoon garlic salt

Black paste food coloring

36 butter-flavored crackers

18 cherry tomatoes, quartered

18 large pitted ripe olives

72 fresh chive pieces (about 1-1/2 inches long)

1. In a small mixing bowl, beat the cream cheese until smooth. Add sour cream, chives, parsley and garlic salt; mix well. Place 1 tablespoon in a small plastic bag and tint black; set aside.

2. Spread remaining cream cheese mixture on crackers. Arrange two tomato quarters on each for the ladybug wings. For heads, halve the olives widthwise; place one half on each cracker. Insert two chives into olives for antennae. Use tinted cream cheese mixture to pipe spots onto wings. **Yield:** 3 dozen.

Honey Granola

~Sharon Mensing, Greenfield, Iowa

1/4 cup honey

1/4 cup butter, melted

1 tablespoon brown sugar

1/4 teaspoon ground cinnamon

2 cups rolled oats

1/2 cup unprocessed bran

1/2 cup raisins, optional

In a 9-in. square baking pan, combine honey, butter, brown sugar and cinnamon. Stir in oats and bran. Bake at 350° for 25-30 minutes, stirring occasionally, until golden brown. Stir in raisins if desired. Cool. Store in covered container. **Yield:** about 3 cups.

Pizza Corn Dog Snacks

~Linda Knopp, Camas, Washington

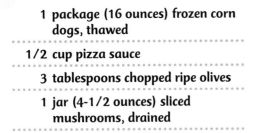

1 package (16 ounces) frozen corn dogs, thawed

1/2 cup pizza sauce

3 tablespoons chopped ripe olives

1 jar (4-1/2 ounces) sliced mushrooms, drained

1/4 cup shredded mozzarella cheese

1. Remove stick from each corn dog; cut into 1-in. slices. Place on an ungreased baking sheet. Spread with pizza sauce. Top with olives, mushrooms and cheese.

2. Bake at 350° for 15-20 minutes or until the cheese is melted and corn dogs are heated through. **Yield:** 30 snacks.

Apple Pie Sandwiches

~Gloria Jarrett, Loveland, Ohio

2 cups diced peeled tart apples

1 cup water

1/2 cup plus 1 tablespoon sugar, divided

5 teaspoons cornstarch

1/2 teaspoon ground cinnamon

1/4 teaspoon ground nutmeg

2 teaspoons lemon juice

12 slices day-old bread

3 eggs

2/3 cup milk

2 teaspoons vanilla extract

Confectioners' sugar, optional

1. In a saucepan, cook apples and water over medium heat for 10 minutes or until apples are tender. Combine 1/2 cup sugar, cornstarch, cinnamon and nutmeg; stir into apple mixture. Bring to a boil; cook and stir for 2 minutes or until thickened.

2. Remove from the heat; stir in lemon juice. Spread six slices of bread with 1/3 cup filling each; top with remaining bread.

3. In a shallow bowl, beat the eggs, milk, vanilla and remaining sugar. Dip sandwiches in egg mixture. Cook on a lightly greased hot griddle until golden brown on both sides. Dust with confectioners' sugar if desired. **Yield:** 6 servings.

Fruity Lemonade

~Taste of Home Test Kitchen

2 cans (12 ounces *each*) frozen lemonade concentrate, thawed

2 cans (12 ounces *each*) fruit punch concentrate *or* juice concentrate of your choice

Ice cubes

3 quarts club soda, chilled

In a bowl or pitcher, combine the lemonade concentrate and fruit punch concentrate. For each serving, pour 1/2 cup of the mixture into a glass. Add ice and 1 cup of club soda; stir well. **Yield:** 12 servings.

Stuffed Celery Sticks

~Opal Schmidt, Battle Creek, Iowa

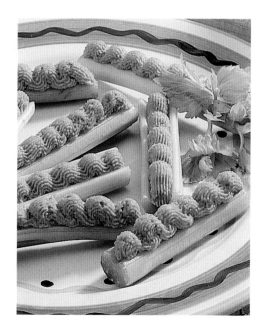

1 package (3 ounces) cream cheese, softened

1/4 cup creamy peanut butter

1 tablespoon milk

2 teaspoons soy sauce

4 celery ribs, cut into serving-size pieces

In a small mixing bowl, beat the cream cheese, peanut butter, milk and soy sauce until smooth. Transfer to a small resealable plastic bag. Cut a small hole in the corner of the bag; pipe mixture into celery pieces. **Yield:** 4 servings.

Peanut Butter Teddies

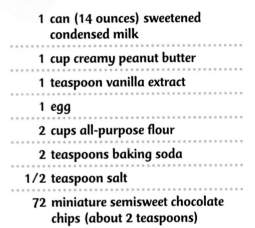

~Cynthia Kolberg, Syracuse, Indiana

1 can (14 ounces) sweetened condensed milk

1 cup creamy peanut butter

1 teaspoon vanilla extract

1 egg

2 cups all-purpose flour

2 teaspoons baking soda

1/2 teaspoon salt

72 miniature semisweet chocolate chips (about 2 teaspoons)

1. In a large mixing bowl, beat the milk, peanut butter, vanilla and egg until smooth. Combine the flour, baking soda and salt; add to peanut butter mixture and mix well.

2. For each bear, shape the dough into one 1-in. ball, one 3/4-in. ball, six 1/2-in. balls and one 1/4-in. ball. On an ungreased baking sheet, slightly flatten the 1-in. ball to form the body. Place the 3/4-in. ball above body for head. For ears, place two 1/2-in. balls above head. For limbs, place four 1/2-in. balls next to the body.

3. For nose, place the 1/4-in. ball in the center of the head. Add two chocolate chips for eyes and one chip for belly button. Bake at 350° for 6-8 minutes or until lightly browned. Cool on baking sheets. **Yield:** 2 dozen.

Orange Fruit Dip

~Tiffany Anderson-Taylor, Gulfport, Florida

1 cup sugar

2 tablespoons plus 1 teaspoon cornstarch

1/4 teaspoon salt

1 cup orange juice

1/2 cup water

1/4 cup lemon juice

1/2 teaspoon grated orange peel

1/2 teaspoon grated lemon peel

Assorted fresh fruit

In a small saucepan, combine the sugar, cornstarch and salt; stir in the orange juice, water, lemon juice, and orange and lemon peel until blended. Bring to a boil; cook and stir for 2 minutes or until thickened. Cover and refrigerate until chilled. Serve with fruit. **Yield:** 2 cups.

Stuffed Apple Treats

~Margaret Slocum, Ridgefield, Washington

2 tablespoons mayonnaise *or* softened cream cheese

2 tablespoons chopped nuts

2 tablespoons raisins, dried cranberries *or* dates

2 apples

Combine mayonnaise or cream cheese, nuts and raisins, cranberries or dates; set aside. Core each apple. Stuff cavity with mixture. **Yield:** 2 servings.

Garden Salsa

~Tammy Mahlke, La Crescent, Minnesota

✓ Uses less fat, sugar or salt. Includes Nutritional Analysis and Diabetic Exchanges.

1 medium green pepper, chopped

2 celery ribs, chopped

1 medium tomato, diced

1 small onion, chopped

1 medium carrot, chopped

1/4 cup minced fresh cilantro

1 can (14-1/2 ounces) diced tomatoes, drained

1/2 cup water

1/2 cup tomato sauce

1/3 cup tomato paste

3 garlic cloves, minced

1 tablespoon lemon juice

1/4 teaspoon pepper

Tortilla chips

In a bowl, combine the first seven ingredients. In another bowl, combine the water, tomato sauce, tomato paste, garlic, lemon juice and pepper; stir into the vegetable mixture. Serve with chips. Refrigerate leftovers. **Yield:** about 3 cups.

Nutritional Analysis: One serving (1/4 cup salsa) equals 29 calories, trace fat (trace saturated fat), 0 cholesterol, 122 mg sodium, 7 g carbohydrate, 2 g fiber, 1 g protein. **Diabetic Exchange:** 1 vegetable.

Tumbleweeds

~Victoria Johnson, Venice, Florida

1 can (12 ounces) salted peanuts

1 can (7 ounces) potato sticks

3 cups butterscotch chips

3 tablespoons peanut butter

1. Combine peanuts and potato sticks in a bowl; set aside. In a microwave, heat butterscotch chips and peanut butter at 70% power for 1-2 minutes or until melted, stirring every 30 seconds. Add to peanut mixture; stir to coat evenly.

2. Drop by rounded tablespoonfuls onto waxed paper-lined baking sheets. Refrigerate until set, about 5 minutes. Store in an airtight container. **Yield:** about 4-1/2 dozen.

Grape Ice

~Sharron Kemp, High Point, North Carolina

3-1/2 cups water

3/4 cup sugar

1 can (12 ounces) frozen grape juice concentrate, thawed

1 tablespoon lemon juice

1. In a microwave-safe bowl, combine the water and sugar. Cover and microwave on high for 1-2 minutes; stir until the sugar is dissolved. Stir in the grape juice concentrate and lemon juice. Pour into a 1-1/2-qt. freezer container.

2. Cover and freeze for at least 12 hours, stirring several times. May be frozen for up to 3 months. Just before serving, break apart with a large spoon. **Yield:** 6 servings.

Editor's Note: This recipe was tested in an 850-watt microwave.

Lemonade Stand Snack

~Taste of Home Test Kitchen

3 cups animal crackers

2 cups peanuts

2 cups raisins

2 cups milk chocolate M&M's

In a large bowl, combine all of the ingredients. Store in snack-size resealable plastic bags. **Yield:** 9 cups.

Sunny Orange Lemonade

~Martha Schwartz, Sarasota, Florida

4-1/4 cups water, *divided*

1 cup sugar

3/4 cup lemon juice (about 4 lemons)

3/4 cup orange juice (about 3 oranges)

2 teaspoons grated lemon peel

1 teaspoon grated orange peel

Ice cubes

In a saucepan, bring 1-1/4 cups water and sugar to a boil. Reduce heat. Simmer for 10 minutes; cool. Transfer to a pitcher; add lemon and orange juices and peels. Cover and refrigerate for at least 1 hour. Stir in the remaining water. Serve over ice. **Yield:** 6-8 servings.

Cranberry Cinnamon Roll-Ups

~Dorothy Pritchett, Wills Point, Texas

12 slices bread, crusts removed

7 tablespoons butter, softened, *divided*

2/3 cup whole-berry cranberry sauce

1/3 cup sugar

1-1/2 teaspoons ground cinnamon

1. Spread bread with 2 tablespoons butter. Spread each buttered slice with about 1 tablespoon cranberry sauce. Roll up jelly-roll style; secure with a toothpick if desired.

2. In a shallow microwave-safe bowl, heat the remaining butter in the microwave until melted. Combine sugar and cinnamon in another shallow bowl. Dip roll-ups in butter, then roll in cinnamon-sugar. Place seam side down on an ungreased baking sheet.

3. Bake at 400° for 6-8 minutes or until browned. Remove toothpicks before serving. **Yield:** 12 servings.

Cheesy Soft Pretzels

~Ruth Ann Stelfox, Raymond, Alberta

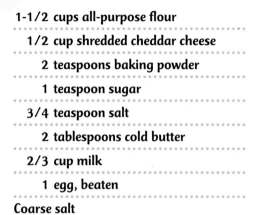

1-1/2 cups all-purpose flour

1/2 cup shredded cheddar cheese

2 teaspoons baking powder

1 teaspoon sugar

3/4 teaspoon salt

2 tablespoons cold butter

2/3 cup milk

1 egg, beaten

Coarse salt

1. In a bowl, combine flour, cheese, baking powder, sugar and salt. Cut in butter until crumbly. Stir in milk just until moistened. Knead on a floured surface for 1 minute; divide in half.

2. Roll each portion into a 12-in. x 8-in. rectangle; cut each into 8-in.-long strips. Fold strips in half, pinching the edges, and twist into pretzel shapes. Place on greased baking sheets.

3. Brush with egg and sprinkle with coarse salt. Bake at 400° for 12-15 minutes or until golden brown. Serve immediately. **Yield:** 1-1/2 dozen.

Peanut Butter-Jelly Spread

~Connie Bell, Wagoner, Oklahoma

1 cup peanut butter

1/4 cup butter

3/4 cup strawberry jam or preserves

1/4 cup honey

2 tablespoons maple syrup

Warm biscuits or toast

In a microwave-safe bowl, combine the peanut butter and butter. Microwave, uncovered, on high for 1 to 1-1/2 minutes or until melted. Stir until smooth. Add jam, honey and syrup; mix well. Serve on biscuits or toast. **Yield:** 2-1/2 cups.

Editor's Note: This recipe was tested in an 850-watt microwave.

Chocolate Malts

~Marion Lowery, Medford, Oregon

3/4 cup milk

1/2 cup caramel ice cream topping

2 cups chocolate ice cream, softened

3 tablespoons malted milk powder

2 tablespoons chopped pecans, optional

Grated chocolate, optional

In a blender, combine the first five ingredients; cover and process until blended. Pour into chilled glasses. Sprinkle with grated chocolate if desired. **Yield:** 2-1/2 cups.

Gingersnap Dip

—Tessie Hughes, Marion, Virginia

1 package (8 ounces) cream cheese, softened

1 cup confectioners' sugar

2 teaspoons pumpkin pie spice

1 carton (8 ounces) frozen whipped topping, thawed

1 package (16 ounces) gingersnaps

In a small mixing bowl, combine the cream cheese, confectioners' sugar and pumpkin pie spice. Beat in whipped topping until blended. Refrigerate until serving. Serve with cookies. **Yield:** 3 cups.

Kiddie Crunch Mix

~Kara De la Vega, Somerset, California

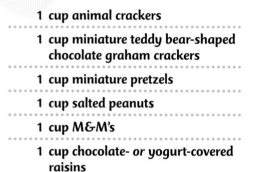

- **1 cup animal crackers**
- **1 cup miniature teddy bear-shaped chocolate graham crackers**
- **1 cup miniature pretzels**
- **1 cup salted peanuts**
- **1 cup M&M's**
- **1 cup chocolate- or yogurt-covered raisins**

In a bowl, combine all ingredients; mix well. Store in an airtight container. **Yield:** 6 cups.

Chewy Granola Bars

~Taste of Home Test Kitchen

- **6 cups quick-cooking oats**
- **1-1/2 cups dried fruit bits**
- **1 cup packed brown sugar**
- **1 cup butter, melted**
- **1 cup corn syrup**
- **1/2 cup miniature chocolate chips**
- **1/2 cup flaked coconut**
- **Vanilla frosting and yellow food coloring, optional**

1. In a large bowl, combine the first seven ingredients; mix well. Spread into a greased 15-in. x 10-in. x 1-in. baking pan. Bake at 350° for 20-25 minutes or until edges are golden brown. Cool on a wire rack.

2. Use a knife to cut into squares or cookie cutters to cut into shapes. If desired, tint frosting and frost bars. Store in a covered container or wrap individually. **Yield:** about 3 dozen.

Bake Sale

Orange Taffy

~Christine Olson, Horse Creek, California

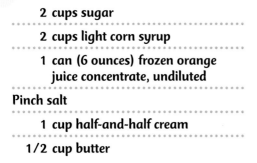

2 cups sugar

2 cups light corn syrup

1 can (6 ounces) frozen orange
juice concentrate, undiluted

Pinch salt

1 cup half-and-half cream

1/2 cup butter

1. In a heavy saucepan, combine first four ingredients. Cook and stir over medium heat until sugar is dissolved. Bring to a rapid boil and cook until a candy thermometer reads 245° (firm-ball stage). Add cream and butter; heat and stir until mixture reaches 245° again.

2. Pour into a greased 15-in. x 10-in. x 1-in. pan; cool. When cool enough to handle, roll into 1-1/2-in. logs or 1-in. balls. Wrap individually in foil or waxed paper; twist ends. **Yield:** about 6 dozen.

Editor's Note: We recommend that you test your candy thermometer before each use by bringing water to a boil; the thermometer should read 212°. Adjust your recipe temperature up or down based on your test.

Peanut Butter Bread

~Linda Muir, Big Lake, Minnesota

2 cups all-purpose flour

1/3 cup sugar

2 teaspoons baking powder

1 teaspoon salt

1 egg

1 cup milk

3/4 cup peanut butter

Grape jelly, optional

1. In a mixing bowl, combine the flour, sugar, baking powder and salt. Add egg, milk and peanut butter; stir just until combined. Pour into a greased 8-in. x 4-in. x 2-in. loaf pan.

2. Bake at 350° for 50-60 minutes or until a toothpick inserted near the center comes out clean. Cool for 10 minutes before removing from pan to a wire rack. Serve with jelly if desired. **Yield:** 1 loaf.

Editor's Note: Reduced-fat or generic brands of peanut butter are not recommended for this recipe.

Mr. Taco Bean Dip

~Taste of Home Test Kitchen

1 can (15 ounces) white kidney *or* cannellini beans, rinsed and drained

1 package (8 ounces) cream cheese, softened

1 cup (8 ounces) sour cream

1 envelope taco seasoning

1 round loaf (9 inches) white *or* whole wheat bread

Curly endive *or* leaf lettuce

1 small sweet red pepper

Wooden toothpicks

1 cherry *or* grape tomato

1 hard-cooked egg, halved

2 pitted ripe olives

Celery leaves

Tortilla chips and additional vegetables

1. In a food processor or blender, process the beans until smooth. In a small mixing bowl, beat the cream cheese, sour cream and taco seasoning until combined. Beat in beans. Cover and refrigerate for at least 20 minutes.

2. Cut the top fourth off the loaf of bread; carefully hollow out bottom, leaving a 1-1/2-in. shell. Cube removed bread; set aside. Place bread bowl on an endive-lined plate.

3. Cut red pepper into two rings for ears and a thick slice for mouth; attach to bread bowl, using toothpicks and referring to photo. Attach tomato for nose, egg and olives for eyes, and celery leaves for eyelashes. Fill bread bowl with bean dip. Serve with bread cubes, tortilla chips and vegetables. **Yield:** 3 cups.

Taco Dip Dragon

~Taste of Home Test Kitchen

1 can (16 ounces) refried beans

2 tablespoons taco seasoning

1 cup (8 ounces) sour cream

1 cup (4 ounces) shredded cheddar cheese

1 cup chopped fresh tomatoes

1/2 cup sliced ripe olives

1 cup guacamole

2 cups torn lettuce

1 whole ripe olive

Tortilla chips

1/2 medium sweet red pepper

1. In a bowl, combine the beans and taco seasoning. Cut a large hole in the corner of a pastry or plastic bag; fill with bean mixture. Trace a dragon shape (about 16 in. x 10 in.) onto waxed paper (see diagram below); cut out. Place pattern on an 18-in. x 12-in. covered board. Pipe bean mixture around pattern. Remove pattern. Pipe remaining bean mixture within dragon outline; spread to fill.

2. Set aside 1 tablespoon sour cream. Spread remaining sour cream over bean mixture. Top with cheese, tomatoes, olives, guacamole and lettuce. For the eye, spoon reserved sour cream onto head; top with the olive.

3. Place Dragon Dippers along back and top of head. With a sharp knife, cut red pepper into a flame shape (see diagram); position below mouth. Serve with additional dippers. **Yield:** 6-8 servings.

Dragon Dippers

~Taste of Home Test Kitchen

2 tablespoons butter, melted

10 flour tortillas (7 inches)

3/4 teaspoon garlic salt

3/4 teaspoon ground cumin

3/4 teaspoon chili powder

Brush butter on one side of each tortilla. Combine the seasonings; sprinkle over tortillas. Cut each into eight wedges. Place on ungreased baking sheets. Bake at 400° for 6-8 minutes or until crisp. **Yield:** 6-1/2 dozen.

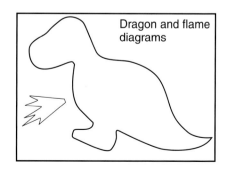

Dragon and flame diagrams

Nutty Toffee Popcorn

~Glenna Hale, Sceptre, Saskatchewan

10 cups popped popcorn

1 cup pecan halves, toasted

1 cup whole unblanched almonds, toasted

1-1/3 cups packed brown sugar

1 cup butter

1/2 cup light corn syrup

1/2 teaspoon cream of tartar

1/2 teaspoon baking soda

1/2 teaspoon rum extract

1. In a large bowl, combine the popcorn and nuts. In a heavy saucepan, combine the brown sugar, butter, corn syrup and cream of tartar; stir until sugar is dissolved. Cook, without stirring, over medium heat until a candy thermometer reads 300°-310° (hard-crack stage). Remove from the heat; stir in baking soda and extract. Immediately pour over popcorn mixture; toss gently.

2. Spread into two greased 15-in. x 10-in. x 1-in. baking pans. Press gently to flatten. Cool completely. Break into pieces. **Yield:** about 2 quarts.

Editor's Note: We recommend that you test your candy thermometer before each use by bringing water to a boil; the thermometer should read 212°. Adjust your recipe temperature up or down based on your test.

Sweet Sausage Rolls

~Lori Cabuno, Poland, Ohio

1 tube (8 ounces) refrigerated crescent rolls

24 miniature smoked sausage links

1/2 cup butter, melted

1/2 cup chopped nuts

3 tablespoons honey

3 tablespoons brown sugar

1. Unroll crescent dough and separate into triangles; cut each lengthwise into three triangles. Place a sausage on the long end and roll up tightly; set aside.

2. Combine the remaining ingredients in an 11-in. x 7-in. x 2-in. baking dish. Arrange sausage rolls, seam side down, in butter mixture. Bake, uncovered, at 400° for 15-20 minutes or until golden brown. **Yield:** 2 dozen.

Cooking for Kids :: Snacks 83

Apple Brickle Dip

(Pictured on page 83)

~Karen Wydrinski, Woodstock, Georgia

1 package (8 ounces) cream cheese, softened

1/2 cup packed brown sugar

1/4 cup sugar

1 teaspoon vanilla extract

1 package almond brickle chips (7-1/2 ounces) *or* English toffee bits (10 ounces)

3 medium tart apples, cut into chunks

In a mixing bowl, beat cream cheese, sugars and vanilla. Fold in brickle chips. Serve with apples. Refrigerate any leftovers. **Yield:** 2 cups.

Pizza Snacks

~Ruby Williams, Bogalusa, Louisiana

1/2 cup shredded cheddar cheese

1/2 cup shredded mozzarella cheese

1 jar (4-1/2 ounces) sliced mushrooms, drained

1/3 cup chopped pepperoni

1/3 cup mayonnaise

1/4 cup chopped onion

3 tablespoons chopped ripe olives

5 English muffins, split

In a bowl, combine the first seven ingredients; mix well. Spread over the cut side of each muffin half. Cover and freeze for up to 2 months. **Yield:** 10 snacks.

To use frozen Pizza Snacks: Place on an ungreased baking sheet. Bake at 350° for 20 minutes or until cheese is melted.

Two-Cheese Quesadillas

~Sharron Kemp, High Point, North Carolina

4 flour tortillas (8 inches)

1 cup (4 ounces) shredded cheddar cheese

1 cup (4 ounces) shredded mozzarella cheese

2 small tomatoes, diced

1/2 cup finely chopped green pepper

1/4 cup chopped onion

Salsa and sour cream

Sprinkle each tortilla with cheeses, tomatoes, green pepper and onion. Fold in half and press edges lightly to seal. On a griddle, cook quesadillas over low heat for 1-2 minutes on each side or until cheese is melted. Cut into wedges. Serve with salsa and sour cream. **Yield:** 2-4 servings.

Chewy Bread Pretzels

~Marilyn Strickland, Williamson, New York

1 package (1/4 ounce) active dry yeast

1-1/2 cups warm water (110° to 115°)

1 tablespoon sugar

2 teaspoons salt

4 cups all-purpose flour

1 egg, beaten

Coarse salt, optional

1. In a large bowl, dissolve yeast in water. Add sugar and salt. Blend in flour, 1 cup at a time, to form a soft dough. Turn out onto a floured surface; knead until smooth and elastic, about 5 minutes.

2. Place dough in a greased bowl, turning once to grease top. Cover and let rise in a warm place until doubled, about 1 hour. Punch dough down and divide into 15 equal portions. Roll each portion into a 14-in. rope. Shape into the traditional pretzel shape and place on a greased baking sheet.

3. Brush pretzels with egg and sprinkle with salt if desired. Cover and let rise 15 minutes. Bake at 425° for 15 minutes. **Yield:** 15 pretzels.

Apple-Raisin Ladybug

~Sherry Masters, Cincinnati, Ohio

- 2 lettuce or kale leaves
- 1 medium Red Delicious apple, quartered and cored
- 2 teaspoons creamy peanut butter
- 2 tablespoons raisins
- 5 red grapes

1. Place lettuce leaves on two salad plates. Arrange two apple quarters, peel side up, on the lettuce. Use dabs of peanut butter to place raisins in the space between apple quarters. Place one grape at the stem end of apple for head.

2. For legs, cut the remaining grapes lengthwise into four pieces; place three on each side of ladybugs. Place small dabs of peanut butter on remaining raisins; gently press onto apples for spots. **Yield:** 2 servings.

Banana-Pear Caterpillar

~Kendra Paige-Wrischnik, Cincinnati, Ohio

- 1 lettuce leaf
- 1 medium banana, peeled
- 1/2 medium red pear, cored and cut into 1/4-inch slices
- 2 raisins

Place lettuce on a salad plate; top with the banana. Cut 1/4-in. V-shaped slices halfway through the banana, spacing cuts 1 in. apart. Place a pear slice, peel side up, in each cut. For eyes, gently press raisins into one end of banana. Serve immediately. **Yield:** 1 serving.

Fruit Cocktail Ice Pops

~Jeanie Beers, Montgomery, New York

✓ Uses less fat, sugar or salt. Includes Nutritional Analysis and Diabetic Exchanges.

- 12 Popsicle molds *or* 12 paper cups (3 ounces *each*) and Popsicle sticks
- 1 can (29 ounces) fruit cocktail in extra light syrup, undrained

Fill molds or cups with about 1/4 cup fruit cocktail; top with holders or insert sticks into cups. Freeze. **Yield:** 1 dozen.

Nutritional Analysis: One serving equals 31 calories, 3 mg sodium, 0 cholesterol, 8 g carbohydrate, trace protein, trace fat. **Diabetic Exchange:** 1/2 fruit.

·.Dinner·.

Octopus and Seaweed

~Kerry Tittle, Little Rock, Arkansas

1 package (3 ounces) beef ramen noodles

4 hot dogs

5 drops liquid green food coloring, optional

Prepared mustard

1. In a saucepan, bring 1-1/2 cups water to a boil. Add the noodles and contents of seasoning packet. Boil for 3-4 minutes or until noodles are tender.

2. Meanwhile, add 4 in. of water to a large saucepan; bring to a boil. Cut each hot dog lengthwise into eight strips to within 2 in. of one end. Drop into boiling water; cook until heated through.

3. Add food coloring to noodles if desired. Drain if necessary. Place noodles on serving plates; top with a hot dog. Add eyes and mouth with dabs of mustard. **Yield:** 4 servings.

Chicken Nugget Casserole

~Tylene Loar, Mesa, Arizona

1 package (13-1/2 ounces) frozen chicken nuggets

1/3 cup grated Parmesan cheese

1 can (26-1/2 ounces) spaghetti sauce

1 cup (4 ounces) shredded mozzarella cheese

1 teaspoon Italian seasoning

Place chicken nuggets in a greased 11-in. x 7-in. x 2-in. baking dish. Sprinkle with Parmesan cheese. Top with spaghetti sauce, mozzarella cheese and Italian seasoning. Cover and bake at 350° for 30-35 minutes or until chicken is heated through and cheese is melted. **Yield:** 4-6 servings.

Chicken Broccoli Shells

~Karen Jagger, Columbia City, Indiana

1 jar (16 ounces) Alfredo sauce

2 cups frozen chopped broccoli, thawed

2 cups diced cooked chicken

1 cup (4 ounces) shredded cheddar cheese

1/4 cup shredded Parmesan cheese

21 jumbo pasta shells, cooked and drained

In a large bowl, combine the Alfredo sauce, broccoli, chicken and cheeses. Spoon into pasta shells. Place in a greased 13-in. x 9-in. x 2-in. baking dish. Cover and bake at 350° for 30-35 minutes or until heated through. **Yield:** 7 servings.

Franks 'n' Beans Supper

~Marlene Muckenhirn, Delano, Minnesota

2 bacon slices, diced

6 hot dogs, cut into thirds

1 small onion, chopped

1 can (10-3/4 ounces) condensed cream of chicken soup, undiluted

1/2 cup water

1/4 teaspoon dried thyme

1/8 to 1/4 teaspoon pepper

3 cups sliced cooked potatoes

1 cup frozen cut green beans, thawed

1. In a skillet, cook bacon until crisp. Remove with a slotted spoon and set aside; drain, reserving 1 tablespoon drippings. Saute hot dogs and onion in drippings until onion is tender.

2. Combine soup, water, thyme and pepper; add to skillet with potatoes and beans. Mix well; bring to a boil. Reduce heat; cover and simmer for 10 minutes or until heated through. Top with bacon. **Yield:** 4-6 servings.

Three-Cheese Spirals

~Deb Collette, Holland, Ohio

1 package (16 ounces) spiral pasta

1 egg

1-1/2 cups (12 ounces) sour cream

1-1/2 cups (12 ounces) small-curd cottage cheese

1 pound process American cheese, cubed

2 cups (8 ounces) shredded cheddar cheese

1. Cook pasta according to package directions. Meanwhile, in a blender, combine the egg, sour cream and cottage cheese; cover and process until smooth. Transfer to a large bowl; add American and cheddar cheeses. Drain pasta; stir into cheese mixture until evenly coated.

2. Transfer to a greased shallow 3-qt. baking dish. Bake, uncovered, at 350° for 15 minutes; stir. Bake 15-20 minutes longer or until bubbly and edges begin to brown. **Yield:** 8-10 servings.

Pizza Roll-Ups

~Donna Klettke, Wheatland, Missouri

1/2 pound ground beef

1 can (8 ounces) tomato sauce

1/2 cup shredded mozzarella cheese

1/2 teaspoon dried oregano

2 tubes (8 ounces *each*) refrigerated crescent rolls

1. In a skillet, cook beef over medium heat until no longer pink; drain. Remove from the heat. Add tomato sauce, mozzarella cheese and oregano; mix well.

2. Separate crescent dough into eight rectangles, pinching seams together. Place about 3 tablespoons of meat mixture along one long side of each rectangle. Roll up jelly-roll style, starting with a long side.

3. Cut each roll into three pieces. Place, seam side down, 2 in. apart on greased baking sheets. Bake at 375° for 15 minutes or until golden brown. **Yield:** 2 dozen.

Spaghetti Mac

~Linda Sawin, Sterling, Massachusetts

2 cups uncooked elbow macaroni

1/2 pound ground beef

1 can (10-3/4 ounces) condensed tomato soup, undiluted

1 can (8 ounces) tomato sauce

1 teaspoon dried minced onion

1 teaspoon dried parsley flakes

1/2 teaspoon salt

1/2 teaspoon dried oregano

1/4 cup shredded Parmesan cheese

Cook macaroni according to package directions. Meanwhile, in a saucepan, cook beef over medium heat until no longer pink; drain. Stir in soup, tomato sauce, onion, parsley, salt and oregano; heat through. Drain macaroni; top with the beef mixture and sprinkle with cheese. **Yield:** 4 servings.

Kids' Breadsticks

~Mary Miller, Fairfield, California

8 hot dog buns, split

6 tablespoons butter, melted

1 cup grated Parmesan cheese

2 to 3 tablespoons poppy *or* sesame seeds

Brush the cut sides of buns with butter. Place on ungreased baking sheets. Combine cheese and poppy or sesame seeds; sprinkle over buns. Bake at 450° for 7-9 minutes or until golden brown. **Yield:** 16 breadsticks.

Southwestern Hot Dogs

~Marion Stanley, Joseph, Oregon

1 cup (4 ounces) finely shredded cheddar cheese

1/2 cup crushed tortilla chips

2 green onions, thinly sliced

3 tablespoons salsa

2 tablespoons mayonnaise

1/2 teaspoon chili powder

10 hot dogs

10 hot dog buns, split

In a bowl, combine the first six ingredients. Cut a 1/2-in.-deep lengthwise slit in each hot dog. Spoon about 2 tablespoons cheese mixture into each. Broil for 2-3 minutes or until cheese is melted. Serve on buns. **Yield:** 10 servings.

Potato Chip Chicken Strips

~Sister Judith LaBrozzi, Canton, Ohio

1 cup (8 ounces) sour cream

1/8 teaspoon garlic salt

1/8 teaspoon onion salt

1/8 teaspoon paprika

1 package (12 ounces) potato chips, crushed

2 pounds boneless skinless chicken breasts, cut into 1-inch strips

1/4 cup butter, melted

Salsa, barbecue sauce or sweet-and-sour sauce

1. In a shallow bowl, combine sour cream and seasonings. Place crushed potato chips in another shallow bowl. Dip chicken strips in sour cream mixture, then coat with potato chips.

2. Place in a greased 15-in. x 10-in. x 1-in. baking pan. Drizzle with butter. Bake at 400° for 20-22 minutes or until chicken is no longer pink. Serve with salsa or sauce. **Yield:** 6 main-dish or 10 appetizer servings.

Monterey Ranch Bread

~Shirley Privratsky, Dickinson, North Dakota

2 cups (8 ounces) shredded
   Monterey Jack cheese

3/4 cup ranch salad dressing with
   bacon

1 loaf (1 pound) unsliced French
   bread

2 tablespoons butter, melted

Minced fresh parsley

In a bowl, combine the cheese and salad dressing; set aside. Cut bread in half lengthwise; brush with butter. Place on baking sheets. Broil 4 in. from the heat until golden brown. Spread with cheese mixture. Bake at 350° for 10-15 minutes or until cheese is melted. Sprinkle with parsley. Cut into 1-1/2-in. slices. **Yield:** 6-8 servings.

Cheesy Potato Beef Bake

~Nicole Rute, Fall River, Wisconsin

1 pound ground beef

2 cans (4 ounces *each*) mushroom stems and pieces, drained, optional

2 packages (5-1/4 ounces *each*) au gratin potatoes

4 cups boiling water

1-1/3 cups milk

2 teaspoons butter

1 teaspoon salt

1/2 teaspoon seasoned salt

1/2 teaspoon pepper

1 cup (4 ounces) shredded cheddar cheese

1. In a skillet over medium heat, cook beef until no longer pink; drain. Place in a greased 13-in. x 9-in. x 2-in. baking pan. Top with mushrooms if desired. Combine potatoes and contents of sauce mix packets, water, milk, butter, salt, seasoned salt and pepper. Pour over beef and mushrooms.

2. Cover and bake at 400° for 30 minutes or until heated through. Sprinkle with cheese. Bake, uncovered, for 5 minutes or until cheese is melted. Let stand 10 minutes before serving. **Yield:** 8 servings.

Tuna Boats

~Janell Aguda, Chicago, Illinois

2 cans (6 ounces *each*) tuna, drained and flaked

1 hard-cooked egg, chopped

3 tablespoons finely chopped celery

1 tablespoon finely chopped onion

1/2 cup mayonnaise

1 teaspoon sweet pickle relish

4 submarine sandwich *or* hoagie buns

4 lettuce leaves

4 slices cheddar cheese

8 wooden skewers

Fish-shaped crackers

1. In a bowl, combine the tuna, egg, celery and onion. Stir in the mayonnaise and pickle relish; set aside. Make a 2-in.- wide V-shaped cut in the center of each bun to within an inch of the bottom. Remove cut portion and save for another use. Line each bun with a lettuce leaf and fill with tuna mixture.

2. Cut cheese slices in half diagonally. For sails, carefully insert a wooden skewer into the top center of each cheese triangle. Bend cheese slightly; push skewer through bottom center of cheese. Insert two skewers into each sandwich. Place on a serving plate. Sprinkle fish crackers around boats. **Yield:** 4 servings.

Kids' Favorite Biscuits

~Dustin Chasteen, Weaverville, North Carolina

1 tube (7-1/2 ounces) refrigerated buttermilk biscuits, separated into 10 biscuits

1/2 cup peanut butter

1/2 cup jelly

Pat each biscuit onto the bottom and up the sides of a greased muffin cup. In a small bowl, combine peanut butter and jelly until smooth; place a rounded tablespoonful into each biscuit cup. Bake at 450° for 8-10 minutes or until golden brown. **Yield:** 10 servings.

Seasoned Fish Sticks

~Taste of Home Test Kitchen

1 teaspoon paprika

1 teaspoon chili powder

1/2 teaspoon garlic powder

1/2 teaspoon onion powder

1/2 teaspoon ground cumin

1/4 teaspoon cayenne pepper

2 tablespoons vegetable oil, *divided*

2 packages (8 ounces *each*) frozen breaded fish sticks

1. In a small bowl, combine the first six ingredients; mix well. Transfer half of the seasoning mix to a large resealable plastic bag; set aside.

2. Place 1 tablespoon oil in a large resealable plastic bag; add half of fish sticks and shake to coat. Transfer fish to resealable bag with seasonings and shake to coat.

3. Place in a single layer on an ungreased baking sheet. Repeat with remaining ingredients. Bake at 400° for 18-22 minutes or until golden brown. **Yield:** 4 servings.

Bacon Cheeseburger Rice

~Joyce Whipps, West Des Moines, Iowa

1 pound ground beef

1-3/4 cups water

2/3 cup barbecue sauce

1 tablespoon prepared mustard

2 teaspoons dried minced onion

1/2 teaspoon pepper

2 cups uncooked instant rice

1 cup (4 ounces) shredded cheddar cheese

1/3 cup chopped dill pickles

5 bacon strips, cooked and crumbled

In a large saucepan over medium heat, cook the beef until no longer pink; drain. Add water, barbecue sauce, mustard, onion and pepper. Bring to a boil; stir in the rice. Sprinkle with cheese. Reduce heat; cover and simmer for 5 minutes. Sprinkle with pickles and bacon. **Yield:** 4-6 servings.

Mexican Beef Burgers

~Stanny Barta, Pisek, North Dakota

2 eggs, beaten

2 cans (4 ounces *each*) chopped green chilies

1/4 cup finely minced onion

1/3 cup salsa

1 teaspoon salt

1/2 teaspoon pepper

1 garlic clove, minced

3/4 cup finely crushed corn chips

2 pounds ground beef

8 flour tortillas (10 inches), warmed

TOPPINGS:
Chopped tomatoes

Chopped ripe olives

Shredded cheddar cheese

Shredded lettuce

Salsa

Sour cream

In a bowl, combine the first seven ingredients. Add chips and beef; mix well. Shape into eight patties. Pan-fry, grill or broil until no longer pink. Wrap burgers and desired toppings in tortillas. **Yield:** 8 servings.

Teddy Bear Biscuits

~Berra Bleem, Walsh, Illinois

1 tube (7-1/2 ounces) refrigerated buttermilk biscuits, separated into 10 biscuits

1 egg, beaten

2 tablespoons sugar

1/4 teaspoon ground cinnamon

9 miniature semisweet chocolate chips

1. For each bear, shape one biscuit into an oval for the body and place on a greased baking sheet. Cut one biscuit into four pieces; shape into balls for arms and legs. Place next to body. Cut one biscuit into two small pieces and one large piece; shape into head and ears and place above body.

2. Brush with egg. Combine sugar and cinnamon; sprinkle over bears. Bake at 425° for 8-10 minutes (the one remaining biscuit can be baked with the bears). Place chocolate chips on head for eyes and nose while the biscuits are still warm. **Yield:** 3 bears.

Two-Tater Shepherd's Pie

~Cindy Rebain, Robertsdale, Alabama

1-1/2 pounds ground beef

1 can (10-3/4 ounces) condensed cream of mushroom soup, undiluted

1/2 teaspoon garlic salt

1/4 teaspoon pepper

6 cups frozen Tater Tots

2 cups frozen French-style green beans, thawed

3 cups hot mashed potatoes

1 cup (4 ounces) shredded Colby cheese

1. In a large skillet, cook beef over medium heat until no longer pink; drain. Stir in soup, garlic salt and pepper.

2. Place Tater Tots in a greased 13-in. x 9-in. x 2-in. baking dish. Top with beef mixture and green beans. Spread mashed potatoes over the top; sprinkle with cheese. Bake, uncovered, at 350° for 40-45 minutes or until heated through. **Yield:** 8 servings.

No-Noodle Lasagna

~Mary Moore, Omaha, Nebraska

1-1/2 pounds ground beef

1/2 cup chopped onion

1 can (6 ounces) tomato paste

1 tablespoon dried parsley flakes

1/2 teaspoon dried basil

1/2 teaspoon dried oregano

1/2 teaspoon salt

1/2 teaspoon pepper

Dash garlic salt

1 egg

1-1/2 cups (12 ounces) small-curd cottage cheese

1/4 cup grated Parmesan cheese

2 tubes (8 ounces *each*) refrigerated crescent rolls

1/2 pound sliced mozzarella cheese

1 tablespoon milk

1 tablespoon sesame seeds

1. In a large skillet, cook beef and onion over medium heat until meat is no longer pink; drain. Add tomato paste and seasonings; mix well. In a bowl, combine the egg, cottage cheese and Parmesan.

2. Roll out each tube of crescent dough between waxed paper into a 15-in. x 10-in. rectangle. Transfer one rectangle to a greased 15-in. x 10-in. x 1-in. baking pan. Spread with half of the meat mixture to within 1 in. of edges; top with half of the cheese mixture. Repeat meat and cheese layers.

3. Top with mozzarella. Carefully place second dough rectangle on top and press edges to seal. Brush with milk and sprinkle with sesame seeds. Bake, uncovered, at 350° for 25-30 minutes or until golden brown. **Yield:** 6 servings.

Pizza Pancakes

~Maxine Smith, Owanka, South Dakota

2 cups biscuit/baking mix

2 teaspoons Italian seasoning

2 eggs

1 cup milk

1/2 cup shredded mozzarella cheese

1/2 cup chopped pepperoni

1/2 cup chopped plum tomatoes

1/4 cup chopped green pepper

1 can (8 ounces) pizza sauce, warmed

1. In a large bowl, combine the biscuit mix and Italian seasoning. Combine eggs and milk; stir into dry ingredients just until moistened. Fold in the cheese, pepperoni, tomatoes and green pepper.

2. Pour batter by 1/4 cupfuls onto a lightly greased hot griddle. Turn when bubbles form on top; cook until the second side is golden brown. Serve with pizza sauce. **Yield:** 14 pancakes.

Sloppy Joe Wagon Wheels

~Lou Ellen McClinton, Jacksonville, North Carolina

1 package (16 ounces) wagon wheel pasta

2 pounds ground beef

1 medium green pepper, chopped

1 medium onion, chopped

1 jar (28 ounces) meatless spaghetti sauce

1 jar (15-1/2 ounces) sloppy joe sauce

Cook pasta according to package directions. Meanwhile, in a large skillet, cook beef, green pepper and onion until meat is no longer pink; drain. Stir in the spaghetti sauce and sloppy joe sauce; heat through. Drain pasta; top with beef mixture. **Yield:** 8 servings.

Grilled Cheeseburger Pizza

~Tanya Gutierro, Beacon Falls, Connecticut

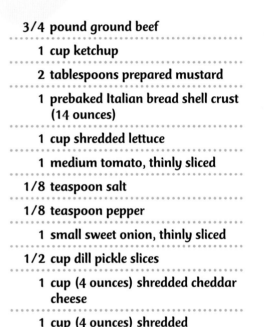

3/4 pound ground beef

1 cup ketchup

2 tablespoons prepared mustard

1 prebaked Italian bread shell crust (14 ounces)

1 cup shredded lettuce

1 medium tomato, thinly sliced

1/8 teaspoon salt

1/8 teaspoon pepper

1 small sweet onion, thinly sliced

1/2 cup dill pickle slices

1 cup (4 ounces) shredded cheddar cheese

1 cup (4 ounces) shredded mozzarella cheese

1. Shape beef into three 1/2-in.-thick patties. Grill, covered, over medium-hot heat for 5 minutes on each side or until meat is no longer pink. Meanwhile, combine ketchup and mustard; spread over the crust to within 1 in. of edge. Sprinkle with lettuce; top with tomato. Sprinkle with salt and pepper. When beef patties are cooked, cut into 1/2-in. pieces; arrange over tomato slices. Top with onion, pickles and cheeses.

2. Place pizza on a 16-in. square piece of heavy-duty foil; transfer to grill. Grill, covered, over indirect medium heat for 12-15 minutes or until cheese is melted and crust is lightly browned. Remove from the grill. Let stand for 5-10 minutes before slicing. **Yield:** 4-6 servings.

Chicken in a Haystack

~Helle Watson, Thornton, Colorado

1 can (10-3/4 ounces) condensed cream of chicken soup, undiluted

2 cups cubed cooked chicken

1/2 cup water

Hot cooked rice

TOPPINGS:
Cooked peas, raisins, pineapple tidbits, shredded cheddar cheese, sliced ripe olives, chow mein noodles *and/or* mandarin oranges

In a microwave-safe bowl, combine soup, chicken and water; mix well. Cover and microwave on high for 3-5 minutes or until heated through. Serve over rice. Top with toppings of your choice. **Yield:** 4-6 servings.

Cola Chicken

~Keri Scofield Lawson, Fullerton, California

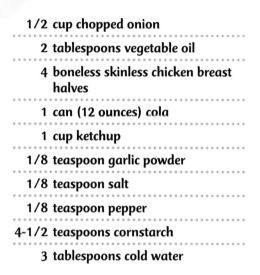

1/2 cup chopped onion

2 tablespoons vegetable oil

4 boneless skinless chicken breast halves

1 can (12 ounces) cola

1 cup ketchup

1/8 teaspoon garlic powder

1/8 teaspoon salt

1/8 teaspoon pepper

4-1/2 teaspoons cornstarch

3 tablespoons cold water

1. In a skillet, saute onion in oil until tender. Add chicken; brown on all sides. Carefully add cola, ketchup, garlic powder, salt and pepper. Cover and simmer for 25-30 minutes or until chicken juices run clear. Remove the chicken and keep warm.

2. Combine the cornstarch and cold water until smooth; add to the skillet. Bring to a boil; cook and stir for 2 minutes or until thickened. Return chicken to pan; heat through. **Yield:** 4 servings.

Pepperoni Hopple-Popple

~Jaycee Gfeller, Russell, Kansas

2-1/2 cups frozen shredded hash brown potatoes

1/3 cup chopped onion

3 tablespoons butter

5 eggs

1/2 cup milk

1 teaspoon Italian seasoning

1/2 teaspoon salt

1/2 teaspoon pepper

25 slices pepperoni

1 cup (4 ounces) shredded Mexican-cheese blend

1. In a large skillet, cook potatoes and onion in butter until tender and lightly browned. In a bowl, beat eggs, milk, Italian seasoning, salt and pepper. Pour over potato mixture. Sprinkle with pepperoni.

2. Cover and cook on medium-low heat for 10-12 minutes or until eggs are set. Remove from the heat. Sprinkle with cheese; cover and let stand for 2 minutes. Cut into wedges. **Yield:** 6 servings.

Sailboat Salads

~Lee Nelson, Waco, Texas

1 package (3 ounces) berry blue gelatin

1 cup boiling water

1 cup cold water

1 can (29 ounces) peach halves, drained

4 toothpicks

2 thick slices process American cheese

2 cups torn lettuce

1. Place gelatin in a bowl; add boiling water and stir until gelatin is dissolved. Stir in cold water. Pour gelatin onto four salad plates; refrigerate until firm.

2. For boat, place a peach half, cut side up, in the center of each plate (refrigerate any remaining peaches for another use). Cut cheese slices in half diagonally.

3. For sail, carefully insert a toothpick into the top center of each cheese triangle. Bend cheese slightly; push toothpick through bottom center of cheese. Insert toothpick into edge of peach. Arrange lettuce around plate. **Yield:** 4 servings.

Pizza Meat Loaf Cups

~Susan Wollin, Marshall, Wisconsin

1 egg, beaten

1/2 cup pizza sauce

1/4 cup seasoned bread crumbs

1/2 teaspoon Italian seasoning

1-1/2 pounds ground beef

1-1/2 cups (6 ounces) shredded
    mozzarella cheese

Additional pizza sauce, optional

1. In a bowl, combine the egg, pizza sauce, bread crumbs and Italian seasoning. Crumble beef over mixture and mix well. Divide between 12 greased muffin cups; press onto the bottom and up the sides. Fill center with cheese.

2. Bake at 375° for 15-18 minutes or until meat is no longer pink. Serve immediately with additional pizza sauce if desired. Or cool, place in freezer bags and freeze for up to 3 months. **Yield:** 1 dozen.

To use frozen pizza cups: Thaw in the refrigerator for 24 hours. Heat on a microwave-safe plate on high for 2-3 minutes or until heated through.

Pizza Biscuit Bears

~Taste of Home Test Kitchen

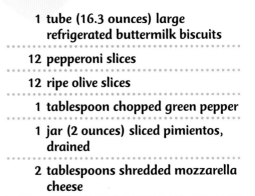

1 tube (16.3 ounces) large
   refrigerated buttermilk biscuits

12 pepperoni slices

12 ripe olive slices

1 tablespoon chopped green pepper

1 jar (2 ounces) sliced pimientos,
   drained

2 tablespoons shredded mozzarella
   cheese

1 can (8 ounces) pizza sauce,
   warmed

1. Separate biscuits; place six biscuits 3 in. apart on an ungreased baking sheet. Cut each remaining biscuit into six pieces; roll each into balls. Attach two balls to each whole biscuit for ears; pinch dough to seal.

2. Decorate each bear with a pepperoni slice on each ear, olive slices for eyes, green pepper for nose, two pimiento strips for mouth and mozzarella cheese for furry forelock. Bake at 375° for 15-20 minutes or until golden brown. Serve with pizza sauce. **Yield:** 6 servings.

Tender Turkey Meatballs

~Jane Thoma, Monroe, Michigan

☑ Uses less fat, sugar or salt. Includes Nutritional
   Analysis and Diabetic Exchanges.

1/2 cup chopped onion

1/4 cup egg substitute

1/4 cup toasted wheat germ

1/4 cup chopped green pepper

1/4 cup ketchup

1 teaspoon chili powder

1/2 teaspoon dried marjoram

1/2 teaspoon pepper

1 pound lean ground turkey

1 package (12 ounces) spaghetti

5 cups meatless spaghetti sauce

1. In a bowl, combine the first eight ingredients. Crumble turkey over mixture and mix well. Shape into 30 balls, about 1 in. each. Place in a 15-in. x 10-in. x 1-in. baking pan coated with nonstick cooking spray. Bake at 400° for 13-16 minutes or until juices run clear.

2. Meanwhile, cook spaghetti according to package directions. Transfer meatballs to a large saucepan; add spaghetti sauce. Heat through. Drain spaghetti; top with meatballs and sauce. **Yield:** 6 servings.

Nutritional Analysis: One serving (5 meatballs with sauce and 1 cup spaghetti) equals 312 calories, 7 g fat (2 g saturated fat), 60 mg cholesterol, 1,047 mg sodium, 40 g carbohydrate, 5 g fiber, 22 g protein. **Diabetic Exchanges:** 2-1/2 starch, 2 lean meat.

Tummy Dogs

~Myra Innes, Auburn, Kansas

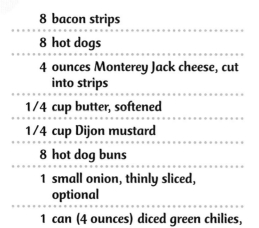

8 bacon strips

8 hot dogs

4 ounces Monterey Jack cheese, cut into strips

1/4 cup butter, softened

1/4 cup Dijon mustard

8 hot dog buns

1 small onion, thinly sliced, optional

1 can (4 ounces) diced green chilies, optional

1. Partially cook bacon; drain on paper towels. Cut a 1/4-in. lengthwise slit in each hot dog; place cheese in each slit. Starting at one end, wrap bacon in a spiral around hot dog; secure with toothpicks. Split buns just halfway. Combine butter and mustard; spread inside buns. Set aside.

2. On a covered grill over medium heat, cook hot dogs with cheese side down for 2 minutes. Turn and grill 3-4 minutes longer or until bacon is crisp and cheese is melted. Place buns on grill with cut side down; grill until lightly toasted. Remove toothpicks from the hot dogs; serve in buns with onion and chilies if desired. **Yield:** 8 sandwiches.

String Cheese Meat Loaf

~Laura Lawrence, Salinas, California

1 cup meatless spaghetti sauce, divided

1 egg, lightly beaten

1 cup seasoned bread crumbs

2 garlic cloves, minced

1-1/2 teaspoons dried rosemary, crushed

1 pound lean ground beef

8 ounces bulk Italian sausage

3 pieces string cheese

1. In a bowl, combine 1/2 cup spaghetti sauce, egg, bread crumbs, garlic and rosemary. Crumble meat over mixture and mix well. Press half into a greased 8-in. x 4-in. x 2-in. loaf pan. Place two pieces of cheese, side by side, near one end of loaf. Cut the remaining piece of cheese in half; place side by side on opposite end of loaf. Top with remaining meat mixture; press down firmly to seal.

2. Bake, uncovered, at 350° for 1-1/4 to 1-1/2 hours or until meat is no longer pink and a meat thermometer reads 160°; drain. Drizzle with the remaining spaghetti sauce; bake 10 minutes longer. Let stand for 10 minutes before slicing. **Yield:** 6 servings.

Editor's Note: 3 ounces of mozzarella cheese, cut into 4- x 1/2-inch sticks may be substituted for the string cheese.

Taco Chicken Rolls

~Kara De la Vega, Suisun City, California

1 cup finely crushed cheese-flavored crackers

1 envelope taco seasoning

6 boneless skinless chicken breast halves (about 2 pounds)

2 ounces Monterey Jack cheese, cut into six 2-inch x 1/2-inch sticks

1 can (4 ounces) chopped green chilies

1. In a shallow dish, combine the cracker crumbs and taco seasoning; set aside. Flatten chicken between two sheets of waxed paper to 1/4-in. thickness. Place a cheese stick and about 1 tablespoon of chilies on each piece of chicken. Tuck ends of chicken in and roll up; secure with a toothpick.

2. Coat chicken with crumb mixture. Place in a greased 13-in. x 9-in. x 2-in. baking dish. Bake, uncovered, at 350° for 35-40 minutes or until chicken juices run clear. Remove toothpicks. **Yield:** 6 servings.

Fancy Joes

~Linda Emery, Tuckerman, Arkansas

1 pound ground chicken *or* turkey

1 large onion, chopped

1 medium green pepper, chopped

2 cans (15-1/2 ounces *each*) sloppy joe sauce

3 cups cooked rice

8 English muffins, split and toasted

In a large skillet, cook the chicken, onion and green pepper over medium heat until chicken is no longer pink; drain. Stir in the sloppy joe sauce. Bring to a boil. Reduce heat; cover and simmer for 10 minutes. Stir in rice; cook 5 minutes longer or until heated through. Spoon 1 cup onto each English muffin. **Yield:** 8 servings.

Circle-O Skillet Supper

~Anna Mayer, Fort Branch, Indiana

5 hot dogs, sliced

1/4 cup chopped onion

1 tablespoon vegetable oil

1-1/2 cups water

1/2 cup chili sauce

1 tablespoon prepared mustard

1 tablespoon sugar

1-1/2 teaspoons cornstarch

1/2 teaspoon salt

Pinch pepper

1-1/4 cups elbow macaroni, cooked and drained

In a skillet, cook hot dogs and onion in oil until lightly browned. Combine the next seven ingredients; mix well. Stir into skillet; bring to a boil. Reduce heat; cook and stir for 2 minutes. Add macaroni; cook on low until heated through. **Yield:** 4-5 servings.

Baked Potato Strips

~Mae Dean Williams, Charlotte, North Carolina

✓ Uses less fat, sugar or salt. Includes Nutritional Analysis and Diabetic Exchanges.

3 large baking potatoes

2 egg whites

2 tablespoons grated Parmesan cheese

1 teaspoon garlic powder

1. Cut potatoes lengthwise into thin 1/4-in. strips. Pat dry with paper towels. In a bowl, combine the egg whites, Parmesan cheese and garlic powder. Add the potatoes; toss to coat. Place in a single layer in a 15-in. x 10-in. x 1-in. baking pan coated with nonstick cooking spray.

2. Bake, uncovered, at 375° for 35-40 minutes or until potatoes are golden brown and tender, turning several times. **Yield:** 4 servings.

Nutritional Analysis: One serving equals 190 calories, 98 mg sodium, 2 mg cholesterol, 39 g carbohydrate, 7 g protein, 1 g fat. **Diabetic Exchange:** 2-1/2 starch.

Turkey Pita Tacos

~Ann Bergstrom, Warrenville, Illinois

1 tablespoon vegetable oil

1 tablespoon cider vinegar

1 teaspoon chili powder

1 teaspoon ground cumin

1/4 teaspoon salt

1/4 teaspoon pepper

1 cup cubed cooked turkey *or* chicken

1 medium green pepper, chopped

1 medium sweet red pepper, chopped

1 small tomato, chopped

1 cup chunky salsa

3 green onions, thinly sliced

1 can (2-1/4 ounces) sliced ripe olives, drained

1 garlic clove, minced

1 cup (4 ounces) shredded cheddar cheese

5 pita breads (6 inches), halved

In a small bowl, combine the first six ingredients; set aside. In a large bowl, combine the turkey, peppers, tomato, salsa, onions, olives and garlic. Stir the oil mixture; pour over the turkey mixture and mix well. Stir in cheese. On a lightly greased griddle, heat pita breads on both sides. Spoon about 1/2 cup turkey mixture into each half. **Yield:** 5 servings.

Bacon Cheese Fries

~Marilyn Dutkus, Laguna Beach, California

1 package (32 ounces) frozen French fries

1 cup (4 ounces) shredded cheddar cheese

1/2 cup thinly sliced green onions

1/4 cup cooked crumbled bacon

Ranch salad dressing

Cook French fries according to package directions. Place fries on a broiler-proof dish or platter. Sprinkle with cheese, onions and bacon. Broil for 1-2 minutes or until cheese is melted. Serve with ranch dressing. **Yield:** 8-10 servings.

Meat-za Pie

~Denise Albers, Freeburg, Illinois

1 can (5 ounces) evaporated milk

1/2 cup plain *or* seasoned dry bread crumbs

3/4 teaspoon garlic salt

1 pound lean ground beef

1/4 cup ketchup

1 teaspoon sugar

1/2 cup canned sliced mushrooms

3 slices process American cheese, cut into thin strips

1/4 teaspoon dried oregano

2 tablespoons grated Parmesan cheese

1. In a bowl, combine milk, bread crumbs and garlic salt; add beef. Stir with a fork just until mixed. Press onto the bottom and 1/2 in. up the sides of an ungreased 9-in. pie plate.

2. Combine the ketchup and sugar; spread over beef mixture. Sprinkle with mushrooms. Arrange cheese in a lattice pattern on top. Sprinkle with oregano and Parmesan cheese.

3. Bake at 400° for 20 minutes or until meat is no longer pink and the cheese is lightly browned. Drain. Cut into wedges. **Yield:** 4 servings.

Mini Chicken Kabobs

~Norma Wells, Cookson, Oklahoma

1/4 cup soy sauce

2 teaspoons sugar

1/2 teaspoon salt

Dash *each* pepper, garlic powder and ground ginger

1/2 pound boneless skinless chicken breasts, cut into 1-inch cubes

1 small green pepper, cut into 1/2-inch pieces

2 cans (8 ounces *each*) pineapple chunks, drained

1 teaspoon honey

1. In a bowl, combine the soy sauce, sugar, salt, pepper, garlic powder and ginger. Remove half of the marinade to a small bowl; set aside for basting. Add chicken to the remaining marinade; stir to coat. Cover and refrigerate for 20-30 minutes.

2. Drain and discard marinade from the chicken. Thread chicken, green pepper and pineapple onto wooden toothpicks. Place on a microwave-safe plate. Add honey to the reserved marinade. Microwave kabobs on high for 5-6 minutes or until chicken juices run clear, turning occasionally. Baste with reserved marinade during the last minute of cooking. **Yield:** 3 dozen.

Editor's Note: This recipe was tested in an 850-watt microwave.

Nutty Chicken Fingers

~Beba Cates, Pearland, Texas

1/2 cup finely chopped pecans

1/3 cup crushed cornflakes

1 tablespoon dried parsley flakes

1/8 teaspoon garlic powder

1/8 teaspoon salt

2 tablespoons milk

3/4 pound boneless skinless chicken breasts, cut into 1-inch strips

In a shallow bowl, combine the first five ingredients. Place milk in another shallow bowl. Dip chicken in milk, then roll in pecan mixture. Place in a single layer in an ungreased 15-in. x 10-in. x 1-in. baking pan. Bake, uncovered, at 400° for 12-15 minutes or until juices run clear. **Yield:** about 2 dozen.

Waffle Fry Nachos

~Debra Morgan, Idaho Falls, Idaho

1 package (22 ounces) frozen waffle fries

10 bacon strips, cooked and crumbled

3 green onions, sliced

1 can (6 ounces) sliced ripe olives, drained

2 medium tomatoes, seeded and chopped

2/3 cup salsa

1-1/2 cups (6 ounces) shredded cheddar cheese

1-1/2 cups (6 ounces) shredded Monterey Jack cheese

Sour cream

Bake fries according to package directions. Transfer to a 10-in. ovenproof skillet. Top with the bacon, onions, olives, tomatoes, salsa and cheeses. Return to the oven for 5 minutes or until cheese is melted. Serve with sour cream. **Yield:** 6-8 servings.

Pinto Bean Turnovers

~Sue Seymour, Valatie, New York

3/4 cup pinto bean dip

1/3 cup chopped onion

1/3 cup chopped green pepper

Pastry for a double-crust pie (9 inches)

1/2 cup finely shredded cheddar cheese

1/2 teaspoon chili powder

Salsa and sour cream, optional

1. In a bowl, combine bean dip, onion and green pepper; set aside. On a lightly floured surface, roll pastry to 1/8-in. thickness. Sprinkle with half of cheese; press lightly with fingers. Turn pastry over; sprinkle with remaining cheese and press lightly. Cut into 3-in. circles.

2. Place about 2 teaspoons bean mixture in the center of each circle. Fold over; press edges with a fork to seal. Sprinkle with chili powder. Place on lightly greased baking sheets. Bake at 350° for 15-18 minutes or until golden brown. Serve with salsa and sour cream if desired. **Yield:** 2-1/2 dozen.

Editor's Note: This recipe was tested with La Preferida canned bean dip.

Mini Hamburgers

~Judy Lewis, Sterling Heights, Michigan

1/2 cup chopped onion

1 tablespoon butter

1 pound lean ground beef

1 egg, beaten

1/4 teaspoon seasoned salt

1/4 teaspoon rubbed sage

1/4 teaspoon salt

1/8 teaspoon pepper

40 mini rolls, split

8 ounces process American cheese slices, cut into 1-1/2-inch squares, optional

40 dill pickle slices, optional

1. In a skillet, saute onion in butter. Transfer to a bowl; add meat, egg and seasonings. Spread over bottom halves of the rolls; replace tops. Place on baking sheets; cover with foil.

2. Bake at 350° for 20 minutes. If desired, place a cheese square and pickle on each hamburger; replace tops and foil and return to the oven for 5 minutes. **Yield:** 40 mini burgers.

Tater Taco Casserole

~Ronna Lewis, Plains, Kansas

2 pounds ground beef

1/4 cup chopped onion

1 envelope taco seasoning

2/3 cup water

1 can (11 ounces) whole kernel corn, drained

1 can (11 ounces) condensed fiesta nacho cheese soup, undiluted

1 package (32 ounces) frozen Tater Tots

1. In a skillet, cook beef and onion over medium heat until meat is no longer pink; drain. Stir in taco seasoning and water. Simmer, uncovered, for 5 minutes. Add corn and soup; mix well.

2. Transfer to a greased 13-in. x 9-in. x 2-in. baking dish. Arrange Tater Tots in a single layer over the top. Bake, uncovered, at 350° for 30-35 minutes or until potatoes are crispy and golden brown. **Yield:** 8 servings.

Li'l Cheddar Meat Loaves

~Katy Bowron, Cocolalla, Idaho

1 egg

3/4 cup milk

1 cup (4 ounces) shredded cheddar cheese

1/2 cup quick-cooking oats

1/2 cup chopped onion

1 teaspoon salt

1 pound lean ground beef

2/3 cup ketchup

1/2 cup packed brown sugar

1-1/2 teaspoons prepared mustard

1. In a bowl, beat the egg and milk. Stir in cheese, oats, onion and salt. Add beef and mix well. Shape into eight loaves; place in a greased 13-in. x 9-in. x 2-in. baking dish.

2. Combine ketchup, brown sugar and mustard; spoon over loaves. Bake, uncovered, at 350° for 45 minutes or until the meat is no longer pink and a meat thermometer reads 160°. **Yield:** 8 servings.

Jazzy Mac 'n' Cheese

~Taste of Home Test Kitchen

1 package (7-1/4 ounces) macaroni and cheese dinner mix

1 can (10 ounces) diced tomatoes and green chilies, undrained

1/4 cup butter

1/2 cup grated Parmesan cheese

1/2 cup shredded mozzarella cheese

In a medium saucepan, bring 6 cups water to a boil. Add macaroni; set aside cheese packet. Reduce heat; simmer, uncovered, for 6-8 minutes or until pasta is tender. Drain and return to saucepan. Add tomatoes and butter; mix until butter is melted. Add the reserved cheese packet; mix well. Remove from heat; add Parmesan and mozzarella cheese. **Yield:** 4 cups.

·Desserts·

Strawberry Muffin Cones

~Barb Kietzer, Niles, Michigan

2 cups all-purpose flour

1/2 cup sugar

2 teaspoons baking powder

1/2 teaspoon baking soda

1/2 teaspoon salt

2 eggs

1 carton (6 ounces) strawberry yogurt

1/2 cup vegetable oil

1 cup chopped fresh strawberries

15 cake ice cream cones (about 3 inches tall)

1 cup (6 ounces) semisweet chocolate chips

1 tablespoon shortening

Colored sprinkles

1. In a large bowl, combine the first five ingredients. In another bowl, beat eggs, yogurt, oil and strawberries; stir into dry ingredients just until moistened. Place the ice cream cones in muffin cups; spoon about 3 tablespoon batter into each cone.

2. Bake at 375° for 19-21 minutes or until a toothpick inserted near the center comes out clean. Cool completely.

3. In a saucepan over low heat, melt chocolate chips and shortening; stir until smooth. Dip muffin tops in chocolate; decorate with sprinkles. **Yield:** 15 servings.

Editor's Note: These muffin cones are best served the same day they're prepared. Muffins can be baked in paper liners instead of ice cream cones.

PB&J Bars

~Mitzi Sentiff, Alexandria, Virginia

1 package (18 ounces) refrigerated sugar cookie dough, *divided*

2/3 cup strawberry jam

3/4 cup granola cereal without raisins

3/4 cup peanut butter chips

1. Line a 9-in. square baking pan with foil and grease the foil. Press two-thirds of the cookie dough into prepared pan. Spread jam over dough to within 1/4 in. of edges. In a mixing bowl, beat the granola, peanut butter chips and remaining dough until blended. Crumble over jam.

2. Bake at 375° for 25-30 minutes or until golden brown. Cool on a wire rack. Using foil, lift out of pan. Cut into bars and remove from foil. **Yield:** 9-12 servings.

Elephant Ears

~Suzanne McKinley, Lyons, Georgia

1 package (1/4 ounce) active dry yeast

1 cup warm water (110° to 115°)

1 cup warm milk (110° to 115°)

3 tablespoons sugar

1 tablespoon salt

3 tablespoons shortening

4 to 4-1/2 cups all-purpose flour

Oil for deep-fat frying

TOPPING:

1 cup sugar

1 teaspoon ground cinnamon

1. Dissolve yeast in water. Add milk, sugar, salt, shortening and 2 cups flour; beat until smooth. Stir in enough remaining flour to form a soft dough.

2. Turn onto a floured surface, knead until smooth and elastic, about 6-8 minutes. Place in a greased bowl; turn once to grease top. Cover and let rise in a warm place until doubled, about 1 hour. Punch down and shape into 15 ovals, 5-1/2 in. round by 1/8 in. thick.

3. Heat 3-4 in. of oil to 375° in deep-fat fryer. Fry ovals, one at a time, 3 minutes per side or until golden brown. Drain. Mix sugar and cinnamon; sprinkle over warm pastries. **Yield:** 15 servings.

Tropical Island Dessert

~Ashley Walls, New Iberia, Louisiana

3 packages (3 ounces *each*) berry blue gelatin

2 cups boiling water

2-1/2 cups cold water

4 tablespoons fish-shaped gummy candies, *divided*

2 cups cold milk

1 package (3.4 ounces) instant vanilla pudding mix

1 medium lime

2 cinnamon sticks

1 round wooden toothpick

2 tablespoons graham cracker crumbs

6 whole allspice

1 disposable cup (2-ounce size)

Fresh blueberries and additional gummy candies, optional

1. In a bowl, dissolve gelatin in boiling water. Stir in cold water. Pour in-to a 6-cup ring mold coated with nonstick cooking spray. Add 2 tablespoons gummy candies. Chill 1 hour. Stir in remaining candies. Chill 1-2 hours or until set. In a bowl, whisk milk and pudding. Cover; chill until ready to use.

2. To make palm tree leaves, cut lime in half; remove and discard pulp. Place lime halves, cut side down, on a cutting board. With pencil, sketch five leaves on each half. Cut out leaves, leaving center intact; make little cuts to create a palm leaf appearance. To create a base for trees, turn dis-posable cup upside down; cut two small slits in bottom. Insert a cinna-mon stick in each slit for tree trunks. Break toothpick in half. Insert point-ed ends into center of lime halves; insert broken ends into cinnamon sticks.

3. Unmold gelatin onto a 12-in. serving platter. Place cup in the center of gelatin ring. Spoon vanilla pudding over cup, filling center of ring. Sprin-kle with graham cracker crumbs for sand. Place allspice at base of trees for coconuts (discard allspice before serving). Garnish with blueberries and additional gummy fish if desired. **Yield:** 12-16 servings.

Cookie Burgers

~Cheryl Reitz, Hershey, Pennsylvania

DOUGH:

1 package (22.3 ounces) golden sugar cookie mix

2 eggs

1/3 cup vegetable oil

1 teaspoon water

1 package (10 ounces) peanut butter chips, chopped

TOPPING:

3/4 cup flaked coconut

5 to 6 drops green food coloring

FILLING:

1/2 cup butter, softened

2-2/3 cups confectioners' sugar

1/2 cup baking cocoa

1/4 cup milk

1 teaspoon vanilla extract

1. In a large bowl, combine cookie mix, eggs, oil and water; mix well. Stir in peanut butter chips. Shape into 1-1/4-in. balls; place 2 in. apart on ungreased baking sheets. Bake at 375° for 9-11 minutes or until lightly browned. Remove to wire racks to cool.

2. Toss coconut and food coloring until coated; set aside. In a mixing bowl, cream butter. Add sugar, cocoa, milk and vanilla; beat until smooth. Frost the bottoms of 22 cookies; sprinkle with coconut. Top with remaining cookies and gently squeeze together. **Yield:** 22 sandwich cookies.

Editor's Note: You may substitute your favorite sugar cookie recipe for the cookie mix, eggs, oil and water; just add the peanut butter chips.

Peanutty Fries

~Cheryl Reitz, Hershey, Pennsylvania

1 package (10 ounces) peanut butter chips

1 cup sweetened condensed milk

Paper muffin cup liners (2-1/2-inch diameter)

Red icing, optional

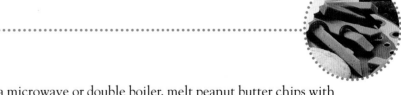

1. In a microwave or double boiler, melt peanut butter chips with milk; stir until smooth. Pour into a 9-in. baking pan lined with foil and greased. Cool completely at room temperature.

2. Lift out of the pan and invert onto a cutting board. Remove foil; cut into 3-in. x 1/4-in. strips. Fold muffin cup liners in half, pressing out creases; fold in half again. Fold point under; use as holders for fries. Use icing for ketchup if desired. **Yield:** about 3-1/2 dozen.

Surefire Sugar Cookies

~Victoria Zmarzley-Hahn, Northampton, Pennsylvania

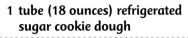

1 tube (18 ounces) refrigerated
   sugar cookie dough

1-1/2 cups semisweet chocolate chips

4-1/2 teaspoons shortening

Colored sprinkles, chopped nuts *or*
   flaked coconut

1. Slice and bake the sugar cookies according to package directions. Cool on wire racks.

2. In a microwave-safe bowl, combine the chocolate chips and shortening. Microwave on high for 1-2 minutes or until melted; stir until smooth. Dip each cookie halfway in melted chocolate. Place on waxed paper; immediately sprinkle with colored sprinkles, nuts or coconut. Let stand until chocolate is completely set. **Yield:** 2 dozen.

Orange Brownies

~Rosella Peters, Gull Lake, Saskatchewan

1/2 cup butter

1/4 cup baking cocoa

2 eggs

1 cup sugar

3/4 cup all-purpose flour

1/2 cup chopped pecans

2 tablespoons orange juice
   concentrate

1 tablespoon grated orange peel

1/8 teaspoon salt

FROSTING:

1-1/2 cups confectioners' sugar

3 tablespoons butter, softened

2 tablespoons orange juice
   concentrate

1 tablespoon grated orange peel,
   optional

1. In a small saucepan, melt butter. Stir in cocoa until smooth. Remove from the heat. In a bowl, beat eggs until frothy. Without stirring, add the sugar, flour, pecans, orange juice concentrate, peel and salt. Pour cocoa mixture over the top; mix well. Transfer to a greased 8-in. square baking pan.

2. Bake at 350° for 28-32 minutes or until edges begin to pull away from sides of pan. Cool completely on a wire rack.

3. For frosting, combine confectioners' sugar, butter and orange juice concentrate; mix well. Spread over the brownies. Cut into bars; garnish with orange peel if desired. **Yield:** 16 servings.

Banana Split Shortcake

~Christi Gillentine, Tulsa, Oklahoma

8 slices pound cake (1/2 inch thick) or 4 individual round sponge cakes

2 medium firm bananas, cut into 1/4-inch slices

4 scoops vanilla ice cream

1/4 cup chocolate sauce

Place cake slices on four dessert plates. Top each with bananas and ice cream. Drizzle with chocolate sauce. **Yield:** 4 servings.

Cinnamon Caramel Apples

~Taste of Home Test Kitchen

2 packages (14 ounces *each*) caramels

3 tablespoons milk chocolate chips

3 tablespoons water

1 teaspoon ground cinnamon

3/4 teaspoon vanilla extract

8 Popsicle sticks

8 large tart apples

Chocolate-covered toffee bits, finely chopped salted peanuts and cashews, flaked coconut, M&M miniature baking bits *and/or* chocolate sprinkles

1. In a microwave-safe bowl, combine the caramels, chocolate chips, water, cinnamon and vanilla. Microwave, uncovered, on high for 1-1/2 minutes; stir. Microwave 30-60 seconds longer or until caramels are melted.

2. Insert Popsicle sticks into the apples; dip into caramel mixture, turning to coat. Roll in or press on desired toppings. Place on waxed paper; let stand until set. **Yield:** 8 servings.

Editor's Note: This recipe was tested in an 850-watt microwave.

Fun Marshmallow Bars

~Debbie Brunssen, Randolph, Nebraska

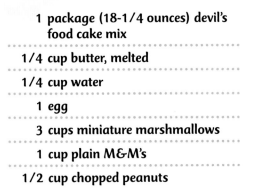

1 package (18-1/4 ounces) devil's food cake mix

1/4 cup butter, melted

1/4 cup water

1 egg

3 cups miniature marshmallows

1 cup plain M&M's

1/2 cup chopped peanuts

1. In a mixing bowl, combine dry cake mix, butter, water and egg; mix well. Press into a greased 13-in. x 9-in. x 2-in. baking pan.

2. Bake at 375° for 20-22 minutes or until a toothpick inserted near the center comes out clean. Sprinkle with marshmallows, M&M's and peanuts. Bake 2-3 minutes longer or until the marshmallows begin to melt. Cool on a wire rack before cutting. **Yield:** 3-1/2 dozen.

Snickers Cookies

~Kari Pease, Conconully, Washington

1 tube (18 ounces) refrigerated chocolate chip cookie dough

24 to 30 bite-size Snickers candy bars

Cut dough into 1/4-in.-thick slices. Place a candy bar on each slice and wrap dough around it. Place 2 in. apart on ungreased baking sheets. Bake at 350° for 8-10 minutes or until lightly browned. Cool on wire racks. **Yield:** 2 to 2-1/2 dozen.

Editor's Note: 2 cups of any chocolate chip cookie dough can be substituted for the refrigerated dough. Use 1 tablespoon of dough for each cookie.

Fudgy Fruit Dip

~Wilma Knobloch, Steen, Minnesota

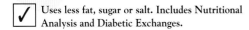

✓ Uses less fat, sugar or salt. Includes Nutritional Analysis and Diabetic Exchanges.

1/3 cup fat-free sugar-free hot fudge topping

1/3 cup fat-free vanilla yogurt

1-1/2 teaspoons orange juice concentrate

Fresh strawberries

In a bowl, combine fudge topping, yogurt and orange juice concentrate. Cover and refrigerate for at least 30 minutes. Serve with strawberries. **Yield:** about 1/2 cup.

Nutritional Analysis: One serving (2 tablespoons of dip) equals 67 calories, trace fat (trace saturated fat), trace cholesterol, 32 mg sodium, 15 g carbohydrate, trace fiber, 1 g protein. **Diabetic Exchanges:** 1/2 starch, 1/2 fruit.

Coconut Orange Cupcakes

~Donna Justin, Sparta, Wisconsin

1 cup sugar

2/3 cup vegetable oil

2 eggs

1 cup orange juice

3 cups all-purpose flour

1 tablespoon baking powder

1 teaspoon baking soda

3/4 teaspoon salt

1 can (11 ounces) mandarin oranges, drained

1 cup vanilla chips

TOPPING:

1 cup flaked coconut

1/3 cup sugar

2 tablespoons butter, melted

1. In a mixing bowl, combine the sugar, oil, eggs and orange juice; mix well. Combine dry ingredients; stir into orange juice mixture just until moistened. Fold in oranges and chips.

2. Fill greased or paper-lined muffin cups two-thirds full. Combine topping ingredients; sprinkle over cupcakes. Bake at 375° for 15-20 minutes or until golden brown. **Yield:** 2 dozen.

Creamy Center Cupcakes

~*Caroline Anderson, Waupaca, Wisconsin*

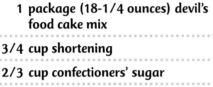

1 package (18-1/4 ounces) devil's
   food cake mix

3/4 cup shortening

2/3 cup confectioners' sugar

1 cup marshmallow creme

1 teaspoon vanilla extract

2 cans (16 ounces *each*) chocolate
   frosting

1. Prepare and bake cake according to package directions for cupcakes, using paper-lined muffin cups. Cool for 10 minutes before removing from pans to wire racks to cool completely.

2. Meanwhile, in a mixing bowl, cream shortening and sugar. Add marshmallow creme and vanilla; mix well.

3. Insert a very small pastry tip into a pastry or plastic bag; fill with cream filling. Insert tip halfway into the center of each cupcake and fill with a small amount. Frost with chocolate frosting. **Yield:** 2 dozen.

Candy Bar Pie

~*Sharlie Hanson, Tulsa, Oklahoma*

1 package (8 ounces) cream cheese,
   softened

1 carton (8 ounces) frozen whipped
   topping, thawed

4 Butterfinger candy bars
   (2.1 ounces *each*)

1 prepared graham cracker crust
   (9 inches)

In a small mixing bowl, beat the cream cheese until smooth. Fold in whipped topping. Crush the candy bars; fold 1 cup into cream cheese mixture. Spoon into crust. Sprinkle with remaining candy bar crumbs. Refrigerate for 2-4 hours before slicing. **Yield:** 6-8 servings.

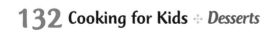

Mini Apple Pies

~Marsha Dingbaum, Aurora, California

1 tube (7-1/2 ounces) refrigerated
  biscuits
1 tart apple, peeled and finely
  chopped
1/4 cup raisins
3 tablespoons sugar
1 teaspoon ground cinnamon
2 tablespoons butter

1. Using a rolling pin, flatten each biscuit to a 3-in. to 4-in. circle. Combine the apple, raisins, sugar and cinnamon; place a tablespoonful on each biscuit. Dot with butter. Bring up sides of biscuit to enclose filling and pinch to seal.

2. Place in ungreased muffin cups. Bake at 375° for 11-13 minutes or until golden brown. **Yield:** 10 servings.

Crackle Cookies

~Ruth Cain, Hartselle, Alabama

1/2 cup sugar
1 egg
2 tablespoons vegetable oil
1 square (1 ounce) unsweetened chocolate, melted and cooled
1/2 teaspoon vanilla extract
1/2 cup all-purpose flour
1/2 to 3/4 teaspoon baking powder
1/8 teaspoon salt
Confectioners' sugar

1. In a mixing bowl, combine sugar, egg, oil, chocolate and vanilla; mix well. Combine flour, baking powder and salt; gradually add to creamed mixture and mix well. Chill dough for at least 2 hours.

2. With sugared hands, shape dough into 1-in. balls. Roll in confectioners' sugar. Place 2 in. apart on greased baking sheets. Bake at 350° for 10-12 minutes or until set. Remove to a wire rack to cool. **Yield:** about 1-1/2 dozen.

Watermelon Slice Cookies

~Sue Ann Benham, Valparaiso, Indiana

3/4 cup butter, softened

3/4 cup sugar

1 egg

1/2 teaspoon almond extract

2 cups all-purpose flour

1/4 teaspoon baking powder

1/8 teaspoon salt

Red and green gel food coloring

1/3 cup raisins

1 teaspoon sesame seeds

1. In a mixing bowl, cream butter and sugar. Beat in egg and extract. Combine the flour, baking powder and salt; gradually add to creamed mixture. Set aside 1 cup of dough. Tint remaining dough red; shape into a 3-1/2-in.-diameter log. Wrap in plastic wrap. Tint 1/3 cup of the reserved dough green; wrap in plastic wrap. Wrap remaining plain dough. Refrigerate for 2 hours or until firm.

2. On a lightly floured surface, roll plain dough into an 8-1/2-in. x 3-1/2-in. rectangle. Place red dough log on the end of a short side of the rectangle; roll up. Roll green dough into a 10-in. x 3-1/2-in. rectangle. Place red and white log on the end of a short side on green dough; roll up. Wrap in plastic wrap; refrigerate overnight.

3. Unwrap and cut into 3/16-in. slices (just less than 1/4 in.). Place 2 in. apart on ungreased baking sheets. Cut raisins into small pieces. Lightly press raisin bits and sesame seeds into red dough to resemble watermelon seeds. Bake at 350° for 9-11 minutes or until firm. Immediately cut cookies in half. Remove to wire racks to cool. **Yield:** about 3 dozen.

Puddin' Cones

~Edna Hoffman, Hebron, Indiana

1-1/2 cups cold milk

1 package (3.4 ounces) instant vanilla pudding mix

3 envelopes whipped topping mix

8 cake ice cream cones (about 3 inches)

Chopped nuts, jimmies and miniature color-coated baking chips *or* topping of your choice

In a mixing bowl, beat milk and pudding mix on low speed for 2 minutes. Blend in whipped topping mix; cover and refrigerate for at least 1 hour. Spoon 1/4 cup into each cone; sprinkle with toppings. **Yield:** 8 servings.

Cookie Lollipops

~Jessie Wiggers, Halstead, Kansas

1 package (12 ounces) vanilla chips

2 tablespoons shortening, *divided*

1 package (16 ounces) double-stuffed chocolate cream-filled sandwich cookies

32 wooden Popsicle or craft sticks

1 cup (6 ounces) semisweet chocolate chips

1. In a microwave or double boiler, melt vanilla chips and 1 tablespoon shortening; stir until smooth. Twist apart sandwich cookies. Dip the end of each Popsicle stick into melted chips; place on a cookie half and top with another half. Place cookies on a waxed paper-lined baking sheet; freeze for 15 minutes.

2. Reheat vanilla chip mixture again if necessary; dip frozen cookies into mixture until completely covered. Return to the baking sheet; freeze 30 minutes longer. Melt the chocolate chips and remaining shortening; stir until smooth. Drizzle over cookies. Store in an airtight container. **Yield:** 32 servings.

Cinnamon Brownies

~Christopher Wolf, Belvidere, Illinois

1-2/3 cups sugar

3/4 cup butter, melted

2 tablespoons strong brewed coffee

2 eggs

2 teaspoons vanilla extract

1-1/3 cups all-purpose flour

3/4 cup baking cocoa

1 tablespoon ground cinnamon

1/2 teaspoon baking powder

1/4 teaspoon salt

1 cup chopped walnuts

Confectioners' sugar

1. In a mixing bowl, beat the sugar, butter and coffee. Add eggs and vanilla. Combine the flour, cocoa, cinnamon, baking powder and salt; gradually add to the sugar mixture and mix well. Stir in walnuts.

2. Spread into a greased 13-in. x 9-in. x 2-in. baking pan. Bake at 350° for 18-22 minutes or until a toothpick inserted near the center comes out clean (do not overbake). Cool on a wire rack. Dust with confectioners' sugar. **Yield:** 2 dozen.

Tie-Dyed Cheesecake Bars

~Taste of Home Test Kitchen

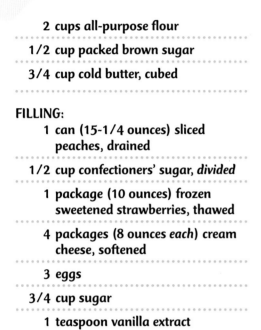

2 cups all-purpose flour

1/2 cup packed brown sugar

3/4 cup cold butter, cubed

FILLING:

1 can (15-1/4 ounces) sliced peaches, drained

1/2 cup confectioners' sugar, *divided*

1 package (10 ounces) frozen sweetened strawberries, thawed

4 packages (8 ounces *each*) cream cheese, softened

3 eggs

3/4 cup sugar

1 teaspoon vanilla extract

1. In a food processor, process the flour, brown sugar and butter until mixture resembles coarse crumbs. Press into a greased 15-in. x 10-in. x 1-in baking pan. Bake at 350° for 15 minutes.

2. In a blender or food processor, combine peaches and 1/4 cup confectioners' sugar; cover and process until smooth. Transfer to a bowl. Repeat with strawberries and remaining confectioners' sugar; set aside.

3. In a large mixing bowl, beat cream cheese until smooth. Add eggs, sugar and vanilla; beat until smooth. Pour over crust. Spoon 1/2 cup peach mixture over the cream cheese layer. Top with 1/2 cup strawberry mixture. With a knife, cut through cream cheese filling to swirl.

4. Bake at 350° for 30-35 minutes or until a knife comes out clean. Cool on a wire rack. Cut into bars; serve with remaining fruit mixtures if desired. Store in the refrigerator. **Yield:** 2 dozen.

Rocky Road Fudge Pops

~Karen Grant, Tulare, California

1 package (3.4 ounces) cook-and-serve chocolate pudding mix

2-1/2 cups milk

1/2 cup chopped peanuts

1/2 cup miniature semisweet chocolate chips

12 plastic cups (3 ounces *each*)

1/2 cup marshmallow creme

12 Popsicle sticks

1. In a large microwave-safe bowl, combine pudding mix and milk. Microwave, uncovered, on high for 6 to 7-1/2 minutes or until bubbly and slightly thickened, stirring every 2 minutes. Cool for 20 minutes, stirring several times.

2. Meanwhile, combine peanuts and chocolate chips; place about 2 tablespoons in each plastic cup. Stir marshmallow creme into pudding; spoon into cups. Insert Popsicle sticks; freeze. **Yield:** 12 servings.

Editor's Note: This recipe was tested in an 850-watt microwave.

Gumdrop Cereal Bars

~Laura Tryssenaar, Listowel, Ontario

5 cups Corn Pops cereal

1 cup gumdrops

4 cups miniature marshmallows

1/4 cup butter

1 teaspoon vanilla extract

Place cereal and gumdrops in a large bowl; set aside. In a microwave-safe bowl, heat the marshmallows and butter on high for 2 minutes; stir until melted. Stir in vanilla. Pour over cereal mixture and toss to coat. Spread into a greased 9-in. square pan. Cool on a wire rack. Cut with a buttered knife. **Yield:** 16 bars.

Editor's Note: This recipe was tested in an 850-watt microwave.

Brownie Turtles

~Taste of Home Test Kitchen

1 package brownie mix (13-inch x 9-inch pan size)

1/2 cup chopped pecans

32 pecan halves

16 butterscotch chips

Caramel ice cream topping

1. Prepare brownie mix according to package directions. Stir chopped pecans into batter. Fill eight greased miniature muffin cups and eight greased regular-size muffin cups two-thirds full. Bake at 350° for 10-12 for miniature brownies and 23-25 minutes for regular-size brownies or until a toothpick comes out with moist crumbs (do not overbake). Cool completely in pans on wire racks.

2. On eight dessert plates, place one regular-size brownie for the turtle's body and one small brownie for the head. Arrange four pecan halves around each body for feet. Insert butterscotch chips for eyes. Drizzle caramel topping over turtles. **Yield:** 8 servings.

Editor's Note: This recipe was tested with Betty Crocker supreme brownie mix.

Fried Egg Candy

~Melanie Hayes, Libby, Montana

- 1 package (15 ounces) pretzel sticks
- 1 package (12 ounces) vanilla *or* white chips
- 48 yellow M&M's

Place pretzel sticks on waxed paper in groups of two, leaving a small space between each. In a microwave-safe bowl, heat vanilla chips at 70% power until melted; stir until smooth. Drop by tablespoonfuls over each pair of pretzel sticks. For "yolks," place one or two M&M's in the center of each "egg." **Yield:** about 3-1/2 dozen.

Root Beer Float Cake

~Kat Thompson, Prineville, Oregon

- 1 package (18-1/4 ounces) white cake mix
- 1-3/4 cups cold root beer, *divided*
- 1/4 cup vegetable oil
- 2 eggs
- 1 envelope whipped topping mix

1. In a mixing bowl, combine dry cake mix, 1-1/4 cups root beer, oil and eggs. Beat on low speed for 2 minutes or stir by hand for 3 minutes. Pour into a greased 13-in. x 9-in. x 2-in. baking pan. Bake at 350° for 30-35 minutes or until a toothpick inserted near the center comes out clean. Cool completely on a wire rack.

2. In a mixing bowl, combine the whipped topping mix and remaining root beer. Beat until soft peaks form. Frost cake. Store in the refrigerator. **Yield:** 12-16 servings.

Pizza Cake

~Caroline Simzisko, Cordova, Tennessee

1 package (18-1/4 ounces) yellow cake mix

1 cup vanilla frosting

Red liquid *or* paste food coloring

3 squares (1 ounce *each*) white baking chocolate, grated

2 strawberry Fruit Roll-Ups

1. Prepare cake mix according to package directions. Pour the batter into two greased and floured 9-in. round baking pans. Bake at 350° for 20 minutes or until a toothpick inserted near the center comes out clean and cake is golden brown. Cool for 10 minutes before removing from pans to wire racks to cool completely.

2. Place each cake on a 10-in. serving platter. Combine the frosting and food coloring; spread over the top of each cake to within 1/2 in. of edges. Sprinkle with grated chocolate for cheese. Unroll Fruit Roll-Ups; use a 1-1/2-in. round cutter to cut into circles for pepperoni. Arrange on cakes. **Yield:** 2 cakes (6-8 servings each).

Cookies and Cream

~Teena Lang, Mt. Vernon, Ohio

1 package (12 ounces) rocky road *or* chocolate chocolate chip cookies

1 carton (8 ounces) frozen whipped topping, thawed

1/2 cup milk

1. Crumble one cookie and set aside. Spoon a fourth of the whipped topping into an 8-in. square pan. Place milk in a shallow bowl. Break remaining cookies in half; dip seven or eight halves into milk for about 30 seconds each. Place over whipped topping. Repeat layers twice.

2. Top with remaining whipped topping; sprinkle with the reserved cookie crumbs. Cover and refrigerate for 4 hours or overnight. **Yield:** 4-6 servings.

Peanut Butter Cup Cupcakes

~Heidi Harrington, Steuben, Maine

1/3 cup shortening

1/3 cup peanut butter

1-1/4 cups packed brown sugar

2 eggs

1 teaspoon vanilla extract

1-3/4 cups all-purpose flour

1-3/4 teaspoons baking powder

1 teaspoon salt

1 cup milk

16 miniature peanut butter cups

1. In a mixing bowl, cream the shortening, peanut butter and brown sugar. Add eggs and vanilla; mix well. Combine flour, baking powder and salt; add to creamed mixture alternately with milk.

2. Fill paper-lined muffin cups with 1/4 cup of batter. Press a peanut butter cup into the center of each until top edge is even with batter. Bake at 350° for 22-24 minutes or until a toothpick inserted on an angle toward the center comes out clean. **Yield:** 16 cupcakes.

No-Bake Bars

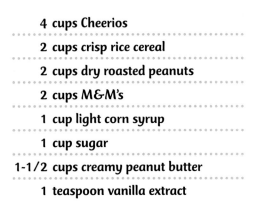

~Susie Wingert, Panama, Iowa

4 cups Cheerios

2 cups crisp rice cereal

2 cups dry roasted peanuts

2 cups M&M's

1 cup light corn syrup

1 cup sugar

1-1/2 cups creamy peanut butter

1 teaspoon vanilla extract

In a large bowl, combine the first four ingredients; set aside. In a saucepan, bring corn syrup and sugar to a boil, stirring frequently. Remove from the heat; stir in peanut butter and vanilla. Pour over cereal mixture and toss to coat evenly. Spread into a greased 15-in. x 10-in. x 1-in. baking pan. Cool. Cut into 3-in. x 3-in. bars. **Yield:** 15 bars.

Frozen Banana Pineapple Cups

~Alice Miller, Middlebury, Indiana

3 cups water	In a 2-qt. freezer container, combine all ingredients; mix well. Cover and freeze for 5 hours or overnight. Remove from the freezer 15 minutes before serving. **Yield:** 9-12 servings.

3 cups water

2-2/3 cups mashed ripe bananas
(5 to 6 medium)

1-1/2 cups sugar

1 can (20 ounces) crushed
pineapple, undrained

1 can (6 ounces) frozen orange
juice concentrate, thawed

In a 2-qt. freezer container, combine all ingredients; mix well. Cover and freeze for 5 hours or overnight. Remove from the freezer 15 minutes before serving. **Yield:** 9-12 servings.

Popcorn Candy Cake

~Roberta Uhl, Summerville, Oregon

1 package (16 ounces) miniature marshmallows

3/4 cup vegetable oil

1/2 cup butter

5 quarts popped popcorn

1 package (24 ounces) spiced gumdrops

1 cup salted peanuts

1. In a large saucepan, melt marshmallows, oil and butter until smooth. In a large bowl, combine popcorn, gumdrops and peanuts. Add marshmallow mixture and mix well. Press into a greased 10-in. tube pan. Cover and refrigerate for 5 hours or overnight.

2. Dip pan in hot water for 5-10 seconds to unmold. Slice cake with an electric or serrated knife. **Yield:** 16-18 servings.

Editor's Note: A two-piece tube pan is not recommended for this recipe.

Ice Cream Brownie Mountain

~Mirien Church, Aurora, Colorado

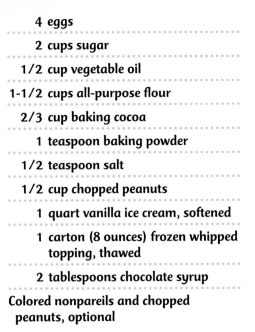

4 eggs

2 cups sugar

1/2 cup vegetable oil

1-1/2 cups all-purpose flour

2/3 cup baking cocoa

1 teaspoon baking powder

1/2 teaspoon salt

1/2 cup chopped peanuts

1 quart vanilla ice cream, softened

1 carton (8 ounces) frozen whipped topping, thawed

2 tablespoons chocolate syrup

Colored nonpareils and chopped peanuts, optional

1. In a mixing bowl, beat the eggs, sugar and oil. Combine flour, cocoa, baking powder and salt; gradually add to sugar mixture and mix well. Stir in peanuts. Spread into a greased 13-in. x 9-in. x 2-in. baking pan. Bake at 350° for 25-28 minutes or until a toothpick inserted near center comes out with moist crumbs (do not overbake). Cool on a wire rack.

2. Line a 2-1/2-qt. bowl with a double layer of plastic wrap. Break brownies into pieces about 2 in. square; set aside a third of the pieces. Line the bottom and sides of prepared bowl with remaining brownie pieces, pressing firmly to completely cover to within 1 in. of rim. Fill brownie-lined bowl with ice cream, pressing down firmly. Top with reserved brownie pieces, covering ice cream completely. Cover and freeze overnight.

3. To serve, uncover and invert onto a serving plate. Let stand for 10 minutes before removing bowl and plastic wrap. Spread whipped topping over top and sides of dessert; drizzle with chocolate syrup. Garnish with nonpareils and peanuts if desired. Cut into wedges with a sharp knife. **Yield:** 10-12 servings.

Chilly Peanut Butter Pie

~Marietta Slater, Augusta, Kansas

1 carton (8 ounces) frozen whipped topping, thawed, *divided*

1 graham cracker crust (9 inches)

1/2 cup strawberry jelly *or* jam

1 cup cold milk

1 package (3.4 ounces) instant vanilla pudding mix

1/2 cup peanut butter

1. Spread 1 cup whipped topping over the bottom of the crust. Drop jelly by tablespoonfuls onto topping; spread carefully. In a bowl, whisk milk and pudding mix until thickened. Add peanut butter; mix well. Fold in the remaining whipped topping. Spread over jelly.

2. Cover and freeze for 4 hours or until firm. Remove from the freezer 10 minutes before serving. **Yield:** 6-8 servings.

Chocolate Chip Cookie Tart

~Peg Gerhard, Latrobe, Pennsylvania

1 tube (18 ounces) refrigerated chocolate chip cookie dough

1 package (8 ounces) cream cheese, softened

2 tablespoons creamy peanut butter

1 tablespoon butter, softened

2 cups confectioners' sugar

1/4 cup milk chocolate chips, melted and cooled

1. Press cookie dough onto the bottom of an ungreased 9-in. springform pan. Bake at 350° for 20-24 minutes or until golden brown. Cool on a wire rack.

2. In a small mixing bowl, beat cream cheese, peanut butter and butter until smooth. Beat in confectioners' sugar. Remove sides of springform pan; place crust on a serving plate. Spread cream cheese mixture over crust to within 1/2 in. of edge. Drizzle with melted chocolate. Refrigerate for 1 hour or until set. **Yield:** 10-12 servings.

Homemade Fudge Pops

~Mary Detweiler, West Farmington, Ohio

1/4 cup cornstarch

1/8 teaspoon salt

3 cups milk

1/2 cup light corn syrup

1 teaspoon vanilla extract

1 cup milk chocolate chips

12 disposable plastic cups (3 ounces)

12 Popsicle sticks

1. In a heavy saucepan, combine the cornstarch and salt. Gradually stir in milk until smooth. Stir in corn syrup and vanilla. Bring to a boil; cook and stir for 1 minute or until thickened. Reduce heat; stir in chocolate chips until melted. Pour into cups.

2. Cover each cup with heavy-duty foil; insert sticks through foil. Place in a 13-in. x 9-in. x 2-in. pan. Freeze until firm. Remove foil and cups before serving. **Yield:** 1 dozen.

Kids PARTY Food

·:·Contents·:·

Kids Party Food

Birthdays

Birthday Blocks

~Ethel Ledbetter, Canton, North Carolina

POUND CAKE:
1-1/2 cups butter, softened

1 package (8 ounces) cream cheese, softened

3 cups sugar

6 eggs, room temperature

3 cups all-purpose flour

1 teaspoon coconut extract

1 teaspoon vanilla extract

1/2 teaspoon lemon extract

FROSTING/DECORATING:
1/3 cup butter, softened

9 cups confectioners' sugar, *divided*

1/2 cup milk

3 teaspoons vanilla extract

Additional milk

Tinted icing and pastry bag or tubes of tinted icing

1. In a large mixing bowl, cream butter and cream cheese. Gradually add the sugar, beating until light and fluffy, about 5-7 minutes. Add eggs, one at a time, beating well after each addition. Gradually add flour; beat just until blended. Stir in extracts. Pour into two greased and floured 9-in. x 5-in. x 3-in. loaf pans. Bake at 325° for 1 hour and 20 minutes or until a toothpick inserted near center comes out clean. Cool in pan 15 minutes before removing to a wire rack; cool completely.

2. For frosting, cream butter in a mixing bowl until fluffy. Gradually beat in 4 cups of sugar. Slowly add milk and vanilla. Beat in remaining sugar. Add additional milk, 1 tablespoon at a time, until frosting reaches desired spreading consistency; set aside.

3. To make building blocks, cut each cake in half, then cut each half into four blocks for a total of 16 blocks. Gently trim crusts of each; blocks should measure 2 in. x 2 in. Frost sides and top of blocks. Smooth frosting using a warm spatula. Using tinted icing, decorate with letters and numbers. Carefully stack blocks on a serving platter. **Yield:** 16 servings.

Xylophone Cakes

~Michele Cascais, Mendham, New Jersey

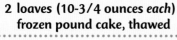

2 loaves (10-3/4 ounces *each*)
   frozen pound cake, thawed

Yellow, green, orange and red gel food
   coloring

1 can (16 ounces) vanilla frosting

M&M miniature baking bits

28 miniature marshmallows

28 pretzel sticks

1. Cut each cake widthwise into seven 1-in. slices. Trim a diagonal slice from the long sides of each slice, angling slightly, leaving 1 in. wide at a short end.

2. Use food coloring to tint the frosting. Carefully spread or pipe stripes on cake slices; top with miniature baking bits. For mallets, press a miniature marshmallow into one end of each pretzel stick. **Yield:** 14 cakes.

One-Bowl Chocolate Cake

~Coleen Martin, Brookfield, Wisconsin

2 cups all-purpose flour

2 cups sugar

1/2 cup baking cocoa

2 teaspoons baking soda

1 teaspoon baking powder

1/2 teaspoon salt

1 cup vegetable oil

1 cup buttermilk

2 eggs

1 cup hot water

Frosting of your choice

Colored sprinkles, optional

1. In a large bowl, combine dry ingredients. Stir in oil, buttermilk and eggs. Add water and stir until combined. Pour into a greased 13-in. x 9-in. x 2-in. baking pan.

2. Bake at 350° for 35-38 minutes or until a toothpick inserted near the center comes out clean. Cool completely. Frost. Decorate with sprinkles if desired. **Yield:** 12-16 servings.

Kite Birthday Cake

~Mildred Sharp, Jackson, Michigan

1/2 cup shortening

1-1/2 cups sugar

2 eggs

1 teaspoon vanilla extract

1 cup milk

1 tablespoon vinegar

2-2/3 cups all-purpose flour

2 teaspoons baking powder

1 teaspoon baking soda

1 teaspoon salt

1 cup mashed ripe bananas
(about 2 medium)

FROSTING:

3 tablespoons plus 2 teaspoons
cake flour

3/4 cup milk

6 tablespoons butter, softened

6 tablespoons shortening

3/4 cup sugar

1-1/2 teaspoons vanilla extract

Soft gel paste food coloring—pink,
yellow, purple and blue

Pastry tips—round tip #3 and #7

1. In a mixing bowl, cream shortening and sugar. Add eggs, one at a time, beating well after each. Stir in vanilla. In a bowl, combine milk and vinegar; set aside. Combine flour, baking powder, baking soda and salt; add to creamed mixture alternately with milk mixture and bananas. Pour into a greased 13-in. x 9-in. x 2-in. baking pan. Bake at 350° for 35-40 minutes or until a toothpick inserted near the center comes out clean. Cool on a wire rack for 10 minutes; invert onto rack to cool completely. Transfer to a 15-in. x 12-in. covered board.

2. In a saucepan, combine flour and milk until smooth. Bring to a boil; cook and stir for 2 minutes or until thickened. Cool. In a mixing bowl, cream butter, shortening, sugar and vanilla. Beat in flour mixture until thickened.

3. Place 2 tablespoons frosting each in three bowls; tint one pink, one yellow and one purple. Place 3/4 cup frosting in a bowl; tint blue. Frost top of cake blue and sides white. Form three clouds with some of the white frosting; set remaining white frosting aside.

4. Draw one small kite and one medium kite on waxed paper and cut out. With a sharp knife, trace two of each kite pattern on the blue frosting. Fill in kites with some of the purple, pink and yellow frosting. Cut a small hole in the corner of a pastry or plastic bag; insert round tip #3 (or pipe directly from bag). Fill bag with remaining purple frosting; pipe kite strings on the two small kites. Repeat with yellow and pink frosting on medium kites. Pipe colored bows on the top of kite strings.

5. Cut a small hole in the corner of a pastry or plastic bag; insert round tip #3. Fill bag with remaining white frosting; pipe crossbars and an outline around each kite. Using round tip #7, pipe a border around top edge of cake. **Yield:** 12 servings.

Editor's Note: Use of a coupler ring will allow you to easily change tips for different designs.

Checkerboard Birthday Cake

~Taste of Home Test Kitchen

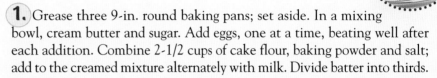

1 cup butter, softened

2 cups sugar

4 eggs

3 cups cake flour, *divided*

4 teaspoons baking powder

1/4 teaspoon salt

1 cup milk

1 square (1 ounce) unsweetened chocolate, melted and cooled

1/2 teaspoon vanilla extract

1/2 teaspoon almond extract

Red liquid food coloring

1/2 teaspoon lemon extract

Yellow liquid food coloring

FROSTING:

6 tablespoons butter, softened

6-1/2 to 7-1/2 cups confectioners' sugar, *divided*

5 squares (1 ounce *each*) unsweetened chocolate, melted and cooled

3/4 cup milk

1-1/2 teaspoons vanilla extract

1. Grease three 9-in. round baking pans; set aside. In a mixing bowl, cream butter and sugar. Add eggs, one at a time, beating well after each addition. Combine 2-1/2 cups of cake flour, baking powder and salt; add to the creamed mixture alternately with milk. Divide batter into thirds.

2. To one portion, fold in melted chocolate and vanilla. To second portion, fold in 1/4 cup flour, almond extract and 3-4 drops red food coloring. To third portion, fold in lemon extract, 3-4 drops yellow food coloring and remaining flour.

3. Spoon a ring of chocolate batter around edge of one prepared pan; spoon a ring of pink batter inside chocolate ring and fill center with yellow batter. Spoon a ring of yellow batter around the edge of the second pan; add a chocolate middle ring and a pink center. Spoon a ring of pink batter around edge of third pan; add a yellow middle ring and a chocolate center.

4. Bake at 350° for 20-25 minutes or until a toothpick inserted near the center comes out clean. Cool for 10 minutes before removing from pans to wire racks to cool completely.

5. For frosting, in a mixing bowl, cream butter and 2 cups confectioners' sugar. Beat in melted chocolate until smooth. Add milk and vanilla. Beat in enough of the remaining confectioners' sugar until frosting achieves spreading consistency. Spread between layers and over top and sides of cake. **Yield:** 12-14 servings.

Tea Party Cake

~Wanda Ward, Louisville, Mississippi

- **1 package (16 ounces) pound cake mix**
- **2 individual round sponge cakes (about 3 inches)**
- **1 can (12 ounces) vanilla frosting**
- **Green food coloring**
- **6 prepared rose decorations**
- **Wooden toothpicks or skewers**
- **1 tube yellow decorating icing with star tip**

1. Prepare cake batter according to package directions. Pour into a greased and floured 1-1/2-qt. ovenproof bowl (about 6-1/2 in. wide x 4 in. tall). Bake at 350° for 65-70 minutes or until a toothpick inserted near the center comes out clean. Cool for 10 minutes before removing from bowl to a wire rack; cool completely.

2. Cut a 1-1/2-in. circle from the center of one sponge cake; discard center. Cut the remaining portion into three pieces, one small, one medium and one large (see diagram below). Freeze until firm.

3. To assemble, place bowl-shaped cake upside down on a serving plate for teapot. For lid, trim the second sponge cake to desired size; place on top of pot. Tint frosting green; spread over teapot and lid. Place prepared roses on sides of cake.

4. For the knob, frost the small frozen sponge cake piece; attach to lid with a toothpick. For spout, trim medium piece to desired size, cutting bottom end at an angle to fit flat against teapot; frost and attach to front of pot with toothpicks. For handle, trim ends of large piece at an angle; frost and attach to back of pot with toothpicks.

5. With yellow icing, pipe a star border around bottom of teapot, lid and knob. **Yield:** 8-10 servings.

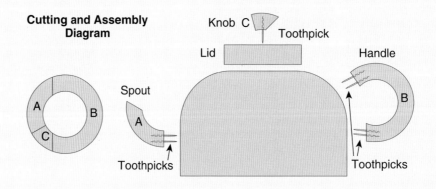

Cutting and Assembly Diagram

'Hoppy' Frog Cake

~Taste of Home Test Kitchen

3/4 cup butter, softened

1-1/4 cups sugar

3 eggs

1 teaspoon vanilla extract

2-1/2 cups all-purpose flour

3 teaspoons baking powder

1/4 teaspoon salt

1 cup milk

FROSTING:

2 tablespoons all-purpose flour

1 cup milk

1/2 cup butter, softened

1/2 cup shortening

1 cup sugar

1 teaspoon vanilla extract

2 Twinkies

2 milk chocolate M&M's

Green paste *or* gel food coloring

Red shoestring licorice

1. In a large mixing bowl, cream butter and sugar. Beat in the eggs and vanilla. Combine the flour, baking powder and salt; add to creamed mixture alternately with milk. Fill 12 greased muffin cups two-thirds full. Pour the remaining batter into a greased 9-in. round baking pan.

2. Bake cupcakes at 350° for 20-25 minutes and cake for 25-30 minutes or until a toothpick inserted near center comes out clean. Cool cupcakes for 5 minutes before removing from pan to a wire rack. Cool cake for 10 minutes before removing from pan to a wire rack. Cool completely.

3. To assemble, place the 9-in. cake in the center of a 15-in. x 13-in. covered board. Place two cupcakes above the cake for eyes. Arrange Twinkies below the cake for legs. For feet, cut one cupcake in half, using a zigzag cut. Place each half with the rounded edge touching a Twinkie. (Save remaining cupcakes for another use.)

4. For frosting, whisk flour and milk in a small saucepan until smooth. Bring to a boil; cook and stir for 2 minutes or until thickened. Cool. In a small mixing bowl, cream butter, shortening, sugar and vanilla. Beat in milk mixture until sugar is dissolved, about 4 minutes.

5. Use 1/3 cup white frosting to frost the bottom two-thirds of eyes; add M&M's for pupils. Tint 1/3 cup frosting dark green; set aside. Tint remaining frosting light green; spread over eyelids and over the top and sides of the rest of frog.

6. Cut a hole in the corner of a pastry or plastic bag. Insert round tip #5 and add dark green frosting. Outline the eyes, head, legs and feet. Arrange one long licorice piece for the mouth. Place two 1-in. licorice pieces at the ends of the mouth. **Yield:** 12-15 servings.

Happy Clown Cake

~Taste of Home Test Kitchen

1 package (18-1/4 ounces) yellow cake mix

1 cup flaked coconut, *divided*

Yellow, blue, green and red liquid food coloring

1 package (5 ounces) red shoestring licorice

1 can (16 ounces) vanilla frosting

2 miniature peanut butter cups

1 package (2.17 ounces) Skittles bite-size candies

1. Prepare cake batter according to package directions. Fill 12 paper-lined muffin cups two-thirds full. Pour remaining batter into a greased 9-in. round baking pan. Bake cake and cupcakes according to package directions. Cool for 10 minutes before removing from pans to wire racks to cool completely.

2. Place 1/2 cup coconut in a plastic bag; sprinkle 5-6 drops of yellow food coloring into bag and shake until color is evenly distributed. Repeat with 1/4 cup coconut and blue coloring, then with remaining coconut and green coloring. Reserve one licorice piece for mouth; cut remaining pieces into 2-in. to 3-in. pieces for hair.

3. Frost round cake with vanilla frosting; place on a large platter or covered board (about 22 in. x 15 in.). Press peanut butter cups upside down in place for eyes. Form long licorice piece into mouth and press into frosting (insert a small piece for smile if desired).

4. Remove liner from one cupcake and cut the top off. Cut the top in half again and press into sides of frosted cake for ears. Tint 2 tablespoons of frosting with red food coloring; frost bottom half of cupcake and press in place for nose.

5. Frost all remaining cupcakes. Remove liners from two cupcakes and cut in half; sprinkle with green coconut. Press flat sides against top of cake to form hat brim. Sprinkle five cupcakes with yellow coconut and one with blue coconut; stack in a pyramid on top of brim to make the hat.

6. Push ends of small licorice pieces into frosting for hair. Place remaining cupcakes at bottom of cake to make a bow tie; decorate those cupcakes with Skittles. **Yield:** 16-20 servings.

Buggy Birthday Cake

~LaVonne Hegland, St. Michael, Minnesota

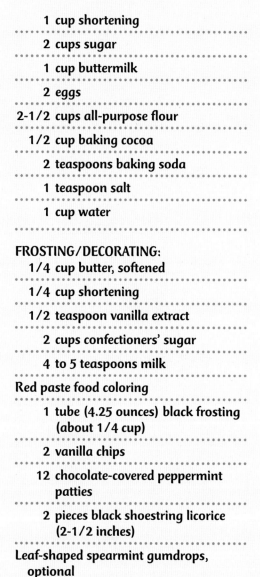

1 cup shortening

2 cups sugar

1 cup buttermilk

2 eggs

2-1/2 cups all-purpose flour

1/2 cup baking cocoa

2 teaspoons baking soda

1 teaspoon salt

1 cup water

FROSTING/DECORATING:

1/4 cup butter, softened

1/4 cup shortening

1/2 teaspoon vanilla extract

2 cups confectioners' sugar

4 to 5 teaspoons milk

Red paste food coloring

1 tube (4.25 ounces) black frosting
(about 1/4 cup)

2 vanilla chips

12 chocolate-covered peppermint
patties

2 pieces black shoestring licorice
(2-1/2 inches)

**Leaf-shaped spearmint gumdrops,
optional**

1. In a mixing bowl, cream shortening and sugar. Beat in milk and eggs. Combine flour, cocoa, baking soda and salt; add to the creamed mixture alternately with water. Pour into a greased and floured 4-qt. oven-proof bowl. Bake at 350° for 80-90 minutes (covering with foil halfway through baking time) or until a toothpick inserted near the center comes out clean. Cool for 10 minutes before removing from bowl to a wire rack to cool completely.

2. For frosting, cream butter, shortening and vanilla in a mixing bowl. Gradually beat in the sugar and enough milk to achieve a spreading consistency. Add food coloring. Set 3 tablespoons of frosting aside.

3. Place the cake on a serving platter. Frost with remaining frosting, leaving an 8-1/2-in. x 6-in. x 6-in. triangle of cake unfrosted. Frost the triangle with some of the black frosting. Fill a small bag with remaining black frosting; cut a small hole in corner of bag. Pipe a line from the tip of the triangle over the top of the cake to the other side, creating wings. With the same frosting, outline the edge of the triangle. For the eyes, pipe a 1/4-in. black dot on the flat side of each vanilla chip; position the chips on black triangle and press gently into frosting.

4. Randomly place peppermint patties over red frosting for ladybug's spots; press down gently. Fill a small bag with reserved red frosting; cut a small hole in corner of bag. Pipe a smile under eyes. Insert licorice pieces above eyes for antennae. Place gumdrops around the edge of the platter if desired. **Yield:** 12-16 servings.

Beehive Cake

~Sheila Bradshaw, Columbus, Ohio

1 package (18-1/4 ounces) spice cake mix

1-1/4 cups water

3 eggs

1/2 cup honey

1/3 cup vegetable oil

1 can (16 ounces) vanilla frosting

9 to 10 drops yellow food coloring

1 chocolate wafer (2-1/2 inches)

1. In a large mixing bowl, beat cake mix, water, eggs, honey and oil on low speed for 2 minutes. Grease and flour a 6-oz. and a 10-oz. custard cup and a 1-1/2-qt. round baking dish. Pour 1/3 cup batter into the 6-oz. cup, 1 cup batter into the 10-oz. cup and the remaining batter into the baking dish.

2. Bake the small cake at 350° for 30-35 minutes, the medium cake for 40-45 minutes and the large cake for 55-60 minutes or until a toothpick inserted near the center comes out clean. Cool for 15 minutes before removing from dishes to wire racks to cool completely.

3. In a mixing bowl, beat frosting and food coloring. Place large cake on a serving plate; spread with frosting. Top with medium cake; frost. Add small cake; frost top and sides of entire cake. Using a wooden spoon and beginning at bottom of cake, make circles in frosting around cake to form the beehive. Position chocolate wafer at the base for the entrance. **Yield:** 10-12 servings.

Treasure Chest Birthday Cake

~Sharon Hanson, Franklin, Tennessee

2 packages (18-1/4 ounces *each*) chocolate cake mix

1-1/3 cups butter, softened

8 squares (1 ounce *each*) unsweetened chocolate, melted and cooled

6 teaspoons vanilla extract

7-1/2 to 8 cups confectioners' sugar

1/3 to 1/2 cup milk

5 wooden skewers (three 4 inches, two 7-1/2 inches)

Foil-covered heavy corrugated cardboard (12 inches x 7-1/2 inches)

Candy necklaces, foil-covered chocolate coins, candy pacifiers *or* candies of your choice

2 pieces berry tie-dye Fruit Roll-Ups

1. In two batches, prepare and bake cakes according to package directions, using two greased and floured 13-in. x 9-in. x 2-in. baking pans. Cool for 10 minutes; remove from pans to cool on wire racks.

2. In a large mixing bowl, cream butter; beat in chocolate, vanilla, confectioners' sugar and enough milk to achieve spreading consistency. Center one cake on a 16-in. x 12-in. covered board; frost top. Top with remaining cake; frost top and sides of cake. With a metal spatula, smooth frosting to resemble boards.

3. For chest lid, insert 4-in. skewers equally spaced 6 in. into one long side of corrugated cardboard lid. Frost top of lid. Cut a small hole in the corner of a pastry or plastic bag; insert star tip #21. Pipe a shell border on edges of lid and for handles on sides of chest.

4. Place one 7-1/2-in. skewer on each side of cake top, about 3-1/2 in. from back of chest. Position lid over cake; gently insert short skewers into cake about 1 in. from back of chest. Rest lid on long skewers.

5. Arrange candy in chest. Cut a small keyhole from a fruit roll-up; center on front of cake. Position strips of fruit roll-ups in front and back of chest. **Yield:** 14-16 servings.

Snowflake Cake

~Lynne Peterson, Salt Lake City, Utah

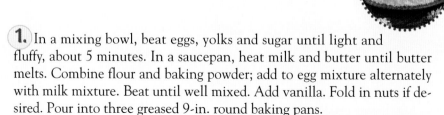

2 eggs plus 4 egg yolks

1-1/2 cups sugar

1 cup milk

1/2 cup butter

2-1/2 cups all-purpose flour

1 tablespoon baking powder

1 teaspoon vanilla extract

1/2 cup chopped nuts, optional

FROSTING:

1-3/4 cups sugar

1/2 cup water

4 egg whites

1/2 teaspoon cream of tartar

1 teaspoon vanilla extract

2 cups flaked coconut

1. In a mixing bowl, beat eggs, yolks and sugar until light and fluffy, about 5 minutes. In a saucepan, heat milk and butter until butter melts. Combine flour and baking powder; add to egg mixture alternately with milk mixture. Beat until well mixed. Add vanilla. Fold in nuts if desired. Pour into three greased 9-in. round baking pans.

2. Bake at 350° for 15-18 minutes or until a toothpick inserted near center comes out clean. Cool in pans 10 minutes before removing to a wire rack to cool completely.

3. For frosting, in a saucepan, bring sugar and water to a boil. Boil 3-4 minutes or until a candy thermometer reads 242° (firm-ball stage). Meanwhile, beat egg whites and cream of tartar in a mixing bowl until foamy. Slowly pour in hot sugar mixture and continue to beat on high for 6-8 minutes or until stiff peaks form. Add vanilla.

4. Frost the tops of two cake layers and sprinkle with coconut; stack on a cake plate with plain layer on top. Frost sides and top of cake; sprinkle with coconut. Refrigerate for several hours. **Yield:** 12-16 servings.

Elephant Cake

~Kristen Proulx, Canton, New York

1 package (18-1/4 ounces) yellow cake mix

1 package (18-1/4 ounces) devil's food cake mix

1-1/2 cups shortening

1-1/2 cups butter, softened

12 cups confectioners' sugar

1 tablespoon vanilla extract

4 to 7 tablespoons milk

Black and blue paste food coloring

1. Line two 9-in. round baking pans and one 13-in. x 9-in. x 2-in. baking pan with waxed paper; grease the paper. Prepare both cake batters and bake according to package directions, using the 9-in. pans for the yellow cake and the 13-in. x 9-in. pan for the chocolate. Cool 10 minutes; remove from pans to wire racks to cool completely. Level cake tops if necessary.

2. Referring to Fig. 1 (below left) and using a serrated knife, cut out a trunk and two feet from one yellow cake. Referring to Fig. 3, cut out an ear and tail from second yellow cake. (Discard leftover cake pieces or save for another use.)

3. Center chocolate cake on a 28-in. x 16-in. covered board. Referring to Fig. 2, position trunk along left bottom edge of cake and tail on right side. Place feet at bottom corners of cake. Place ear 2 in. from left side of cake.

4. For frosting, in a large mixing bowl, cream shortening and butter until fluffy. Gradually add the confectioners' sugar, beating well. Add vanilla and enough milk to achieve a spreading consistency. Tint 1/4 cup of frosting black; set aside. Set aside 1/2 cup white frosting. Tint remaining frosting blue-gray, using small amounts of black and blue food coloring. Spread 2 cups of the blue-gray frosting over top and sides of cake.

5. Trace a 1-1/2-in. x 1-1/4-in. oval for the eye. Cut a small hole in the corner of a plastic bag; insert round tip #4. Fill bag with black frosting. Outline eye and fill in pupil; pipe eyelashes and mouth. Using star tip #25 and reserved white frosting, pipe stars to fill in eye; add nostril and toes.

6. With blue-gray frosting and star tip #16, pipe stars over top and sides of elephant. **Yield:** 24-30 servings.

Fig. 1

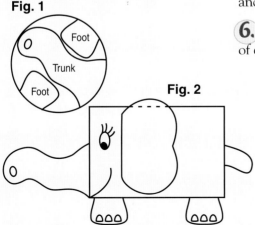

Fig. 2

Fig. 3

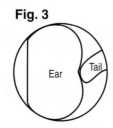

Volcano Cake

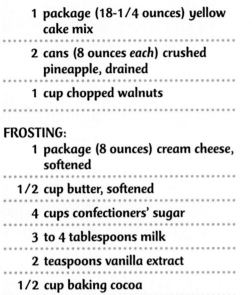

~*Carol Wakley, North East, Pennsylvania*

1 package (18-1/4 ounces) yellow cake mix

2 cans (8 ounces *each*) crushed pineapple, drained

1 cup chopped walnuts

FROSTING:

1 package (8 ounces) cream cheese, softened

1/2 cup butter, softened

4 cups confectioners' sugar

3 to 4 tablespoons milk

2 teaspoons vanilla extract

1/2 cup baking cocoa

Orange and red food coloring

1. Prepare cake batter according to package directions. Stir in pineapple and walnuts. Pour 2 cups into a greased 9-in. round baking pan and 2 cups into a greased 8-in. round baking pan. Pour remaining batter into a greased 1-1/2-qt. ovenproof bowl.

2. Bake the layer cakes at 350° for 18-22 minutes or until a toothpick inserted near the center comes out clean. Bake the bowl cake for 35-40 minutes or until a toothpick comes out clean. Cool for 10 minutes before removing from pans to wire racks to cool completely.

3. In a mixing bowl, beat cream cheese and butter. Add confectioners' sugar alternately with milk. Beat in vanilla. Set aside 3/4 cup frosting. Add cocoa to the remaining frosting; beat until smooth. Place the 9-in. layer on a serving plate; frost with chocolate frosting. Top with 8-in. layer and bowl cake, frosting between layers. Spread remaining chocolate frosting over top and sides of cake.

4. Divide reserved white frosting in half; tint half orange and half red. Drop by spoonfuls over the top and down the sides of cake. **Yield:** 12-14 servings.

Cupcakes with Whipped Cream Frosting

~*Taste of Home Test Kitchen*

1 package (18-1/4 ounces) cake mix

1-1/4 teaspoons unflavored gelatin

5 teaspoons cold water

1-1/4 cups heavy whipping cream

5 tablespoons confectioners' sugar

1/4 teaspoon vanilla extract

Red and yellow food coloring

1. Prepare and bake cake mix according to package directions for cupcakes. Cool on wire racks. In a saucepan, sprinkle gelatin over water; let stand for 1 minute to soften. Cook and stir over low heat until gelatin is dissolved. Remove from the heat; cool. In a mixing bowl, beat cream until soft peaks form. Add sugar, vanilla and gelatin mixture; beat until well combined.

2. Set aside 1 cup for decorating. Spread remaining frosting over tops of cupcakes. Divide reserved frosting in half; tint one portion pink and the other yellow. Use a toothpick to outline shape of heart, flower or sunburst on tops of cupcakes. Use medium star tip to pipe pink or yellow stars along outline. Fill in shape with piped stars as desired. **Yield:** 2 dozen.

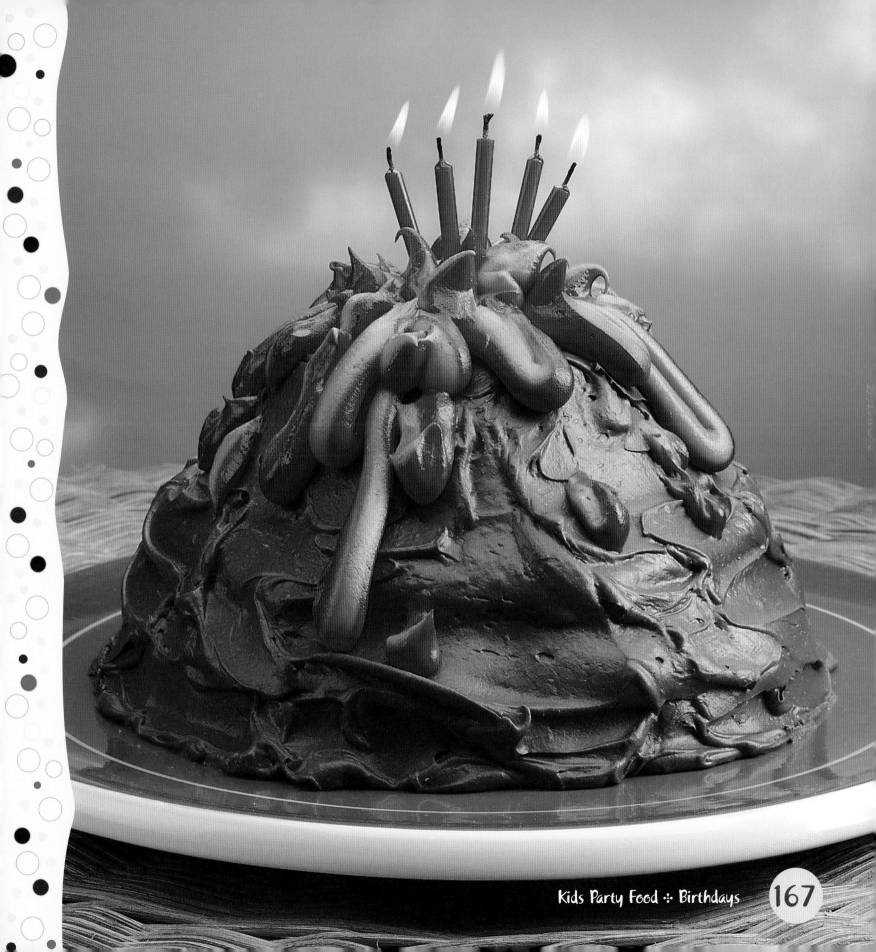

:Christmas:.

Sugar Cone Spruce Trees

~Carla Harris, Trenton, Tennessee

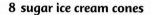

8 sugar ice cream cones

1 can (16 ounces) vanilla frosting, *divided*

1/2 cup confectioners' sugar

Green gel food coloring

Assorted candy decorations

1. Using a serrated knife, carefully score and cut ice cream cones to desired heights. In a small bowl, combine 3/4 cup frosting and confectioners' sugar; tint green. Set remaining frosting aside.

2. Cut a hole in the corner of a pastry or plastic bag; insert star tip #77. Fill with green frosting. Pipe frosting in overlapping rows over cones. Decorate with candies. When frosting on trees is dry, spread white frosting over a large serving platter to resemble snow. Arrange trees on frosted platter. **Yield:** 8 trees.

Sledding Snacks

~Taste of Home Test Kitchen

3 whole graham crackers (about 5 inches x 2-1/2 inches)

1/2 cup vanilla frosting

24 miniature candy canes

Assorted candy decorations

12 pieces red shoestring licorice (12 inches *each*)

Break or cut each graham cracker along perforations into four pieces. Spread a small amount of frosting over both sides of crackers. Immediately press two candy canes into frosting on one side; press assorted decorations into the other side. Let stand until set. Tie ends of licorice together and loop around candy canes. **Yield:** 1 dozen.

Peanut Butter Christmas Mice

~Nancy Rowse, Bella Vista, Arkansas

1 cup creamy peanut butter

1/2 cup butter, softened

1/2 cup sugar

1/2 cup packed brown sugar

1 egg

1 teaspoon vanilla extract

1-1/2 cups all-purpose flour

1/2 teaspoon baking soda

1/2 cup peanut halves

2 tablespoons green and red M&M miniature baking bits

4 teaspoons miniature semisweet chocolate chips

Cake decorator holly leaf and berry candies

60 to 66 pieces red shoestring licorice (2 inches each)

1. In a large mixing bowl, cream peanut butter, butter, sugar and brown sugar. Beat in egg and vanilla. Combine the flour and baking soda; gradually add to the creamed mixture. Refrigerate for 1 hour or until easy to handle.

2. Roll into 1-in. balls. Place 2 in. apart on ungreased baking sheets. Pinch each ball at one end to taper. Insert two peanut halves in center of each ball for ears. Add one M&M baking bit for nose and two chocolate chips for eyes. Arrange holly and berry candies in front of one ear.

3. Bake at 350° for 8-10 minutes or until set. Gently insert one licorice piece into each warm cookie for tail. Remove to wire racks to cool completely. **Yield:** about 5 dozen.

Christmas Wreaths

~Taste of Home Test Kitchen

20 large marshmallows

2 tablespoons butter, cubed

Green food coloring

3 cups cornflakes

72 red M&M miniature baking bits

1. In a microwave-safe bowl, combine the marshmallows and butter. Microwave, uncovered, on high for 1 minute or until butter is melted and marshmallows are puffed. Add the food coloring; mix well. Stir in the cornflakes.

2. Shape into 3-in. wreaths on a waxed paper-lined baking sheet. Immediately press M&M's in three clusters of three for berries. Let stand until set. **Yield:** 8 wreaths.

Santa Claus Cookies

~Mary Kaufenberg, Shakopee, Minnesota

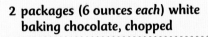

2 packages (6 ounces *each*) white baking chocolate, chopped

1 package (1 pound) Nutter Butter sandwich cookies

Red colored sugar

32 vanilla *or* white chips

64 miniature semisweet chocolate chips

32 red-hot candies

1. In a heavy saucepan over low heat, melt the white chocolate, stirring occasionally. Dip one end of each cookie into melted chocolate. Place on wire racks. For Santa's hat, sprinkle red sugar on top part of chocolate. Press one vanilla chip off-center on hat for pom-pom; let stand until set.

2. Dip other end of each cookie into melted chocolate for beard, leaving center of cookie uncovered. Place on wire racks. With a dab of melted chocolate, attach semisweet chips for eyes and a red-hot for nose. Place on waxed paper until chocolate sets. **Yield:** 32 cookies.

Candy Christmas Tree

~Kathryn Luna, Dana Point, California

1 cup vanilla frosting

Green liquid *or* paste food coloring

1 Styrofoam cone (12 inches high)

15 hard peppermint candies

15 hard spearmint candies

19 large red gumdrops

19 large green gumdrops

25 to 35 pieces crimped ribbon candy

23 pieces cut rock candy

1. Tint frosting green. Place cone on a 9-in. plate; frost the sides and top of cone. Starting at the bottom, alternate peppermint and spearmint candies around the cone in a single row. Alternate red and green gumdrops in a row above candies.

2. Arrange remaining candies in rows around the cone until reaching the top. Position a mint candy on the tip of the cone; top with a gumdrop. **Yield:** 1 tree.

Snowman Party Stew

~Taste of Home Test Kitchen

1 pound ground beef

1 package (16 ounces) frozen vegetables for stew, *divided*

1 can (10-1/4 ounces) beef gravy

2 cups mashed potatoes (prepared with a small amount of milk)

16 whole black peppercorns

1/4 cup ketchup

1. In a skillet, cook beef over medium heat until no longer pink; drain. Remove 24 peas and one carrot chunk from the stew vegetables; set aside. Add the remaining vegetables to beef. Cook until vegetables are thawed. Add gravy; mix well. Pour into an ungreased 9-in. pie plate. Top with eight mashed potato snowmen, using 1 tablespoon of potatoes for each head and 3 tablespoons for each body.

2. Bake, uncovered, at 350° for 20 minutes. Meanwhile, with a sharp knife, cut the reserved carrot into eight strips. Insert one strip into each snowman for a nose. Place three reserved peas on each for buttons. Add peppercorns for eyes. Drizzle ketchup between head and body to form a scarf. **Yield:** 6-8 servings.

Editor's Note: If serving small children, remove the peppercorns.

Cauliflower Snowman

~Taste of Home Test Kitchen

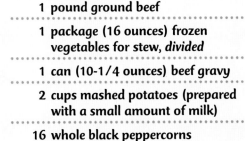

6 cups cauliflowerets

1/4 cup diced white onion

1/4 cup butter

1/3 cup all-purpose flour

2 cups milk

1 cup (4 ounces) shredded Swiss cheese

1 teaspoon salt

1/4 teaspoon garlic salt

1/4 teaspoon white pepper

10 whole ripe olives

1 baby carrot

1. In a large saucepan, cook cauliflower in a small amount of water for 6-7 minutes or until crisp-tender; drain well.

2. In a medium saucepan, saute onion in butter for 2 minutes. Stir in flour until blended; gradually add milk. Bring to a boil; boil for 2 minutes, stirring constantly. Remove from the heat; stir in cheese until melted. Add salt, garlic salt and pepper.

3. Place half of the cauliflower in a greased 2-1/2-qt. baking dish; top with half of the sauce. Repeat. Bake, uncovered, at 350° for 20 minutes or until bubbly. Add olives for eyes and mouth and a carrot for the nose. **Yield:** 6-8 servings.

Sweet Snowman

(Pictured on page 172)

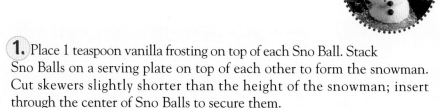

~Taste of Home Test Kitchen

2 tablespoons vanilla frosting

3 Sno Balls

3 wooden skewers (8 inches)

1 chocolate wafer (2-1/2 inches)

2 chocolate cream-filled sandwich cookies

1 piece red shoestring licorice (12 inches)

2 brown M&M's

1 piece candy corn

5 miniature chocolate chips

3 semisweet chocolate chips

Confectioners' sugar, optional

1. Place 1 teaspoon vanilla frosting on top of each Sno Ball. Stack Sno Balls on a serving plate on top of each other to form the snowman. Cut skewers slightly shorter than the height of the snowman; insert through the center of Sno Balls to secure them.

2. Place chocolate wafer on top to form hat brim. Place a dollop of frosting on top of one sandwich cookie; top with other cookie. Attach to wafer with frosting to create the hat. Carefully tie licorice around snowman for a scarf.

3. Use frosting to attach M&M's for eyes, candy corn for nose, miniature chips for mouth and semisweet chips for buttons. Dust confectioners' sugar around base of snowman if desired. **Yield:** 1 snowman (3 servings).

Editor's Note: Hostess brand Sno Balls are coconut marshmallow-covered chocolate cakes with cream filling.

Edible Evergreens

~Taste of Home Test Kitchen

6 green Fruit Roll-Ups, unrolled

2 sugar ice cream cones

With a scissors, cut roll-ups widthwise into thirds. Gather each piece, beginning with a long side, to form ruffles. Place ice cream cones on a serving plate. Starting at base of cone, attach ruffles by wrapping around cone. Pinch at top to form a point. **Yield:** 2 trees.

Editor's Note: This recipe was tested with Fruit Roll-Ups brand, which has fruit pieces measuring approximately 5 x 5 inches. If roll-ups have precut designs in them, place unrolled fruit between two sheets of greased waxed paper. Microwave on high for 10-15 seconds. Roll fruit flat with a rolling pin. Remove waxed paper.

White Chocolate Party Mix

~Norene Wright, Manilla, Indiana

- 1 package (10 ounces) mini pretzels
- 5 cups Cheerios
- 5 cups Corn Chex
- 2 cups salted peanuts
- 1 pound M&M's
- 2 packages (12 ounces *each*) vanilla chips
- 3 tablespoons vegetable oil

1. In a large bowl, combine first five ingredients; set aside. In a microwave-safe bowl, heat chips and oil on medium-high for 2 minutes, stirring once. Microwave on high for 10 seconds; stir until smooth. Pour over cereal mixture and mix well.

2. Spread onto three waxed paper-lined baking sheets. Cool; break apart. Store in an airtight container. **Yield:** 5 quarts.

Editor's Note: This recipe was tested using a 700-watt microwave.

Reindeer Cookies

~Gretchen Vandenberghe, Toledo, Ohio

- 1 package (17-1/2 ounces) peanut butter cookie mix
- 1/3 cup vegetable oil
- 1 egg
- 60 miniature pretzel twists
- 60 semisweet chocolate chips
- 30 red-hot candies

1. In a mixing bowl, combine dry cookie mix, oil and egg. Beat until well mixed. Shape into a 7-1/2-in. roll; wrap in plastic wrap. Refrigerate for 1 hour. Unwrap and cut into 1/4-in. slices. Place 2 in. apart on ungreased baking sheets.

2. Using thumb and forefinger, make a slight indention one-third of the way down the sides of each slice. Press in pretzels for antlers, chocolate chips for eyes and a red-hot for the nose. Bake at 350° for 9-11 minutes or until light brown. Remove to wire racks to cool. **Yield:** 2-1/2 dozen.

Editor's Note: You may substitute any peanut butter cookie recipe for the cookie mix, oil and egg.

Ho-Ho-Ho Sandwiches

~Taste of Home Test Kitchen

1/2 cup mayonnaise

2 tablespoons chopped ripe olives

1 tablespoon spicy brown *or* horseradish mustard

8 slices white bread

1/4 pound thinly sliced deli ham

4 slices provolone cheese

1/4 pound thinly sliced deli salami

4 slices mozzarella cheese

In a small bowl, combine the mayonnaise, olives and mustard. Spread about 1 tablespoon over each slice of bread. Layer the ham, provolone cheese, salami and mozzarella cheese on four slices of bread; top with remaining bread. Serve immediately. **Yield:** 4 servings.

Reindeer Snack Mix

~Taste of Home Test Kitchen

2 cups Bugles

2 cups cheese-flavored snack crackers

2 cups pretzel sticks

1 cup Corn Chex

1 cup bite-size Shredded Wheat

1 cup pecan halves

1/2 cup butter, melted

1 tablespoon maple syrup

1-1/2 teaspoons Worcestershire sauce

3/4 teaspoon Cajun seasoning

1/4 teaspoon cayenne pepper

1. In a large bowl, combine the first six ingredients. In another bowl, combine the butter, syrup, Worcestershire sauce, Cajun seasoning and cayenne; pour over cereal mixture and toss to coat.

2. Transfer to an ungreased 15-in. x 10-in. x 1-in. baking pan. Bake, uncovered, at 250° for 1 hour, stirring every 15 minutes. Cool; store in an airtight container. **Yield:** about 9 cups.

for Santa

Santa's Cup O' Mousse

(Pictured on page 177)

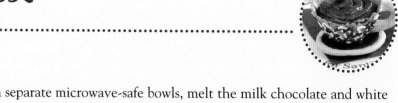

~*Taste of Home Test Kitchen*

3 ounces milk chocolate candy coating

1-1/2 ounces white candy coating

4 waffle bowls

1 tube (18 ounces) refrigerated sugar cookie dough

2 packages (2.8 ounces *each*) mocha mousse mix

1. In separate microwave-safe bowls, melt the milk chocolate and white candy coatings. Transfer each to a resealable plastic bag; cut a small hole in corner of bag. Invert waffle bowls; drizzle with coatings. Set aside.

2. For saucers, cut four 1/4-in. slices of cookie dough. Place on an ungreased baking sheet. Bake at 350° for 8-10 minutes or until edges are golden brown. Drape each warm cookie over an inverted 8-oz. custard cup; cool.

3. For cup handles, roll remaining cookie dough to 1/4-in. thickness. Cut out two hearts with a 2-1/4-in. heart-shaped cookie cutter. Cut a small heart in the center of each large heart with a 1-in. heart-shaped cutter. Remove center cutout; add to the remaining dough and save for another use. Place hearts on an ungreased baking sheet. Bake at 350° for 5-7 minutes. Cut hearts in half. Remove to wire racks to cool completely.

4. Turn waffle bowls right side up. Attach handles, using remaining white candy coating. Spread center of saucers with the remaining milk chocolate coating; let stand until set. Place cups on saucers. Prepare mousse mix according to package directions. Transfer to a large resealable plastic bag. Cut a hole in the corner of the bag; pipe mousse into cups. **Yield:** 4 servings.

Melted Frosty

~*Taste of Home Test Kitchen*

1 quart vanilla ice cream

2 cups buttermilk

2 teaspoons vanilla extract

1 teaspoon ground cinnamon

1/2 cup miniature chocolate chips, optional

In a blender, place half of the ice cream, buttermilk, vanilla and cinnamon; cover and blend until smooth. Repeat. Pour into glasses. Stir in chocolate chips if desired. **Yield:** 8 servings.

Snowman Cake

~Betsey Ross, Chebeague Island, Maine

2 packages (18-1/4 ounces *each*) chocolate cake mix

3 cups vanilla frosting

1 can (16 ounces) chocolate frosting

5 to 6 drops blue food coloring

1 green Fruit Roll-Up, unrolled

3 red-coated tiny tarts

1 red candy coin

4 black gumdrops

6 black licorice bites

1. Prepare cake mixes according to package directions. Divide batter among two greased and floured 9-in. round baking pans, one 9-in. square baking pan and 12 cupcakes. Bake cakes at 350° for 20-25 minutes and cupcakes for 18-20 minutes or until a toothpick inserted near the center comes out clean. Cool for 10 minutes before removing from pans to wire racks to cool completely.

2. Place one round cake off center and 1 in. from the bottom of a 25-in. x 16-in. covered board. Place second round cake above it. Set aside 1 cup vanilla frosting. Frost round cakes with remaining vanilla frosting.

3. Cut the square cake into two rectangles—one 8 in. x 2 in. and one 8 in. x 4 in. (save remaining piece for another use). For hat brim, place the smaller rectangle (B) above the top round cake. Cut a 5-3/4-in. x 4-in. piece from the large rectangle; place (A) above hat brim. For scarf, cut the remaining cake piece in half diagonally (C and D); position on left side of top circle. (Save the cupcakes for another use.)

4. Frost hat with chocolate frosting. Tint reserved vanilla frosting blue; frost a stripe on hat for ribbon and frost the scarf. Cut three holly leaves from fruit roll-up; place on hat ribbon. Top with tiny tarts for berries. Position red candy coin for nose; add black gumdrops for eyes and buttons. Add licorice bites for mouth. **Yield:** 16-20 servings plus 12 cupcakes.

Snowman Cutting Pattern and Assembly Diagram

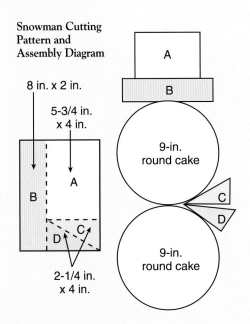

8 in. x 2 in.

5-3/4 in. x 4 in.

A

B

C

D

9-in. round cake

9-in. round cake

2-1/4 in. x 4 in.

Popcorn Christmas Trees

~Nicole Clayton, Las Vegas, Nevada

6 cups popped popcorn

1/2 cup sugar

1/2 cup light corn syrup

1/4 cup creamy peanut butter

10 to 12 drops green food coloring

2 to 3 tablespoons red M&M miniature baking bits

1. Place popcorn in a large bowl; set aside. In a heavy saucepan over medium heat, bring sugar and corn syrup to a boil, stirring occasionally. Boil and stir for 1 minute. Remove from the heat; stir in the peanut butter and food coloring until blended. Pour over popcorn and stir to coat.

2. With wet hands, shape mixture by 3/4 cupfuls into evergreen tree shapes. While warm, press a few baking bits into each tree. Place on a greased baking sheet; let stand until firm, about 30 minutes. **Yield:** 8 servings.

Snowmen Cookies

~Sherri Johnson, Burns, Tennessee

1 package (16 ounces) Nutter Butter cookies

1-1/4 pounds white candy coating, melted

Miniature chocolate chips

M&M miniature baking bits

Pretzel sticks, halved

Orange and red decorating gel or frosting

Using tongs, dip cookies in candy coating; shake off excess. Place on waxed paper. Place two chocolate chips on one end of cookies for eyes. Place baking bits down middle for buttons. For arms, dip ends of two pretzel stick halves into coating; attach one to each side. Let stand until hardened. Pipe nose and scarf with gel or frosting. **Yield:** 32 cookies.

Starry Cheese Spread

~Taste of Home Test Kitchen

6 cups (24 ounces) shredded sharp cheddar cheese

1 package (3 ounces) cream cheese, softened

1/4 cup butter, softened

2 tablespoons prepared horseradish

2/3 cup apple juice

2 tablespoons chopped stuffed olives

Sliced pimientos, yellow pepper strips and one stuffed olive slice

1. In a mixing bowl, beat cheeses, butter, horseradish, apple juice and olives on low speed for 1 minute. Beat on high until almost smooth.

2. Press 3/4 cup into a 4-in. star-shaped mold coated with nonstick cooking spray. Cover and chill for 3 hours or until set. Refrigerate remaining cheese mixture for another use or for the Party Sandwich Tree.

3. Run a sharp knife around mold to loosen cheese spread and unmold. Garnish with pimientos, peppers and olive. **Yield:** about 3-3/4 cups.

Party Sandwich Tree

~Taste of Home Test Kitchen

11 slices thin rye bread

3 cups Starry Cheese Spread (recipe above) or cheese spread of your choice

Chopped pecans

10 slices deli roast beef, halved

Leaf lettuce

Stuffed olives, halved cherry tomatoes and sliced radishes

1. Cut each slice of bread into a 3-1/2-in. x 3-in. rectangle, removing crusts. Spread with cheese spread. Cut each rectangle in half diagonally, forming triangles. On a 24-in. x 18-in. serving tray or covered board, form the tree.

2. Near the top, place two bread triangles 1/2 in. apart with 3-in. sides facing. (Leave room at the top of the tray for the Starry Cheese Spread mold if desired.) For the second, third and fourth rows, place two triangles with long sides together to form six rectangles. Place a triangle on either side of rectangles.

3. Center two remaining triangles under last row for trunk; sprinkle with pecans. Top the rest of the triangles with beef and lettuce. Add olive, tomato and radish "ornaments" with toothpicks. **Yield:** 22 appetizers.

Candy Cane Cookies
(Pictured on page 183)

~Taste of Home Test Kitchen

1/2 cup butter, softened

1/2 cup shortening

1 cup sugar

1/4 cup confectioners' sugar

1/2 cup milk

1 egg

1 teaspoon peppermint extract

1 teaspoon vanilla extract

3-1/2 cups all-purpose flour

1/4 teaspoon salt

Green and red food coloring

1. In a bowl, cream butter, shortening and sugars. Beat in milk, egg and extracts. Gradually add flour and salt. Set aside half of the dough. Divide remaining dough in half; add green food coloring to one portion and red food coloring to the other. Wrap dough separately in plastic wrap. Refrigerate for 1 hour or until easy to handle.

2. Roll 1/2 teaspoonfuls of each color of dough into 3-in. ropes. Place each green rope next to a white rope; press together gently and twist. Repeat with red ropes and remaining white ropes. Place 2 in. apart on ungreased baking sheets. Curve one end, forming a cane.

3. Bake at 350° for 11-13 minutes or until set. Cool for 2 minutes; carefully remove to wire racks. **Yield:** about 6 dozen.

Gelatin Christmas Ornaments
(Pictured on page 183)

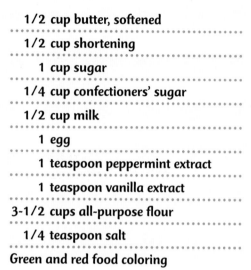

~Taste of Home Test Kitchen

3-1/4 cups white grape juice

1 package (6 ounces) lime gelatin

1 package (6 ounces) raspberry gelatin

6 *each* red and green maraschino cherries with stems

Mayonnaise, sour cream *or* whipped cream in a can

1. In a saucepan, bring the grape juice to a boil. Place lime gelatin in a bowl; add half of the juice and stir until completely dissolved. Repeat with raspberry gelatin. Pour lime gelatin into six muffin cups (about 1/3 cup in each) coated with nonstick cooking spray. Repeat, filling six more cups with raspberry gelatin. Refrigerate for 4 hours or until firm.

2. Loosen gelatin around the edges with a sharp knife; invert muffin tin onto waxed paper. Use a metal spatula to transfer to serving plates. Fill a small plastic bag with mayonnaise; cut a small hole in corner of bag. Pipe a small circle near one edge of each ornament; place cherry in center. Decorate ornaments with additional mayonnaise if desired. **Yield:** 1 dozen.

Popcorn Sleigh

~Donna Torres, Grand Rapids, Minnesota

1/2 cup sugar

1/2 cup light corn syrup

1/4 cup water

1 tablespoon butter

4 drops green food coloring

2 quarts popped popcorn

4 candy canes

2 large green gumdrops

6 red-hot candies

Assorted wrapped peppermint candies

1. In a large saucepan, combine the sugar, corn syrup and water. Bring to a boil; cook without stirring until a candy thermometer reaches 250° (firm-ball stage). Remove from the heat; add the butter and food coloring. Set aside 2 tablespoons. Place the popcorn in a large bowl; drizzle with remaining syrup. Stir until well coated.

2. For sleigh, press popcorn mixture onto the bottom and all the way up the sides of a greased 8-in. x 4-in. x 2-in. loaf pan, forming a 1-in.-thick shell. Beginning 3 in. from one corner, remove a small amount of popcorn mixture from a long side, so side tapers toward front end, as shown in photo at left. Repeat on the other side. Remove from the pan. Curve the sleigh front toward the back.

3. Microwave the reserved syrup for 20 seconds or until melted. Cut the rounded ends from two candy canes (save rounded ends for another use). For runners, attach a whole candy cane and a straight candy cane piece with syrup to the bottom of each long side of sleigh.

4. For holly garnish, flatten gumdrops between waxed paper; cut each into three leaf shapes. Attach leaves and red-hot candies with syrup to each side. Fill sleigh with mint candies. **Yield:** 1 sleigh.

Editor's Note: We recommend that you test your candy thermometer before each use by bringing water to a boil; the thermometer should read 212°. Adjust your recipe temperature up or down based on your test.

Valentine's Day

Heart's Desire Pizza

~Taste of Home Test Kitchen

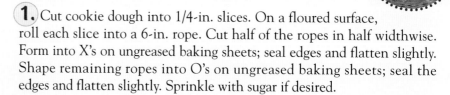

1 tube (17.3 ounces) large refrigerated biscuits

1 jar (14 ounces) pizza sauce

1-1/2 to 2 cups toppings—sliced ripe olives, sliced and quartered pepperoni, chopped fresh mushrooms, chopped green and/or sweet yellow pepper

1-1/2 cups (6 ounces) shredded mozzarella cheese

1-1/2 cups (6 ounces) shredded cheddar cheese

1. Cut eight 6-in.-square pieces of aluminum foil; place on baking sheets. Lightly coat foil with nonstick cooking spray; set aside. On a lightly floured surface, roll each biscuit to a 5-in. square. Cut a 1-in. triangle from center top and place on the center bottom, forming a heart. Press edges to seal. Transfer to foil squares.

2. Spoon pizza sauce over dough to within 1/4 in. of edges. Sprinkle with desired toppings and cheeses. Bake at 425° for 10-15 minutes or until golden brown. **Yield:** 8 individual pizzas.

Hugs 'n' Kisses Cookies

~Taste of Home Test Kitchen

1 package (18 ounces) refrigerated sugar cookie dough

Red colored sugar, optional

1. Cut cookie dough into 1/4-in. slices. On a floured surface, roll each slice into a 6-in. rope. Cut half of the ropes in half widthwise. Form into X's on ungreased baking sheets; seal edges and flatten slightly. Shape remaining ropes into O's on ungreased baking sheets; seal the edges and flatten slightly. Sprinkle with sugar if desired.

2. Bake at 350° for 8-10 minutes or until the edges are lightly browned. Cool for 3 minutes; remove from pans to wire racks to cool completely. **Yield:** about 5 dozen.

Conversation Cupcakes

(Pictured on page 187)

~Taste of Home Test Kitchen

1 package (18-1/4 ounces) white cake mix

1/2 cup butter, softened

1/2 cup shortening

1 teaspoon vanilla extract

1/8 teaspoon butter flavoring, optional

4 cups confectioners' sugar

2 tablespoons milk

1 to 2 drops red food coloring

1 to 2 drops yellow food coloring

1 to 2 drops blue food coloring

1. Prepare cake mix according to package directions. Place paper or foil liners in a heart-shaped or standard muffin tin. Fill cups half full of batter. Bake according to package directions for cupcakes. Cool for 10 minutes; remove from pans to wire racks to cool completely.

2. For frosting, cream butter and shortening in a small mixing bowl. Add vanilla and butter flavoring if desired. Add sugar, 1 cup at a time, beating well after each addition. Beat in milk until light and fluffy.

3. Divide frosting into fourths; place in four separate bowls. Leave one bowl untinted. Add food coloring to the other three bowls; stir until well blended. Frost cupcakes. Pipe untinted frosting around edges and decorate tops with Valentine phrases. **Yield:** 28 cupcakes.

Frosted Valentine Cookies

~Marcy Cella, L'Anse, Michigan

2 cups butter, softened

1 cup confectioners' sugar

4 cups all-purpose flour

2 cups quick-cooking oats

2 teaspoons vanilla extract

1/2 teaspoon almond extract

1/2 teaspoon salt

1/2 pound semisweet or milk chocolate candy coating, melted

Confectioners' sugar icing, optional

1. In a mixing bowl, cream butter and sugar. Add flour, oats, extracts and salt; mix well. Roll out dough to 1/4-in. thickness. Cut with a 3-in. heart-shaped cookie cutter; place on ungreased baking sheets.

2. Bake at 350° for 12-15 minutes. While cookies are warm, spread melted chocolate on tops. Cool. Using a pastry tube, decorate with confectioners' sugar icing if desired. **Yield:** 3-1/2 dozen.

Valentine Cutouts

~*Annette Ellyson, Carolina, West Virginia*

2 packages (6 ounces *each*) cherry
  or raspberry gelatin

2-1/2 cups boiling water

1 cup cold milk

1 package (3.4 ounces) instant
  vanilla pudding mix

In a bowl, dissolve gelatin in water; set aside for 30 minutes. In a small bowl, whisk milk and pudding mix until smooth, about 1 minute. Quickly pour into gelatin; whisk until well blended. Pour into a 13-in. x 9-in. x 2-in. dish coated with nonstick cooking spray. Chill until set. Cut into cubes or use a heart-shaped cookie cutter. **Yield:** 8-10 servings.

Sweetheart Treat

~*Alyssa Harris, Elizabethton, Tennessee*

3 tablespoons butter

1 package (10 ounces) marshmallows

Red gel *or* paste food coloring

6 cups crisp rice cereal

1 cup vanilla *or* white chips

2 teaspoons shortening

1. Line a baking sheet with waxed paper. Draw a 9-in. heart on waxed paper. Coat with nonstick cooking spray; set aside. In a large saucepan, heat butter and marshmallows over medium heat until marshmallows are melted, stirring constantly. Remove from the heat; stir in food coloring and cereal. Shape mixture into a heart on prepared pan. Let stand for 1 hour or until set.

2. In a heavy saucepan or microwave, melt chips and shortening; stir until smooth. Spread a 1-in. border near edge of heart. Place remaining melted chips in a pastry or plastic bag; cut a small hole in the corner of bag. Pipe initials in the center of heart. **Yield:** 6-8 servings.

St. Patrick's Day

Shamrock Sandwiches

~*Taste of Home Test Kitchen*

1 package (8 ounces) cream cheese, softened

1/4 cup mayonnaise

2 tablespoons Dijon mustard

1 package (2-1/2 ounces) thinly sliced cooked corned beef, chopped

2 tablespoons grated red onion

2 teaspoons snipped fresh dill *or* 3/4 teaspoon dill weed

1/4 teaspoon salt

1 pound thinly sliced seedless rye bread

Fresh dill sprigs, optional

1. In a mixing bowl, beat cream cheese, mayonnaise and mustard. Add corned beef, onion, dill and salt; mix well.

2. Using a 2-in. shamrock cookie cutter, cut out two shamrocks from each slice of bread. Spread tablespoonfuls of filling over half of the bread; top with remaining bread. Garnish with dill if desired. **Yield:** about 16 sandwiches.

Leprechaun Lime Drink

~*Taste of Home Test Kitchen*

1 quart lime sherbet, softened

1/2 cup limeade concentrate

2 tablespoons sugar

2 cans (12 ounces *each*) lemon-lime soda, chilled

1 to 2 cups crushed ice

In a mixing bowl, blend sherbet, limeade and sugar. Stir in soda and ice. Pour into glasses. Garnish if desired. **Yield:** 7 cups.

Blarney Stone Bars

(Pictured on page 191)

~Taste of Home Test Kitchen

1/2 cup butter, softened

3/4 cup packed brown sugar

2 eggs

1 tablespoon milk

1 teaspoon vanilla extract

3/4 cup all-purpose flour

3/4 cup quick-cooking oats

1/2 teaspoon baking powder

1/4 teaspoon salt

3/4 cup English toffee bits

1/3 cup chopped pecans

4 drops green food coloring

3/4 cup vanilla frosting

1. In a mixing bowl, cream butter and sugar. Beat in eggs, milk and vanilla. Combine flour, oats, baking powder and salt; add to the creamed mixture. Fold in the toffee bits and pecans.

2. Spread into a greased 9-in. square baking pan. Bake at 350° for 20-24 minutes or until a toothpick comes out clean. Cool on a wire rack. Add food coloring to frosting; spread over the bars. Cut into diamond shapes. **Yield:** about 3-1/2 dozen.

St. Patrick's Day Popcorn

~Karen Weber, Salem, Missouri

4 quarts popped popcorn

1 cup sugar

1/2 cup packed brown sugar

1/2 cup water

1/2 cup light corn syrup

1 teaspoon white vinegar

1/4 teaspoon salt

1/2 cup butter

8 to 10 drops green food coloring

1. Place popcorn in a large roasting pan; place in a 250° oven. Meanwhile, in a large heavy saucepan, combine the sugars, water, corn syrup, vinegar and salt. Cook and stir over medium heat until mixture comes to a boil. Cook, stirring occasionally, until a candy thermometer reads 260° (hard-ball stage).

2. Remove from the heat; stir in butter until blended. Stir in food coloring. Drizzle over warm popcorn and toss to coat. Let stand until cool. Break apart. Store in an airtight container. **Yield:** 6 quarts.

Editor's Note: We recommend that you test your candy thermometer before each use by bringing water to a boil; the thermometer should read 212°. Adjust your recipe temperature up or down based on your test.

Pot o' Gold Potato Soup

(Pictured on page 191)

~Taste of Home Test Kitchen

3/4 cup chopped celery

3/4 cup chopped onion

1/4 cup butter

2 cans (14-1/2 ounces *each*) chicken broth

2-1/3 cups mashed potato flakes

1-1/2 cups milk

1/2 cup cubed process American cheese

3/4 teaspoon garlic salt

1/8 to 1/4 teaspoon chili powder

1/2 cup sour cream

In a 3-qt. saucepan, saute celery and onion in butter for 2-3 minutes. Stir in broth; bring to boil. Reduce heat. Add potato flakes; cook and stir for 5-7 minutes. Add milk, cheese, garlic salt and chili powder. Cook and stir until cheese is melted. Just before serving, add sour cream and heat through (do not boil). **Yield:** 6 servings.

Shamrock Pie

~Gloria Warczak, Cedarburg, Wisconsin

1 cup sugar

1/4 cup cornstarch

1-1/2 cups water

3 egg yolks, lightly beaten

1/4 cup lemon juice

1 tablespoon butter

1-1/2 teaspoons grated lemon peel

5 to 6 drops green food coloring

1 pastry shell (9 inches), baked

MERINGUE:

3 egg whites

1/3 cup sugar

1. Combine sugar, cornstarch and water in a saucepan; stir until smooth. Bring to a boil, stirring constantly. Boil 2 minutes or until thickened. Stir a small amount into egg yolks; return all to the pan. Cook and stir 1 minute. Remove from heat; stir in lemon juice, butter, lemon peel and food coloring until smooth. Pour into crust.

2. For meringue, beat egg whites until foamy. Gradually add sugar and beat until stiff peaks form. Spread over hot filling, sealing to the edges. Bake at 350° for 10-15 minutes or until lightly browned. Cool. **Yield:** 6-8 servings.

Easter

Easter Basket Cake

~Taste of Home Test Kitchen

1 package (18-1/4 ounces) white cake mix

4 cups vanilla frosting

Pink, yellow, blue and purple gel or paste food coloring

3 tablespoons flaked coconut

3 drops green food coloring

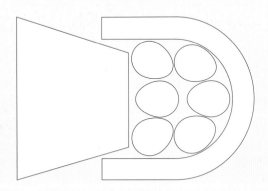

1. Prepare cake mix according to package directions. Pour the batter into a greased 15-in. x 10-in. x 1-in. baking pan. Bake at 350° for 20-25 minutes or until a toothpick inserted near the center comes out clean. Cool on a wire rack for 10 minutes; invert cake onto a wire rack to cool completely.

2. Referring to the diagram below left, cut cake into a basket, handle and six eggs. Arrange basket and handle on a 19-in. x 14-in. covered board. Place 1/4 cup of frosting in each of three bowls; tint one pink, one yellow and one blue. Place 1 cup of frosting in another bowl; tint purple. Leave the remaining frosting white.

3. Frost the basket purple. Frost the sides of the handle white. Cut a hole in the corner of a pastry or plastic bag; insert star tip #32. Fill with white frosting. Pipe a rope border on the handle and on the top and bottom of basket.

4. For grass, place coconut in a resealable plastic bag; add green food coloring. Seal bag and shake to tint. Sprinkle above the top of the basket.

5. Frost and decorate eggs as desired with white and tinted frosting. Arrange in and around basket. **Yield:** 8-10 servings.

Cute Egg Chicks

~Tami Escher, Dumont, Minnesota

12 hard-cooked eggs

1/2 cup mayonnaise

1/2 cup shredded Parmesan cheese

2 teaspoons finely chopped onion

1/2 teaspoon curry powder

1/2 teaspoon prepared mustard

1/8 teaspoon pepper

3 stuffed olives

1 small sweet red pepper

1. Cut a thin slice from the bottom of each egg so it sits flat. Cut a zigzag pattern a third down from the top of each egg. Carefully remove yolks and place in a small bowl; mash with a fork. Add the mayonnaise, Parmesan cheese, onion, curry, mustard and pepper; stir until well blended. Spoon yolk mixture into the egg white bottoms; replace tops.

2. Cut olives into slices for eyes. Cut 12 small triangles from red pepper for beaks. Gently press the eyes and beaks into egg yolk filling. Refrigerate until serving. **Yield:** 1 dozen.

Peanut Butter Eggs

~ Ethel Charles, Elizabethtown, Pennsylvania

1 package (8 ounces) cream cheese, softened

1/2 cup butter, softened

1 jar (17.3 ounces) creamy peanut butter

1 teaspoon vanilla extract

1 package (2 pounds) confectioners' sugar

2 cups flaked coconut, optional

6 cups (36 ounces) semisweet chocolate chips

1/3 cup shortening

1. In a mixing bowl, beat cream cheese, butter, peanut butter and vanilla until smooth. Beat in sugar. Stir in coconut if desired. Form rounded tablespoonfuls into egg shapes. Place on waxed paper-lined baking sheets. Chill for 30 minutes.

2. In a microwave-safe bowl or heavy saucepan, melt chocolate chips and shortening; stir until smooth. Dip eggs until coated; place on waxed paper to harden. For more decorative eggs, place about 1/4 cup melted chocolate in a small plastic bag. Cut a hole in the corner of the bag; pipe chocolate over tops of eggs. Store in the refrigerator. **Yield:** about 5-1/2 dozen.

Easter Bunny Bread

~Taste of Home Test Kitchen

2 loaves (1 pound *each*) frozen bread dough, thawed

2 raisins

2 sliced almonds

1 egg, lightly beaten

Lettuce leaves

Dip of your choice

1. Cut a fourth off of one loaf of dough; shape into a pear to form head. For body, flatten remaining portion into a 7-in. x 6-in. oval; place on a greased baking sheet. Place head above body. Make narrow cuts, about 3/4 in. deep, on each side of head for whiskers.

2. Cut second loaf into four equal portions. For ears, shape two portions into 16-in. ropes; fold ropes in half. Arrange ears with open ends touching head. Cut a third portion of dough in half; shape each into a 3-1/2-in. oval for back paws. Cut two 1-in. slits on top edge for toes. Position on each side of body.

3. Divide the fourth portion of dough into three pieces. Shape two pieces into 2-1/2-in. balls for front paws; shape the remaining piece into two 1-in. balls for cheeks and one 1/2-in. ball for nose. Place paws on each side of body; cut two 1-in. slits for toes. Place cheeks and nose on face. Add raisins for eyes and almonds for teeth. Brush dough with egg. Cover and let rise in a warm place until doubled, about 30-45 minutes. Bake at 350° for 25-30 minutes or until golden brown. Remove to a wire rack to cool.

4. Place bread on a lettuce-lined 16-in. x 13-in. serving tray. Cut a 5-in. x 4-in. oval in center of body. Hollow out bread, leaving a 1/2-in. shell (discard removed bread or save for another use). Line with lettuce and fill with dip. **Yield:** 1 loaf.

Easter Egg Candies

~Taste of Home Test Kitchen

1 package (10 to 12 ounces) vanilla or white chips

1 package (3 ounces) cream cheese, cubed

1 teaspoon water

1/2 teaspoon vanilla extract

Colored sprinkles, colored sugar and/or jimmies

In a microwave-safe bowl, melt the chips at 50% power. Add the cream cheese, water and vanilla; stir until blended. Chill for 1 hour or until easy to handle. Quickly shape into 1-1/4-in. eggs. Roll in sprinkles, colored sugar or jimmies. Store in an airtight container in the refrigerator. **Yield:** about 4 dozen (1-1/2 pounds).

Easter Egg Cookies

~Barbara Neuweg, West Point, Iowa

1 cup butter, softened

1/2 cup packed brown sugar

1 egg

1-1/2 teaspoons vanilla extract

3 cups all-purpose flour

1 cup quick-cooking oats

3/4 teaspoon salt

GLAZE:

1-1/2 cups confectioners' sugar

1/8 teaspoon salt

2-1/2 tablespoons half-and-half cream

Cake decorating gel, optional

1. In a mixing bowl, cream butter and brown sugar. Add egg and vanilla; mix well. Combine flour, oats and salt; stir into creamed mixture.

2. Divide dough into three equal portions. Form 12 egg-shaped cookies from each portion. Place on ungreased baking sheets.

3. Bake at 350° for 20-25 minutes or until set. Cool completely. Combine glaze ingredients until smooth; spoon over cookies. Decorate as desired. **Yield:** 3 dozen.

Meringue Bunnies

~Taste of Home Test Kitchen

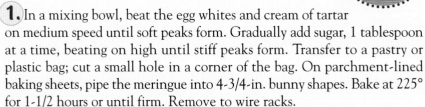

2 egg whites

1/8 teaspoon cream of tartar

1/2 cup sugar

1/4 cup pink candy coating disks

36 heart-shaped red decorating sprinkles

1. In a mixing bowl, beat the egg whites and cream of tartar on medium speed until soft peaks form. Gradually add sugar, 1 tablespoon at a time, beating on high until stiff peaks form. Transfer to a pastry or plastic bag; cut a small hole in a corner of the bag. On parchment-lined baking sheets, pipe the meringue into 4-3/4-in. bunny shapes. Bake at 225° for 1-1/2 hours or until firm. Remove to wire racks.

2. In a microwave, melt candy coating; stir until smooth. Place in a pastry or plastic bag; cut a small hole in a corner of the bag. Pipe ears, whiskers and mouths on bunnies. Attach hearts for eyes and nose with melted candy coating. **Yield:** 1 dozen.

Cupcake Easter Baskets

~Julie Johnston, Shaunavon, Saskatchewan

1/2 cup butter, softened

1 cup sugar

1 egg

1 teaspoon grated orange peel

2 cups cake flour

3/4 teaspoon baking soda

1/2 teaspoon baking powder

1/4 teaspoon salt

2/3 cup buttermilk

FROSTING:

3/4 cup butter, softened

2 packages (3 ounces *each*) cream cheese, softened

1 teaspoon vanilla extract

3 cups confectioners' sugar

1 teaspoon water

4 drops green food coloring

1-1/2 cups flaked coconut

Red shoestring licorice

Jelly beans

1. In a large mixing bowl, cream butter and sugar. Beat in the egg and orange peel. Combine the flour, baking soda, baking powder and salt; add to creamed mixture alternately with buttermilk. Fill paper-lined muffin cups two-thirds full. Bake at 350° for 20-25 minutes or until a toothpick comes out clean. Cool for 10 minutes before removing from pans to wire racks to cool completely.

2. In a small mixing bowl, beat butter, cream cheese and vanilla until smooth. Gradually beat in confectioners' sugar; spread over cupcakes. Combine water and food coloring in a large resealable plastic bag; add coconut. Seal bag and shake to tint. Sprinkle over cupcakes.

3. Using a metal or wooden skewer, poke a hole in the top on opposite sides of each cupcake. Cut licorice into 6-in. strips for handle; insert each end into a hole. Decorate with jelly beans. **Yield:** 1-1/2 dozen.

4th of July

Old Glory Dessert

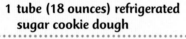

~Taste of Home Test Kitchen

1 tube (18 ounces) refrigerated
  sugar cookie dough

2 packages (one 8 ounces, one 3
  ounces) cream cheese, softened

3/4 cup confectioners' sugar

4-1/2 teaspoons lemon juice

1/2 cup fresh blueberries

2 cups quartered fresh strawberries

1. Press cookie dough into a greased 15-in. x 10-in. x 1-in. baking pan. Bake at 350° for 10-12 minutes or until golden brown. Cool on a wire rack.

2. In a mixing bowl, beat cream cheese, sugar and lemon juice until smooth. Set aside 1/4 cup. Spread remaining cream cheese mixture over crust. Decorate with blueberries and strawberries to resemble a flag.

3. Cut a small hole in a corner of a pastry or plastic bag. Insert star tip #16. Fill with reserved cream cheese mixture. Beginning in one corner, pipe stars in the spaces between the blueberries. **Yield:** 12-15 servings.

Patriotic Picnic Club

~Esther Lehman, Fayetteville, Pennsylvania

1/2 cup mayonnaise

1 to 2 tablespoons chili sauce

1 tablespoon sweet pickle relish

9 slices bread, toasted

3 thin slices deli ham

3 slices Swiss cheese

3 thin slices deli turkey

6 thin slices tomato

3 lettuce leaves

In a bowl, combine the mayonnaise, chili sauce and pickle relish. Spread 1 tablespoonful on each slice of bread. Top three slices of bread with a slice of ham and Swiss cheese. Top each with another slice of bread. Layer with turkey, tomato and lettuce. Top with remaining bread. Secure with toothpicks if necessary. Cut into quarters. **Yield:** 3-6 servings.

Starry Fruit Soup

(Pictured on page 201)

~Edie DeSpain, Logan, Utah

2 medium ripe bananas

1 can (15 ounces) sliced pears, undrained

1 package (10 ounces) frozen sweetened raspberries, thawed

1 can (6 ounces) frozen orange juice concentrate, thawed

1/4 cup lemon juice

1 to 2 teaspoons grated orange peel

1/2 cup sour cream

2 tablespoons confectioners' sugar

1. Cut banana into quarters. In a blender, combine banana and next five ingredients; cover and process until smooth. Strain to remove seeds if desired. Chill until serving.

2. Combine sour cream and sugar until smooth; place in a heavy-duty resealable plastic bag. Cut a small hole in a corner of bag. Pipe two thin concentric circles 1/2 in. apart on top of each bowl of soup. Beginning with the center circle, gently pull a toothpick through both circles toward outer edge. Wipe toothpick clean. Draw toothpick from outer edge of bowl back to center. Repeat to complete star pattern. **Yield:** 6 servings.

Patriotic Gelatin Salad

~Sue Gronholz, Columbus, Wisconsin

2 packages (3 ounces *each*) berry blue gelatin

2 packages (3 ounces *each*) strawberry gelatin

4 cups boiling water, *divided*

2-1/2 cups cold water, *divided*

2 envelopes unflavored gelatin

2 cups milk

1 cup sugar

2 cups (16 ounces) sour cream

2 teaspoons vanilla extract

1. In four separate bowls, dissolve each package of gelatin in 1 cup boiling water. Add 1/2 cup cold water to each and stir. Pour one bowl of blue gelatin into a 10-in. fluted tube pan coated with nonstick cooking spray; chill until almost set, about 30 minutes. Set other three bowls of gelatin aside at room temperature. Soften unflavored gelatin in remaining cold water; let stand 5 minutes.

2. Heat milk in a saucepan over medium heat just below boiling. Stir in softened gelatin and sugar until sugar is dissolved. Remove from heat; stir in sour cream and vanilla until smooth. When blue gelatin in pan is almost set, carefully spoon 1-1/2 cups sour cream mixture over it. Chill until almost set, about 30 minutes. Carefully spoon one bowl of strawberry gelatin over cream layer. Chill until almost set. Carefully spoon 1-1/2 cups cream mixture over strawberry layer. Chill until almost set. Repeat, adding layers of blue gelatin, cream mixture and strawberry gelatin, chilling in between each. Chill several hours or overnight. **Yield:** 16 servings.

Firecracker Roll-Ups

(Pictured on page 201)

~Kathleen Tribble, Buellton, California

1 medium green pepper, cut into 3/4-inch strips

1 medium red onion, cut into 1/2-inch strips

1 medium zucchini, cut into 1/4-inch slices

2 cups quartered fresh mushrooms

3 teaspoons dried basil, *divided*

2 teaspoons garlic powder, *divided*

1/4 teaspoon salt

1/4 teaspoon pepper

1/4 cup mayonnaise

2 teaspoons dried parsley flakes

4 flour tortillas (8 inches)

1-1/3 cups shredded lettuce

1. Place vegetables in a greased 15-in. x 10-in. x 1-in. baking pan. Spritz with nonstick cooking spray. Sprinkle with 2 teaspoons basil, 1 teaspoon garlic powder, salt and pepper.

2. Broil 4-6 in. from the heat for 16 minutes or until vegetables are browned, stirring once.

3. Meanwhile, in a bowl, combine mayonnaise, parsley and remaining basil and garlic powder. Warm the tortillas; spread 1 tablespoon of mayonnaise mixture on each. Spoon 3/4 cup vegetables down the center; top with 1/3 cup lettuce. Fold bottom of tortilla over filling and roll up. **Yield:** 4 servings.

Halloween

Frightening Fingers

~Natalie Hyde, Cambridge, Ontario

1 cup butter, softened

1 cup confectioners' sugar

1 egg

1 teaspoon vanilla extract

1 teaspoon almond extract

2-3/4 cups all-purpose flour

1 teaspoon baking powder

1 teaspoon salt

Red decorating gel

1/2 cup sliced almonds

1. In a mixing bowl, cream butter and sugar. Beat in the egg and extracts. Combine the flour, baking powder and salt; gradually add to the creamed mixture. Divide dough into fourths. Cover and refrigerate for 30 minutes or until easy to handle.

2. Working with one piece of dough at a time, roll into 1-in. balls. Shape balls into 3-in. x 1/2-in. fingers. Using the flat tip of a table knife, make an indentation on one end of each for fingernail. With a knife, make three slashes in the middle of each finger for knuckle.

3. Place 2 in. apart on lightly greased baking sheets. Bake at 325° for 20-25 minutes or until lightly browned. Cool for 3 minutes. Squeeze a small amount of red gel on nail bed; press a sliced almond over gel for nail, allowing gel to ooze around nail. Remove to wire racks to cool. **Yield:** about 5 dozen cookies.

Marshmallow Ghosts

~Nancy Foust, Stoneboro, Pennsylvania

12 ounces white candy coating

1-1/2 cups miniature marshmallows

Chocolate decorating gel or assorted candies

In a microwave, melt candy coating; stir until smooth. Cool slightly. Stir in marshmallows until coated. Drop by heaping tablespoonfuls onto waxed paper; smooth and flatten into ghost shapes. Decorate with gel or candies for eyes. Cool completely. Store in an airtight container. **Yield:** about 15 servings.

Bewitching Ice Cream Cones

(Pictured on page 205)

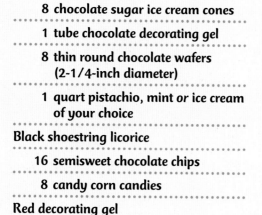

~Edie DeSpain, Logan, Utah

8 chocolate sugar ice cream cones

1 tube chocolate decorating gel

8 thin round chocolate wafers
(2-1/4-inch diameter)

1 quart pistachio, mint *or* ice cream
of your choice

Black shoestring licorice

16 semisweet chocolate chips

8 candy corn candies

Red decorating gel

1. Coat edge of ice cream cones with decorating gel; press chocolate wafer against gel to make brim of hat. Set aside.

2. Drop eight scoops of ice cream onto a waxed paper-lined baking sheet. Cut licorice into strips for hair; press into ice cream. Add chocolate chips for eyes and candy corn for noses. Pipe red gel for mouths.

3. Flatten scoops slightly to hold hats in place; position hats over heads. Freeze for at least 2 hours or until hats are set. Wrap each in plastic wrap after solidly frozen. **Yield:** 8 servings.

Halloween Snack Mix

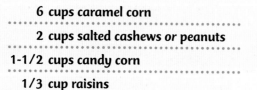

~Barbara Roberts, Middleton, Wisconsin

6 cups caramel corn

2 cups salted cashews *or* peanuts

1-1/2 cups candy corn

1/3 cup raisins

In a large bowl, combine all of the ingredients; mix well. **Yield:** about 2 quarts.

Scaredy Cakes

~*Taste of Home Test Kitchen*

1 package (18-1/4 ounces) yellow cake mix

1 can (16 ounces) vanilla frosting

Green gel food coloring, optional

Assorted candies of your choice (Chiclets, black licorice nips, red shoe-string licorice, Gummi Worms, M&M's, Life Savers, gumballs, strawberry sour belts, Tart 'n' Tangy's, Tic Tacs)

1. Prepare cake batter according to package directions. Fill greased or paper-lined muffin cups two-thirds full. Bake at 350° for 18-24 minutes or until a toothpick inserted near the center comes out clean. Cool for 5 minutes before removing from pans to wire racks to cool completely.

2. Tint some of the frosting green if desired. Frost cupcakes. Decorate with assorted candy to create monster faces. **Yield:** 2 dozen.

Great Pumpkin Sandwiches

~*Taste of Home Test Kitchen*

3 cups (12 ounces) shredded cheddar cheese

3/4 cup butter, softened

3 eggs

1/2 teaspoon garlic salt

1/2 teaspoon onion salt

9 flour tortillas (6 inches)

Paprika

3 celery sticks with leaves, optional

1. In a food processor, blend cheese and butter. Add the eggs, garlic salt and onion salt; process for 1 minute or until creamy. Spread 1/2 cupful on each tortilla.

2. Stack three tortillas, cheese side up, for each sandwich; sprinkle with paprika. Place on an ungreased baking sheet. Bake at 400° for 10-15 minutes or until golden and bubbly. If desired, add celery to resemble a pumpkin stem. Cut sandwiches into halves to serve. **Yield:** 6 servings.

Black Cat Cookies

~Kathy Stock, Levasy, Missouri

1 cup butter, softened

2 cups sugar

2 eggs

3 teaspoons vanilla extract

3 cups all-purpose flour

1 cup baking cocoa

1/2 teaspoon baking powder

1/2 teaspoon baking soda

1/2 teaspoon salt

24 wooden craft or Popsicle sticks

48 candy corn candies

24 red-hot candies

1. In a mixing bowl, cream butter and sugar. Beat in eggs and vanilla. Combine the flour, cocoa, baking powder, baking soda and salt; gradually add to the creamed mixture. Roll dough into 1-1/2-in. balls. Place 3 in. apart on lightly greased baking sheets.

2. Insert a wooden stick into each cookie. Flatten with a glass dipped in sugar. Pinch top of cookie to form ears. For whiskers, press a fork twice into each cookie. Bake at 350° for 10-12 minutes or until cookies are set. Remove from the oven; immediately press on candy corn for eyes and red-hots for noses. Remove to wire racks to cool. **Yield:** 2 dozen.

Boo Beverage

~Taste of Home Test Kitchen

2 cups orange juice

2 cups milk

2 pints orange sherbet

4 medium ripe bananas

2 cups whipped topping

18 miniature chocolate chips

In four batches, process the orange juice, milk, sherbet and bananas in a blender until smooth. Pour into glasses. Cut a hole in the corner of a pastry or plastic bag; fill with whipped topping. Pipe a ghost shape on top of each beverage. Position chocolate chips for eyes. **Yield:** 9 servings.

Haunted House Cake

~*Taste of Home Test Kitchen*

1 package (18-1/4 ounces) chocolate cake mix

1 package (18-1/4 ounces) white cake mix

2 Nutter Butter cookies

3/4 cup shortening

3/4 cup butter, softened

6 cups confectioners' sugar

3 tablespoons plus 1-1/2 teaspoons milk

1-1/2 teaspoons vanilla extract

1 milk chocolate candy bar (1.55 ounces)

1 orange M&M miniature baking bit

Orange liquid *or* paste food coloring

1 cup Golden Grahams cereal

1 stick of orange-striped fruit gum

Chocolate jimmies

1/4 cup gold rock candy

1. Prepare chocolate cake batter according to package directions. Spoon 3 cups into a greased and floured 8- x 4- x 2-in. loaf pan. Set remaining batter aside. Bake at 350° for 55-60 minutes or until a toothpick inserted near the center comes out clean. Cool for 10 minutes before removing from pan to a wire rack to cool completely.

2. Prepare white cake batter and pour into a greased and floured 13- x 9- x 2-in. baking pan. Drop reserved chocolate batter by 1/4 cupfuls onto white batter. Cut through batter with a knife to swirl. Bake at 350° for 35-40 minutes or until a toothpick inserted near the center comes out clean. Cool for 10 minutes before removing from pan to a wire rack to cool completely.

3. Place the 13- x 9-in. cake on a covered 14- x 10-in. serving board. Using a serrated knife, level top of loaf cake and cut it in half widthwise. Place one half on the corner of the 13- x 9-in. cake for the house. For the roof, slice the remaining half of loaf cake in half diagonally. Position the two halves together so they form a triangular shape on top of house. Cut each cookie in half widthwise and set aside.

4. In a mixing bowl, cream shortening and butter. Gradually add the confectioners' sugar, milk and vanilla, mixing until smooth. Frost house, roof, sides of 13- x 9-in. cake and cookie halves.

5. Break candy bar into rectangles. Place one on front of house for door (save remaining pieces for another use). Place a small dot of frosting on left side of door and attach M&M baking bit for doorknob. Tint remaining frosting orange and frost the top of the 13- x 9-in. cake.

6. Place cereal on roof of house for shingles. Cut gum in half widthwise and then lengthwise. Place two pieces above the door for shutters. Use jimmies to outline the window.

7. For tombstones, attach jimmies to the cookies to read "RIP" and "BOO." Place cookies on the cake, lightly pushing them into frosting. Place rock candy in front of door for a walkway. **Yield:** 12-15 servings.

Cream Puff Ghosts

~Dixie Terry, Goreville, Illinois

3/4 cup water

6 tablespoons butter

1 teaspoon sugar

1/4 teaspoon salt

1 cup all-purpose flour

4 eggs

PUMPKIN FILLING:

2 envelopes unflavored gelatin

1/2 cup cold orange juice

1 cup milk

2/3 cup packed brown sugar

1 can (15 ounces) solid-pack pumpkin

1-1/2 teaspoons pumpkin pie spice

1 cup heavy whipping cream, whipped

Confectioners' sugar

Miniature black jelly beans or chocolate chips

1. In a saucepan, bring the water, butter, sugar and salt to a boil. Add flour all at once and stir until a smooth ball forms. Remove from the heat; let stand for 5 minutes. Add eggs, one at a time, beating well after each addition.

2. Continue beating until mixture is smooth and shiny. Drop by 1/3 cupfuls 3 in. apart onto ungreased baking sheets; spread into 4-in. x 3-in. ovals. Using a knife coated with nonstick cooking spray, make a wavy edge at the bottom of the ghost as shown in photo above right. Bake at 400° for 30-35 minutes or until golden brown. Remove to wire racks to cool.

3. Meanwhile, in a saucepan, sprinkle gelatin over orange juice; let stand for 1 minute. Stir in the milk and brown sugar; cook and stir over low heat until gelatin and sugar are completely dissolved. Stir in pumpkin and pumpkin pie spice. Cover and refrigerate for 45-60 minutes or until thickened. Fold in whipped cream.

4. Split cream puffs in half; remove dough from inside. Set aside 1 to 2 tablespoons of filling for eyes. Spoon remaining filling into cream puffs; replace tops. Dust with confectioners' sugar. Place two small dots of reserved filling on each ghost; top with jelly beans. Serve immediately. **Yield:** 9 cream puffs.

Caramel Apple Cupcakes

~Diane Halferty, Corpus Christi, Texas

1 package (18-1/4 ounces) spice or carrot cake mix

2 cups chopped peeled tart apples

20 caramels

3 tablespoons milk

1 cup finely chopped pecans, toasted

12 Popsicle sticks

1. Prepare cake batter according to package directions; fold in apples. Fill 12 greased or paper-lined jumbo muffin cups three-fourths full. Bake at 350° for 20 minutes or until a toothpick comes out clean. Cool for 10 minutes before removing from pans to wire racks to cool completely.

2. In a saucepan, cook the caramels and milk over low heat until smooth. Spread over cupcakes. Sprinkle with pecans. Insert a wooden stick into the center of each cupcake. **Yield:** 1 dozen.

Halloween Cat Cookies

~Taste of Home Test Kitchen

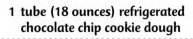

1 tube (18 ounces) refrigerated chocolate chip cookie dough

54 pieces candy corn

1 can (16 ounces) chocolate frosting

Red shoestring licorice, cut into 1-3/8-inch pieces

9 thin chocolate wafers (2-1/4-inch diameter), quartered

1. Bake cookies according to package directions. Cool on wire racks. Cut off yellow tips from 18 pieces of candy corn (discard orange and white portion or save for another use).

2. Frost cookies with chocolate frosting. Immediately decorate with two whole candy corns for eyes, a yellow candy corn tip for nose, six licorice pieces for whiskers and two wafer quarters for ears. **Yield:** 1-1/2 dozen.

Sweet 'n' Spicy Halloween Munch

~Shana Reiley, Theresa, New York

- **1 pound spiced gumdrops**
- **1 pound candy corn**
- **1 can (16 ounces) salted peanuts**

In a bowl, combine the gumdrops, candy corn and peanuts. Store in an airtight container. **Yield:** 2 quarts.

Jumbo Jack-o'-Lantern Cookies

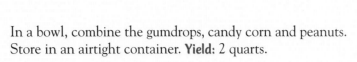

~Marlene Kuiper, Oostburg, Wisconsin

- **1 cup butter, softened**
- **1 cup sugar**
- **1 cup packed brown sugar**
- **1 egg**
- **1 teaspoon vanilla extract**
- **2 cups all-purpose flour**
- **1 cup quick-cooking oats**
- **1 teaspoon baking soda**
- **1 teaspoon ground cinnamon**
- **1/2 teaspoon salt**
- **1 cup canned pumpkin**
- **1 cup (6 ounces) semisweet chocolate chips**
- **Orange and green decorating icing or vanilla frosting and orange and green gel food coloring**

1. In a large mixing bowl, cream the butter and sugars; add the egg and vanilla. Combine the flour, oats, baking soda, cinnamon and salt; add to the creamed mixture alternately with pumpkin. Stir in the chocolate chips.

2. Drop by 1/4 cupfuls onto ungreased baking sheets. Spread into 3-1/2-in. pumpkin shapes. Drop 1/2 teaspoon of dough at the top of each for stem. Bake at 350° for 15-18 minutes or until edges are golden brown. Cool for 1 minute before removing to wire racks to cool completely. Create jack-o'-lantern faces on cookies with decorating icing or tinted frosting. **Yield:** 1-1/2 dozen.

Popcorn Owls

~Emma Magielda, Amsterdam, New York

5 quarts popped popcorn

2 cups sugar

1-1/2 cups water

1/2 cup light corn syrup

1/2 teaspoon salt

3 tablespoons butter

1 teaspoon white vinegar

1 to 2 tablespoons marshmallow creme

20 candy corn candies

20 candy orange slices

10 M&M miniature baking bits

Black shoestring licorice

1. Place popcorn in a large bowl; keep warm in a 200° oven. In a heavy saucepan, combine the sugar, water, corn syrup and salt. Cook over medium heat until a candy thermometer reads 250° (hard-ball stage). Remove from the heat; stir in butter and vinegar until butter is melted. Immediately pour over popcorn; toss to coat.

2. When mixture is cool enough to handle, quickly shape into five 3-1/4-in. balls and five 4-in. balls, dipping hands in cold water to prevent sticking. Flatten bottom of popcorn balls slightly for stability. Place a small ball on top of a large ball, forming the owl's head and body.

3. Immediately decorate owl, using marshmallow creme to attach candies. Add candy corn for claws. Press the orange slices into sides for wings. Flatten and cut additional orange slices to make triangle ears and nose and 3/4-in. circular eyes. Press M&M's into orange circles to complete the eyes. Add a 3-in. licorice strip above eyes. **Yield:** 5 owls.

Editor's Note: This recipe was prepared with popcorn popped in oil. We recommend that you test your candy thermometer before each use by bringing water to a boil; the thermometer should read 212°. Adjust your recipe temperature up or down based on the results of your test.

Chocolate Caramel Apples

(Pictured on page 217)

~Linda Smith, Frederick, Maryland

1 package (14 ounces) caramels

2 tablespoons water

4 wooden sticks

4 large tart apples

2 cups chopped pecans or peanuts

1 cup (6 ounces) semisweet chocolate chips

1 teaspoon shortening

1 cup English toffee bits or almond brickle chips

1. In a microwave-safe bowl, combine the caramels and water. Microwave, uncovered, on high for 1 minute; stir. Microwave 30-45 seconds longer or until the caramels are melted. Insert wooden sticks into apples; dip apples into the caramel mixture, turning to coat. Coat with nuts; set on waxed paper to cool.

2. Melt chocolate chips and shortening; drizzle over apples. Sprinkle with toffee bits. Set on waxed paper to cool. Cut into wedges to serve. **Yield:** 8 servings.

Editor's Note: This recipe was tested in an 850-watt microwave.

Witches' Broomsticks

~Nicole Clayton, Las Vegas, Nevada

2-1/3 cups biscuit/baking mix

2/3 cup milk

1 teaspoon Italian seasoning

3 tablespoons butter, melted

1/4 cup grated Parmesan cheese

1. In a bowl, combine biscuit mix, milk and Italian seasoning. Turn onto a lightly floured surface; knead 10 times. Divide into 30 portions; set half aside. Roll the remaining 15 pieces into 7-in. ropes for broom handles; fold in half and twist. Place on ungreased baking sheets.

2. Shape reserved pieces into 2-1/2-in. circles; cut with scissors to form a bundle of broom twigs. Place below each broom handle; pinch edges to seal. Brush with butter; sprinkle with Parmesan cheese. Bake at 450° for 10-12 minutes or until lightly browned. Serve warm or cool on a wire rack. **Yield:** 15 servings.

Cream Puff Monsters

~Susan Seymour, Valatie, New York

3/4 cup plus 2 tablespoons all-purpose flour

2 tablespoons sugar

2 tablespoons baking cocoa

1 cup water

1/2 cup butter

4 eggs

1 package (3.9 ounces) instant chocolate pudding mix

2 cups cold milk

Yellow, red, blue and green food coloring

1 can (16 ounces) vanilla frosting

Sprinkles, small candies and slivered almonds

1. Combine flour, sugar and cocoa; set aside. In a saucepan over medium heat, bring water and butter to a boil; reduce heat to low. Add flour mixture all at once; stir until a smooth ball forms. Remove from the heat; let stand 5 minutes. Add eggs, one at a time, beating well after each. Beat until smooth.

2. Cover baking sheets with foil; grease foil. Drop batter by tablespoonfuls at least 2 in. apart onto baking sheets. Bake at 400° for 25-30 minutes or until lightly browned. Lift foil and transfer to a wire rack. Immediately cut a slit in each puff to allow steam to escape; cool.

3. Beat pudding mix and milk according to package directions; chill. When puffs are cool; split and remove soft dough from inside. Spoon pudding into puffs; replace tops.

4. Following food coloring package directions, combine red and yellow to make orange, and red and blue to make purple. Divide frosting among three microwave-safe bowls; tint with orange, purple and green food coloring. Microwave frosting until thin (not runny). Spoon one or more colors onto puffs. Add sprinkles and candy for eyes; use almonds for teeth or whiskers. Chill. **Yield:** 2 dozen.

Jack o' Lantern Brownies

~Flo Burtnett, Gage, Oklahoma

1-1/2 cups sugar

3/4 cup butter, melted

1-1/2 teaspoons vanilla extract

3 eggs

3/4 cup all-purpose flour

1/2 cup baking cocoa

1/2 teaspoon baking powder

1/4 teaspoon salt

1 can (16 ounces) vanilla frosting

Orange paste food coloring

Green and black decorating gel

1. In a large mixing bowl, combine the sugar, butter and vanilla. Beat in the eggs until well blended. Combine the flour, cocoa, baking powder and salt; gradually add to sugar mixture.

2. Line a greased 13-in. x 9-in. x 2-in. baking pan with waxed paper; grease the paper. Spread batter evenly in pan. Bake at 350° for 18-22 minutes or until brownies begin to pull away from sides of pan. Cool on a wire rack.

3. Run a knife around edge of pan. Invert brownies onto a work surface and remove waxed paper. Cut brownies with a 3-in. pumpkin cookie cutter, leaving at least 1/8 in. between each shape. (Discard scraps or save for another use.) Tint frosting with orange food coloring; frost brownies. Use green gel to create the pumpkin stems and black gel to decorate the faces. **Yield:** about 1 dozen.

Spooky Spider Snacks

~Andrea Chapman, Helena, Oklahoma

1/2 cup plus 1 tablespoon peanut butter

48 butter-flavored crackers

1/2 cup chow mein noodles

1/4 cup raisins

Spread 1 teaspoon of peanut butter on the tops of 24 crackers. Place three noodles on each side of each cracker; top with the remaining crackers. Spread a small amount of peanut butter on each raisin; place two on each cracker for eyes. **Yield:** 2 dozen.

Thanksgiving

Gobbler Goodies

~Sue Gronholz, Columbus, Wisconsin

1/4 cup butter

4 cups miniature marshmallows

6 cups crisp rice cereal

28 chocolate cream-filled sandwich cookies

1-1/2 cups chocolate frosting

1 package (12-1/2 ounces) candy corn

1. In a large saucepan, melt butter. Add marshmallows; stir over low heat until melted. Stir in cereal. Cool for 10 minutes. With buttered hands, form cereal mixture into 1-1/2-in. balls. Twist apart sandwich cookies; spread frosting on the inside of cookies.

2. Place 28 cookie halves under cereal balls to form the base for each turkey. Place three pieces of candy corn in a fan pattern on remaining cookie halves; press each half onto a cereal ball to form the tail. Attach remaining candy corn with frosting to form turkey's head. **Yield:** 28 servings.

Harvest Apple Cider

~Lesley Geisel, Severna Park, Maryland

8 whole cloves

4 cups apple cider

4 cups pineapple juice

1/2 cup water

1 cinnamon stick (3 inches)

1 individual tea bag

1. Place cloves on a double thickness of cheesecloth; bring up corners of cloth and tie with kitchen string to form a bag. Place the remaining ingredients in a slow cooker; add spice bag.

2. Cover and cook on low for 2 hours or until cider reaches desired temperature. Discard spice bag, cinnamon stick and tea bag before serving. **Yield:** about 2 quarts.

Harvest Stew

~Taste of Home Test Kitchen

1-1/2 pounds boneless pork, cut
    into 1-inch cubes

1 medium onion, chopped

2 garlic cloves, minced

2 tablespoons butter

3 cups chicken broth

3/4 teaspoon salt

1/4 teaspoon dried rosemary, crushed

1/4 teaspoon rubbed sage

1 bay leaf

1 medium butternut squash, peeled
    and cubed (3 cups)

2 medium apples, peeled and cubed

In a large saucepan, cook the pork, onion and garlic in the butter until meat is no longer pink; drain. Add the broth, salt, rosemary, sage and bay leaf. Cover and simmer for 20 minutes. Add squash and apples; simmer, uncovered, for 20 minutes or until squash and apples are tender. Discard bay leaf. **Yield:** 6 servings.

Fruity Apple Salad

~Taste of Home Test Kitchen

1 large green apple, chopped

1 medium red apple, chopped

1/2 cup seedless red grapes, halved

1/2 cup seedless green grapes, halved

1 can (8 ounces) unsweetened
    pineapple tidbits, drained

1/2 cup fresh or frozen blueberries

3/4 cup mandarin oranges

1/4 cup sugar

1/4 cup lemon juice

1/4 cup water

In a serving bowl, combine the apples, grapes, pineapple, blueberries and oranges. In a small bowl, combine the sugar, lemon juice and water; stir until sugar is dissolved. Pour over fruit and toss gently. Serve with a slotted spoon. **Yield:** 6 servings.

Pecan Cheddar Snacks

~Nellie Webb, Athens, Tennessee

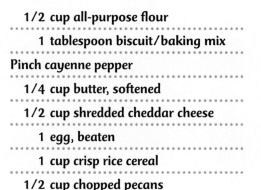

1/2 cup all-purpose flour

1 tablespoon biscuit/baking mix

Pinch cayenne pepper

1/4 cup butter, softened

1/2 cup shredded cheddar cheese

1 egg, beaten

1 cup crisp rice cereal

1/2 cup chopped pecans

1. In a bowl, combine the flour, biscuit mix and cayenne. Stir in butter until crumbly. Add cheese and egg; mix well. Stir in cereal and nuts.

2. Shape into 1-1/2-in. balls; place on an ungreased baking sheet. Bake at 350° for 18-20 minutes or until lightly browned. Serve warm. **Yield:** 2-3 servings.

Pumpkin Spice Cookies

~Taste of Home Test Kitchen

1 package (18-1/4 ounces) yellow cake mix

1/2 cup quick-cooking oats

2 to 2-1/2 teaspoons pumpkin pie spice

1 egg

1 can (15 ounces) solid-pack pumpkin

2 tablespoons vegetable oil

3 cups confectioners' sugar

1 teaspoon grated orange peel

3 to 4 tablespoons orange juice

1. In a bowl, combine the cake mix, oats and pumpkin pie spice. In another bowl, beat the egg, pumpkin and oil; stir into dry ingredients just until moistened. Drop by 2 tablespoonfuls onto baking sheets coated with nonstick cooking spray; flatten with the back of a spoon. Bake at 350° for 18-20 minutes or until the edges are golden brown. Remove to wire racks to cool.

2. In a bowl, combine confectioners' sugar, orange peel and enough orange juice to achieve desired spreading consistency. Frost cooled cookies. **Yield:** 32 cookies.

School Treats

Brownie Pizza

~*Loretta Wohlenhaus, Cumberland, Iowa*

3/4 cup butter, softened

1 cup sugar

1 egg

1 teaspoon vanilla extract

1-1/2 cups all-purpose flour

1/4 cup baking cocoa

1/2 teaspoon baking powder

1/4 teaspoon salt

3/4 cup milk chocolate M&M's, *divided*

1/2 cup chopped walnuts, *divided*

1/4 cup miniature marshmallows

1/4 cup flaked coconut

1. In a mixing bowl, cream butter and sugar. Beat in egg and vanilla. Combine the flour, cocoa, baking powder and salt; gradually add to creamed mixture and mix well. Stir in 1/2 cup M&M's and 1/4 cup walnuts.

2. Spread onto a greased 14-in. pizza pan to within 1/2 in. of edges. Sprinkle with remaining M&M's and walnuts. Top with marshmallows and coconut. Bake at 350° for 15-20 minutes or until a toothpick inserted near the center comes out clean. Cool on a wire rack. Cut into wedges. **Yield:** 10-12 servings.

Fancy Cream Cupcakes

~Merrilee Chambers, Haines Junction, Yukon Territory

1/2 cup shortening

1-1/2 cups sugar

4 egg whites

1 teaspoon vanilla extract

2 cups all-purpose flour

3-1/2 teaspoons baking powder

1 teaspoon salt

1 cup milk

1 cup heavy whipping cream

2 tablespoons confectioners' sugar

4 to 5 drops red food coloring, optional

1/4 teaspoon almond extract

1. In a mixing bowl, cream shortening and sugar. Add egg whites, one at a time, beating well after each addition. Beat in vanilla. Combine dry ingredients; add to creamed mixture alternately with milk. Fill paper- or foil-lined muffin cups two-thirds full. Bake at 350° for 15-20 minutes or until a toothpick comes out clean. Cool for 10 minutes; remove to wire racks to cool completely.

2. For filling, in a mixing bowl, beat cream until soft peaks form. Gradually beat in confectioners' sugar and food coloring if desired until stiff peaks form. Beat in almond extract.

3. Cut a 1-in. cone shape from the center of each cupcake; set cone aside. Fill indentation with filling. Cut each cone in half from top to bottom; place two halves on filling for butterfly wings. If desired, pipe a thin strip of filling between wings for butterfly body. **Yield:** 22 cupcakes.

Peanut Butter Brownies

~Linda Wales, Millerton, Pennsylvania

2/3 cup butter, softened

2/3 cup peanut butter

2 cups sugar

2 teaspoons vanilla extract

4 eggs

1 cup all-purpose flour

2/3 cup baking cocoa

2 teaspoons baking powder

1. In a mixing bowl, cream butter, peanut butter, sugar and vanilla. Add eggs, one at a time, beating well after each addition. Combine flour, cocoa and baking powder; add to creamed mixture just until blended. Pour into a greased 13-in. x 9-in. x 2-in. baking pan.

2. Bake at 350° for 22-28 minutes or until a toothpick inserted near the center comes out with moist crumbs (do not overbake). Cool on a wire rack. Cut into bars. **Yield:** about 2 dozen.

Fudgy Nut Brownies

~Ruth Sparer Stern, Shadow Hills, California

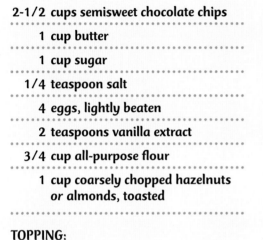

2-1/2 cups semisweet chocolate chips

1 cup butter

1 cup sugar

1/4 teaspoon salt

4 eggs, lightly beaten

2 teaspoons vanilla extract

3/4 cup all-purpose flour

1 cup coarsely chopped hazelnuts *or* almonds, toasted

TOPPING:

12 squares (1 ounce *each*) semisweet chocolate

1 tablespoon shortening

3 squares (1 ounce *each*) white baking chocolate

1. In a saucepan over low heat, melt chocolate chips and butter; remove from the heat. Add sugar and salt; stir until dissolved. Cool for 10 minutes. Stir in eggs, vanilla, flour and nuts. Spread into a greased 15-in. x 10-in. x 1-in. baking pan. Bake at 350° for 25-30 minutes or until a toothpick inserted near the center comes out with moist crumbs (do not overbake). Cool completely on a wire rack.

2. For topping, in a heavy saucepan or microwave, heat semisweet chocolate and shortening just until melted. Spread over brownies.

3. Melt white chocolate. Pour into a small heavy-duty resealable plastic bag; cut a small hole in corner of bag. Pipe thin lines 1 in. apart widthwise. Beginning about 1 in. from a wide side, gently pull a toothpick through the lines to the opposite side. Wipe toothpick clean. Then pull toothpick through lines in opposite direction. Repeat over entire top at 1-in. intervals. Cut into bars. **Yield:** about 2-1/2 dozen.

German Chocolate Cupcakes

~Lettice Charmasson, San Diego, California

1 package (18-1/4 ounces) German chocolate cake mix

1 cup water

3 eggs

1/2 cup vegetable oil

3 tablespoons chopped pecans

3 tablespoons flaked coconut

3 tablespoons brown sugar

1. In a large mixing bowl, combine the cake mix, water, eggs and oil. Beat on medium speed for 2 minutes. Fill paper-lined muffin cups three-fourths full. Combine pecans, coconut and brown sugar; sprinkle over batter.

2. Bake at 400° for 15-20 minutes or until a toothpick comes out clean. Cool for 5 minutes before removing from pans to wire racks. **Yield:** about 2 dozen.

Editor's Note: This recipe was tested with Betty Crocker German chocolate cake mix.

Chocolate Banana Split Cupcakes

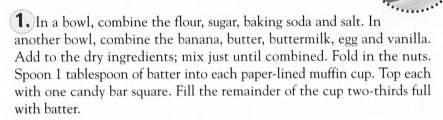

~Lorelie Miller, Benito, Manitoba

1-1/4 cups all-purpose flour

1/2 cup sugar

1/4 teaspoon baking soda

1/4 teaspoon salt

1/2 cup mashed banana (about 1 medium)

1/2 cup butter, melted

1/4 cup buttermilk

1 egg, lightly beaten

1/2 teaspoon vanilla extract

1/2 cup chopped walnuts

2 milk chocolate bars (1.55 ounces each), broken into squares, *divided*

FROSTING:

1 tablespoon butter, melted

1/2 teaspoon vanilla extract

1-1/2 cups confectioners' sugar

1 to 2 tablespoons milk

12 maraschino cherries with stems

1. In a bowl, combine the flour, sugar, baking soda and salt. In another bowl, combine the banana, butter, buttermilk, egg and vanilla. Add to the dry ingredients; mix just until combined. Fold in the nuts. Spoon 1 tablespoon of batter into each paper-lined muffin cup. Top each with one candy bar square. Fill the remainder of the cup two-thirds full with batter.

2. Bake at 350° for 20-25 minutes or until a toothpick inserted in the cupcake comes out clean. Cool for 10 minutes before removing from pan to a wire rack to cool completely.

3. In a bowl, combine the butter, vanilla, confectioners' sugar and enough milk to achieve spreading consistency. Frost. In a microwave, melt the remaining candy bar squares; drizzle over frosting. Top each with a cherry. **Yield:** 1 dozen.

Brownies in a Cone

~Mitzi Sentiff, Alexandria, Virginia

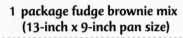

1 **package fudge brownie mix
(13-inch x 9-inch pan size)**

17 **ice cream cake cones
(about 2-3/4-inches tall)**

1 **cup (6 ounces) semisweet
chocolate chips**

1 **tablespoon shortening**

Colored sprinkles

1. Prepare brownie batter according to package directions, using 3 eggs. Place the ice cream cones in muffin cups; spoon about 3 tablespoons batter into each cone. Bake at 350° for 25-30 minutes or until a toothpick comes out clean and top is dry (do not overbake). Cool completely.

2. In a microwave, melt chocolate chips and shortening; stir until smooth. Dip tops of brownies in melted chocolate; decorate with sprinkles. **Yield:** 17 servings.

Editor's Note: This recipe was tested with Keebler ice cream cups. These brownie cones are best served the day they're prepared.

Fast Fudgy Brownies

~Mary Sprick, New Haven, Missouri

1 **cup vegetable oil**

4 **eggs**

1 **teaspoon vanilla extract**

2 **cups sugar**

1-1/3 **cups all-purpose flour**

1/2 **cup baking cocoa**

1 **teaspoon salt**

1 **cup (6 ounces) semisweet
chocolate chips**

1/2 **cup chopped maraschino cherries
or nuts, optional**

1. In a mixing bowl, beat oil, eggs and vanilla on medium speed for 1 minute. Combine the sugar, flour, cocoa and salt; add to egg mixture just until blended. Stir in chocolate chips and cherries. Pour into a greased 13-in. x 9-in. x 2-in. baking pan.

2. Bake at 350° for 30-35 minutes or until a toothpick inserted near the center comes out with moist crumbs (do not overbake). Cool on a wire rack. Cut into bars. **Yield:** 2 dozen.

Orange Applesauce Cupcakes

~Janis Plourde, Smooth Rock Falls, Ontario

6 tablespoons butter, softened

1 cup packed brown sugar

1 egg

1/2 cup unsweetened applesauce

1 teaspoon vanilla extract

1 teaspoon grated orange peel

1 cup all-purpose flour

1 teaspoon baking powder

1/2 teaspoon salt

1/4 teaspoon baking soda

1/2 cup chopped pecans

FROSTING:

1/4 cup butter, softened

2 cups confectioners' sugar

1-1/2 teaspoons grated orange peel

2 to 4 teaspoons orange juice

1. In a mixing bowl, cream the butter and brown sugar. Add egg; beat well. Beat in applesauce, vanilla and orange peel. Combine the flour, baking powder, salt and baking soda; add to creamed mixture. Stir in pecans.

2. Fill paper-lined muffin cups half full. Bake at 350° for 20-25 minutes or until a toothpick comes out clean. Cool for 10 minutes before removing from pan to a wire rack to cool completely.

3. For frosting, in a small mixing bowl, cream butter and confectioners' sugar. Add orange peel and enough orange juice to achieve spreading consistency. Frost cupcakes. **Yield:** 1 dozen.

Cream-Filled Cupcakes

~Edie DeSpain, Logan, Utah

3 cups all-purpose flour

2 cups sugar

1/3 cup baking cocoa

2 teaspoons baking soda

1 teaspoon salt

2 eggs

1 cup milk

1 cup vegetable oil

1 cup water

1 teaspoon vanilla extract

FILLING:

1/4 cup butter, softened

1/4 cup shortening

2 cups confectioners' sugar

3 tablespoons milk

1 teaspoon vanilla extract

Pinch salt

Chocolate frosting

1. In a mixing bowl, combine the first five ingredients. Add eggs, milk, oil, water and vanilla. Beat until smooth, about 2 minutes. Fill paper-lined muffin cups half full.

2. Bake at 375° for 15-20 minutes or until a toothpick inserted near the center comes out clean. Remove from pans to wire racks to cool completely.

3. In a mixing bowl, combine butter, shortening, confectioners' sugar, milk, vanilla and salt; beat until fluffy, about 5 minutes. Insert a very small tip into a pastry or plastic bag; fill with cream filling. Push the tip through the bottom of paper liner to fill each cupcake. Frost tops with chocolate frosting. **Yield:** 3 dozen.

Mint Brownie Cupcakes

~*Carol Maertz, Spruce Grove, Alberta*

1 cup mint chocolate chips

1/2 cup butter

1/2 cup sugar

2 eggs

1/2 cup all-purpose flour

1 teaspoon baking powder

TOPPING:

4 cups miniature marshmallows

3/4 cup milk

1-1/2 teaspoons peppermint extract

Green *or* red food coloring, optional

1-1/2 cups heavy whipping cream, whipped

Additional chocolate chips, optional

1. In a heavy saucepan, melt chips and butter; stir until smooth. Remove from the heat. Stir in sugar and eggs. Combine flour and baking powder; gradually stir into chocolate mixture until smooth. Fill paper-lined muffin cups half full. Bake at 350° for 15-20 minutes or until a toothpick comes out clean (cupcakes will fall in center). Remove to a wire rack.

2. In a saucepan, cook and stir marshmallows and milk over low heat until smooth. Remove from the heat; stir in extract and food coloring if desired. Cover and refrigerate until cool, about 15 minutes. Fold in whipped cream. Spread over cupcakes or top each with a dollop of topping. Chill for at least 1 hour. Sprinkle with chocolate chips if desired. Store in the refrigerator. **Yield:** 16 cupcakes.

Editor's Note: If mint chocolate chips are not available, substitute semisweet chocolate chips and add 1/4 teaspoon peppermint extract.

Peanut Butter Cupcakes

~*Alyce Wyman, Pembina, North Dakota*

1 package (18-1/4 ounces) white cake mix

18 miniature peanut butter cups

1-1/3 cups prepared vanilla frosting

2 tablespoons creamy peanut butter

1. Prepare cake mix according to package directions. Spoon about 2 tablespoons of batter into each paper-lined muffin cup. Place a peanut butter cup in each; fill two-thirds full with remaining batter. Bake at 350° for 20-25 minutes or until lightly browned and a toothpick inserted into cupcake comes out clean. Cool for 10 minutes before removing to wire racks to cool completely.

2. In a bowl, stir together the frosting and peanut butter until smooth. Frost cupcakes. **Yield:** 1-1/2 dozen.

Mocha Truffle Brownies

~Margaret Roberts, Kuna, Idaho

1-1/4 cups semisweet chocolate chips

1/2 cup butter

1 teaspoon instant coffee granules

2 tablespoons hot water

2 eggs

3/4 cup *each* packed brown sugar and all-purpose flour

1/2 teaspoon baking powder

FILLING:

1 tablespoon instant coffee granules

1 tablespoon hot water

1 package (8 ounces) cream cheese, softened

1/3 cup confectioners' sugar

1 cup (6 ounces) semisweet chocolate chips, melted

GLAZE:

1/4 cup semisweet chocolate chips

1 teaspoon shortening

1. In a heavy saucepan or microwave, melt chips and butter. Stir until smooth; cool for 5 minutes. Dissolve coffee granules in hot water; set aside. In a mixing bowl, combine eggs and brown sugar; beat on medium for 1 minute. Stir in chocolate mixture and coffee. Combine flour and baking powder; gradually add to chocolate mixture. Transfer to a greased 9-in. square baking pan. Bake at 350° for 30-35 minutes or until a toothpick comes out with moist crumbs. Cool completely on a wire rack.

2. Dissolve coffee granules in water; set aside. In a mixing bowl, beat cream cheese until smooth. Beat in confectioners' sugar, melted chocolate and coffee. Spread over brownies. For glaze, melt the chips and shortening; stir until smooth. Drizzle over filling. Refrigerate for at least 2 hours before cutting. **Yield:** about 6-1/2 dozen.

Caramel Cashew Brownies

~Judy High, Berryville, Arkansas

18 caramels

1/3 cup butter

2 tablespoons milk

3/4 cup sugar

2 eggs

1/2 teaspoon vanilla extract

1 cup all-purpose flour

1/2 teaspoon baking powder

1/4 teaspoon salt

1 cup chopped salted cashews

1. In a saucepan, cook and stir caramels, butter and milk over low heat until the caramels are melted and mixture is smooth. Remove from the heat; stir in sugar. Combine eggs and vanilla; stir into caramel mixture. Combine flour, baking powder and salt; stir into caramel mixture until blended. Fold in cashews.

2. Transfer to a greased 9-in. square baking pan. Bake at 350° for 24-28 minutes or until a toothpick inserted near the center comes out clean. Cool on a wire rack. Cut into bars. **Yield:** 25 brownies.

Raspberry Crunch Brownies

~Rita Winterberger, Huson, Montana

☑ Uses less fat, sugar or salt. Includes Nutritional Analysis and Diabetic Exchanges.

1/4 cup vegetable oil

1-1/4 cups sugar

4 egg whites

1 cup all-purpose flour

1/2 teaspoon baking powder

1/4 teaspoon salt

2/3 cup baking cocoa

1-1/2 teaspoons vanilla extract

Nonstick cooking spray

1/4 cup raspberry jam

2 tablespoons Grape-Nuts cereal

1. In a mixing bowl, beat oil and sugar. Add egg whites and continue beating until well mixed. Combine flour, baking powder, salt and cocoa; add to mixing bowl and beat until moistened. Stir in vanilla. (Batter will be thick.) Coat a 9-in. square pan with vegetable spray. Spread batter into pan.

2. Bake at 350° for 20-25 minutes or until a toothpick inserted in the center comes out clean. Cool 10 minutes on a wire rack. Spread with jam and sprinkle with Grape-Nuts if desired. Cool completely. **Yield:** 2 dozen.

Nutrition Facts: One serving equals 105 calories, 47 mg sodium, 0 mg cholesterol, 19 gm carbohydrates, 2 gm protein, 3 gm fat. **Diabetic Exchanges:** 1 starch, 1/2 fat.

Out-of-This-World Brownies

~Jeannette Haley, Council, Idaho

1 cup butter, softened

2 cups sugar

4 eggs

2 teaspoons vanilla extract

2 cups all-purpose flour

1/4 cup plus 3 tablespoons baking cocoa

1/8 teaspoon salt

BROWN BUTTER FROSTING:
1/2 cup butter

4 cups confectioners' sugar

1/4 cup plus 2 teaspoons half-and-half cream

2 teaspoons vanilla extract

GLAZE:
1 square (1 ounce) unsweetened chocolate

1 tablespoon butter

1. In a mixing bowl, cream butter and sugar. Add the eggs, one at a time, beating well after each addition. Beat in vanilla. Combine flour, cocoa and salt; gradually add to the creamed mixture.

2. Spread into an ungreased 13-in. x 9-in. x 2-in. baking pan. Bake at 350° for 25-30 minutes or until a toothpick inserted near the center comes out clean (do not overbake). Cool on wire rack.

3. For frosting, in a heavy saucepan, cook and stir butter over medium heat for 5-7 minutes or until golden brown. Pour into a mixing bowl; beat in the confectioners' sugar, cream and vanilla. Frost cooled brownies.

4. For glaze, melt chocolate and butter; drizzle over the frosting. Cut into bars. **Yield:** 3 dozen.

Raspberry Swirl Cupcakes

~Christine Sohm, Newton, Ontario

1 package (18-1/4 ounces) white cake mix

1/4 cup raspberry pie filling

1/2 cup shortening

1/3 cup milk

1 teaspoon vanilla extract

1/4 teaspoon salt

3 cups confectioners' sugar

Fresh raspberries and mint, optional

1. Prepare cake mix according to package directions. Fill paper-lined muffin cups two-thirds full. Drop 1/2 teaspoon of pie filling in the center of each; swirl with a knife. Bake at 350° for 20-25 minutes or until a toothpick comes out clean. Cool for 10 minutes before removing from pans to wire racks to cool completely.

2. In a mixing bowl, cream shortening. Add milk, vanilla, salt and confectioners' sugar; beat until fluffy. Frost cupcakes. Garnish with raspberries and mint if desired. **Yield:** about 1-1/2 dozen.

Favorite Frosted Brownies

~Barbara Birk, St. George, Utah

1 cup butter, softened

2 cups sugar

4 eggs

2 teaspoons vanilla extract

1-3/4 cups all-purpose flour

6 tablespoons baking cocoa

1 teaspoon baking powder

1/4 teaspoon salt

FROSTING:

1/2 cup butter, softened

1/4 cup evaporated milk

1 teaspoon vanilla extract

2 tablespoons baking cocoa

3 cups confectioners' sugar

Decorating sprinkles, optional

1. In a large mixing bowl, cream butter and sugar. Add eggs, one at a time, beating well after each addition. Beat in vanilla. Combine the flour, cocoa, baking powder and salt; gradually add to creamed mixture and mix well.

2. Spread into a greased 13-in. x 9-in. x 2-in. baking pan. Bake at 350° for 25-30 minutes or until a toothpick inserted near the center comes out clean. Cool on a wire rack.

3. For frosting, in a mixing bowl, beat the butter, milk and vanilla; add cocoa. Gradually beat in confectioners' sugar until smooth. Spread over cooled brownies. Decorate with sprinkles if desired. **Yield:** 12-15 servings.

Spring

Caterpillar Cake

~Lee Dean, Boaz, Alabama

1 package (18-1/4 ounces) yellow cake mix

1 can (16 ounces) vanilla frosting

2-1/2 cups flaked coconut, *divided*

2 small purple gumdrops

1 small red gumdrop

2 small orange gumdrops

2 pretzel sticks

Yellow, red and green liquid food coloring

1. Prepare cake batter according to package directions. Fill a greased 8-oz. custard cup three-fourths full. Pour remaining batter into a greased 10-in. fluted tube pan. Bake the custard cup at 350° for 20-25 minutes and the tube cake for 40-45 minutes or until a toothpick inserted near the center comes out clean. Cool for 10 minutes before removing cakes to wire racks; cool completely.

2. Cut large cake in half widthwise. To form caterpillar, place one half on a 15-in. x 10-in. covered board. Place the remaining portion next to the first to form an "S." With a serrated knife, level top and bottom of small cake; place on one end of caterpillar for head.

3. Frost the small cake with vanilla frosting; gently press 1/4 cup coconut into frosting. Add purple gumdrops for eyes. For mouth, flatten red gumdrop with a rolling pin between waxed paper; place below eyes. For antennae, press orange gumdrops onto pretzels; insert into head.

4. Place 3/4 cup coconut each in three small resealable plastic bags. Tint one orange with yellow and red food coloring; tint one green and one yellow. Frost the caterpillar with remaining vanilla frosting. Press alternate colors of coconut into frosting. **Yield:** 8-10 servings.

Ladybug Cookies

~Kendra Barclay, De Kalb, Illinois

1 cup vanilla frosting

1/2 cup vanilla *or* white chips

Red liquid *or* paste food coloring

1 package (12 ounces) chocolate and marshmallow cookies

12 large black gumdrops

3 strips black shoestring licorice, cut into 1-inch pieces

1. In a microwave-safe bowl, melt frosting and vanilla chips; stir until smooth. Stir in food coloring. Spread over the rounded tops of cookies; place on a waxed paper-lined baking sheet.

2. For head, insert two pieces of licorice into gumdrops for antennae. With a toothpick, attach a gumdrop onto the side of each cookie. Use a toothpick or knife to draw a line from the head down the center of each cookie. Insert six pieces of licorice into frosting of each ladybug for legs. Chop remaining licorice into pieces; place on top for spots. **Yield:** 1 dozen.

Editor's Note: This recipe was tested with Nabisco Pinwheels.

Beetle Juice

~Mary Herron, Meshoppen, Pennsylvania

1 cup sugar

1 cup water

2-1/2 cups white grape juice

1-1/2 cups orange juice

1 cup lemon juice

In a large saucepan over medium heat, dissolve sugar in water. Remove from the heat. Stir in the juices; strain to remove pulp. Add enough water or ice to measure 1 gallon; stir well. **Yield:** 16 servings (4 quarts).

Flutter-by Buns

~Kendra Barclay, De Kalb, Illinois

1 tube (12.4 ounces) refrigerated cinnamon rolls with icing

8 maraschino cherries

1. Separate rolls and cut in half. Place on a greased baking sheet with cinnamon side up and curved edges touching to form wings. Cut the cherries into six wedges; place three on each wing. Bake at 400° for 13-17 minutes or until golden brown. Cool on a wire rack.

2. Stir icing until smooth; place in a pastry bag with a round tip (or in a small heavy-duty resealable plastic bag with a small hole cut in the corner). Pipe icing to outline the wings. **Yield:** 8 servings.

Butterfly Cake

~Bonnie Jost, Manitowoc, Wisconsin

1 cup butter, softened

2 cups sugar

3 eggs

1 teaspoon grated orange peel

1 teaspoon orange extract

2 cups all-purpose flour

1/4 teaspoon salt

1/4 teaspoon baking soda

1 cup (8 ounces) sour cream

FROSTING:

3/4 cup butter, softened

2 packages (3 ounces *each*) cream cheese, softened

3 cups confectioners' sugar

1 teaspoon vanilla extract

Yellow gel or paste food coloring

Assorted colored sugars

6 small gumdrops

Orange peel

1. In a large mixing bowl, cream butter and sugar. Add the eggs, orange peel and extract; beat until combined. Combine the flour, salt and baking soda; add to the creamed mixture alternately with sour cream. Spoon into two greased 9-in. heart-shaped baking pans; spread evenly in pans. Bake at 350° for 25-30 minutes or until a toothpick inserted near the center comes out clean. Cool for 10 minutes before removing from pans to wire racks to cool completely.

2. Cut 1-1/2 in. off the pointed ends of each heart cake; set aside. For the butterfly wings, place the cut ends of the heart cakes together on a 17-in. x 15-in. covered board. Trim reserved cake pieces to form the rounded ends of the butterfly's body.

3. In a small mixing bowl, cream butter and cream cheese. Add confectioners' sugar and vanilla. Remove 1/2 cup frosting and tint yellow; set aside. Frost cake sides and top with white frosting. Cut a small hole in the corner of a pastry or plastic bag; insert #6 round tip. Fill bag with remaining white frosting; set aside.

4. Frost a portion of each wing with yellow frosting. Decorate butterfly's body and wings with colored sugars. Pipe white frosting to separate colored sections on wings and to outline the body. Decorate the wings with gumdrops.

5. Using a citrus stripper, cut two 12-in.-long pieces of orange peel. Wrap around the handle of a wooden spoon. Remove from spoon and place above the body for antennae. **Yield:** 8-10 servings.

Pizza Party

Deep-Dish Sausage Pizza

~Michele Madden, Washington Court House, Ohio

1 package (1/4 ounce) active dry yeast

2/3 cup warm water (110° to 115°)

1-3/4 to 2 cups all-purpose flour

1/4 cup vegetable oil

1 teaspoon *each* dried oregano, basil and marjoram

1/2 teaspoon garlic salt

1/2 teaspoon onion salt

TOPPINGS:

4 cups (16 ounces) shredded mozzarella cheese, *divided*

1 large onion, chopped

2 medium green peppers, chopped

1/2 teaspoon *each* dried oregano, basil and marjoram

1 tablespoon olive oil

1 cup grated Parmesan cheese

1 pound bulk pork sausage, cooked and drained

1 can (28 ounces) diced tomatoes, well drained

2 ounces sliced pepperoni

1. In a mixing bowl, dissolve yeast in water. Add 1 cup flour, oil and seasonings; beat until smooth. Add enough remaining flour to form a soft dough. Turn onto a floured surface; knead until smooth and elastic, 6-8 minutes. Place in a greased bowl; turn once to grease top. Cover and let rise in a warm place until doubled, about 1 hour. Punch dough down; roll out into a 15-in. circle.

2. Transfer to a well-greased 12-in. heavy ovenproof skillet, letting dough drape over the edges. Sprinkle with 1 cup mozzarella.

3. In another skillet, saute onion, green peppers and seasonings in oil until tender; drain. Layer half of the mixture over crust. Layer with half of the Parmesan, sausage and tomatoes. Sprinkle with 2 cups mozzarella. Repeat layers. Fold crust over to form an edge.

4. Bake for 400° for 20 minutes. Sprinkle with pepperoni and remaining mozzarella. Bake 10-15 minutes longer or until crust is browned. Let stand 10 minutes before slicing. **Yield:** 8 slices.

Bacon Cheeseburger Pizza

~Cherie Ackerman, Lakeland, Minnesota

1/2 pound ground beef

1 small onion, chopped

1 prebaked Italian bread shell crust (1 pound)

1 can (8 ounces) pizza sauce

6 bacon strips, cooked and crumbled

20 dill pickle coin slices

2 cups (8 ounces) shredded mozzarella cheese

2 cups (8 ounces) shredded cheddar cheese

1 teaspoon pizza or Italian seasoning

In a skillet, cook beef and onion until meat is no longer pink; drain and set aside. Place crust on an ungreased 12-in. pizza pan. Spread with pizza sauce. Top with beef mixture, bacon, pickles and cheeses. Sprinkle with pizza seasoning. Bake at 450° for 8-10 minutes or until cheese is melted. **Yield:** 8 slices.

Baked Potato Pizza

~Gina Pierson, Centralia, Missouri

1 package (6 ounces) pizza crust mix

3 medium unpeeled potatoes, baked and cooled

1 tablespoon butter, melted

1/4 teaspoon garlic powder

1/4 teaspoon Italian seasoning or dried oregano

1 cup (8 ounces) sour cream

6 bacon strips, cooked and crumbled

3 to 5 green onions, chopped

1-1/2 cups (6 ounces) shredded mozzarella cheese

1/2 cup shredded cheddar cheese

1. Prepare crust according to package directions. Press dough into a lightly greased 14-in. pizza pan; build up edges slightly. Bake at 400° for 5-6 minutes or until crust is firm and begins to brown.

2. Cut potatoes into 1/2-in. cubes. In a bowl, combine butter, garlic powder and Italian seasoning. Add potatoes and toss. Spread sour cream over crust; top with potato mixture, bacon, onions and cheeses. Bake at 400° for 15-20 minutes or until cheese is lightly browned. Let stand for 5 minutes before cutting. **Yield:** 8 slices.

Deluxe Turkey Club Pizza

~Philis Bukovcik, Lansing, Michigan

1 tube (10 ounces) refrigerated
    pizza crust

1 tablespoon sesame seeds

1/4 cup mayonnaise

1 teaspoon grated lemon peel

1 medium tomato, thinly sliced

1/2 cup cubed cooked turkey

4 bacon strips, cooked and crumbled

2 medium fresh mushrooms, sliced

1/4 cup chopped onion

1-1/2 cups (6 ounces) shredded
    Colby/Monterey Jack cheese

1. Unroll pizza dough and press onto a greased 12-in. pizza pan; build up edges slightly. Sprinkle with sesame seeds. Bake at 425° for 12-14 minutes or until edges are lightly browned.

2. Combine mayonnaise and lemon peel; spread over crust. Top with tomato, turkey, bacon, mushrooms, onion and cheese. Bake for 6-8 minutes or until cheese is melted. Cut into slices. **Yield:** 8 slices.

Editor's Note: Reduced-fat or fat-free mayonnaise may not be substituted for regular mayonnaise in this recipe.

Pizza with Stuffed Crust

~Sandy McKenzie, Braham, Minnesota

2 teaspoons cornmeal

2 tubes (10 ounces *each*)
    refrigerated pizza crust

8 ounces string cheese

1 tablespoon butter, melted

1-1/2 teaspoons minced fresh basil
    or 1/2 teaspoon dried basil

1 can (8 ounces) pizza sauce

1 package (3-1/2 ounces) sliced
    pepperoni

1 can (4 ounces) mushroom stems
    and pieces, drained

1 can (2-1/4 ounces) sliced ripe
    olives, drained

2 cups (8 ounces) shredded
    mozzarella cheese

1. Sprinkle cornmeal evenly over a greased 15-in. x 10-in. x 1-in. baking pan. Unroll pizza dough and place on pan, letting dough drape 1 in. over the edges. Pinch center seam to seal. Place pieces of string cheese around edges of pan. Fold dough over cheese; pinch to seal. Brush the crust with butter; sprinkle with basil. Bake at 425° for 5 minutes.

2. Spread sauce over crust. Place two-thirds of the pepperoni in a single layer over sauce. Sprinkle with mushrooms, olives and cheese. Top with remaining pepperoni. Bake for 10-12 minutes or until crust and cheese are lightly browned. **Yield:** 8-10 slices.

Editor's Note: 8 ounces of bulk mozzarella cheese, cut into 4-in. x 1/2-in. sticks, may be substituted for the string cheese.

Taco Pan Pizza

~Taste of Home Test Kitchen

1 tube (10 ounces) refrigerated pizza crust

1/2 cup sour cream

1/3 cup mayonnaise

2 tablespoons minced fresh cilantro

1 jalapeno pepper, seeded and chopped

1 teaspoon sugar

1/2 teaspoon chili powder

1/4 teaspoon salt

1/4 teaspoon ground cumin

1 medium ripe avocado, peeled and cubed

2 teaspoons lime juice

2 medium tomatoes, chopped

1/4 cup chopped green onions

1/3 cup sliced ripe olives

1 cup (4 ounces) shredded Mexican cheese blend *or* cheddar cheese

1. Unroll pizza dough and place in a greased 15-in. x 10-in. x 1-in. baking pan; flatten dough and build up edges slightly. Prick dough several times with a fork. Bake at 425° for 10-11 minutes or until lightly browned. Cool on a wire rack.

2. Meanwhile, in a bowl, combine the sour cream, mayonnaise, cilantro, jalapeno, sugar, chili powder, salt and cumin. Spread over cooled crust. Toss avocado with lime juice; arrange over sour cream mixture. Sprinkle with tomatoes, onions, olives and cheese. Refrigerate until serving. Cut into squares. **Yield:** 16-20 slices.

Editor's Note: When cutting or seeding hot peppers, use rubber or plastic gloves to protect your hands. Avoid touching your face.

Games

Cheese Spread Dice

~Taste of Home Test Kitchen

3 packages (8 ounces *each*) cream cheese, softened, *divided*

2 cups (8 ounces) shredded Italian-blend or mozzarella cheese

1 small onion, finely chopped

1 tablespoon Worcestershire sauce

1 tablespoon minced fresh parsley

1 teaspoon milk

8 medium pitted ripe olives

Assorted crackers

1. In a mixing bowl, combine two packages of cream cheese, shredded cheese, onion, Worcestershire sauce and parsley. Press into a plastic wrap-lined 8-in. x 4-in. x 2-in. loaf pan. Cover and refrigerate overnight.

2. Remove from pan; cut in half widthwise. Stack one on top of the other on a serving plate. In a mixing bowl, beat milk and remaining cream cheese until smooth. Spread over cube. Cut olives in half; arrange on top and sides of dice. Serve with crackers. **Yield:** 3 cups.

Chocolate Dominoes

~Cathy Drew, Monroe, Michigan

1/4 cup butter, softened

1/2 cup sugar

2 eggs

3/4 cup chocolate syrup

2/3 cup all-purpose flour

1/2 cup vanilla frosting

Miniature chocolate chips

1. In a mixing bowl, cream the butter and sugar. Add eggs and chocolate syrup; mix well. Gradually add flour. Spread into a greased 8-in. square baking pan.

2. Bake at 350° for 30-35 minutes or until a toothpick inserted near the center comes out clean. Cool completely. Frost brownies; cut into 18 rectangles (2-1/3 in. x 1-1/8 in.). With a toothpick, draw a line dividing each rectangle in half widthwise. Decorate with chocolate chips. **Yield:** 1-1/2 dozen.

Gelatin Game Chips

~Taste of Home Test Kitchen

1/2 cup milk

1/2 cup sugar

3 envelopes unflavored gelatin

3/4 cup cold water

1-1/2 teaspoons vanilla extract

2 cups (16 ounces) sour cream

5 cups lemon-lime soda

4 packages (3 ounces *each*) berry blue gelatin

4 packages (3 ounces *each*) raspberry gelatin

1. In a saucepan, heat milk and sugar over low heat until sugar is dissolved. Soften unflavored gelatin in water; stir into the milk mixture until dissolved. Remove from the heat; add vanilla. Cool to lukewarm; blend in sour cream. Pour into a 13-in. x 9-in. x 2-in. dish. Chill until set.

2. In a saucepan, bring the soda to a boil. Place blue gelatin in a bowl; stir in 2-1/2 cups of soda until gelatin is dissolved. Pour into another 13-in. x 9-in. x 2-in. dish. Repeat with raspberry gelatin and remaining soda. Refrigerate until set. Using a 1-1/2-in. round cookie cutter, cut white, blue and red gelatin into rounds. Stack or scatter on a serving plate. **Yield:** 9 dozen.

Dartboard Pizza

~Taste of Home Test Kitchen

1 tube (10 ounces) refrigerated pizza crust

1 can (8 ounces) pizza sauce

2 cups (8 ounces) shredded mozzarella cheese

1 package (3-1/2 ounces) sliced pepperoni

1-1/2 cups (6 ounces) shredded cheddar cheese

1 cup chopped green pepper

1. Unroll pizza crust onto an ungreased 14-in. pizza pan; flatten dough and build up edges slightly. Prick dough several times with a fork. Bake at 425° for 7 minutes or until lightly browned. Cool on a wire rack. Spread pizza sauce over the crust; sprinkle with mozzarella cheese.

2. Place one pepperoni slice in the center of the pizza; chop remaining pepperoni. Sprinkle some chopped pepperoni around outer edge of pizza, leaving 1/2 in. of crust. Sprinkle remaining pepperoni in a circle between center slice and outer edge. Arrange cheddar cheese and green pepper alternately in a spoke pattern. Bake at 425° for 12 minutes or until cheese is melted and pizza is heated through. **Yield:** 1 pizza (8 slices).

Slumber Party

Starry Night Taco Cups

~Taste of Home Test Kitchen

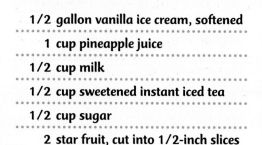

1 pound ground beef

1/2 cup chopped onion

1/4 cup salsa

1/4 cup ketchup

1 tablespoon chili powder

1 teaspoon salt

16 flour tortillas (7 inches)

Toppings: shredded lettuce, chopped tomato, shredded cheddar cheese and/or sour cream

1. In a skillet, cook beef and onion over medium heat until meat is no longer pink; drain. Add salsa, ketchup, chili powder and salt; heat through.

2. Cut each tortilla into a 4-in. square; set scraps aside. Microwave eight squares at a time for 20 seconds. Press onto the bottom and up the sides of greased muffin cups; set aside. Cut tortilla scraps into stars with a 1-in. cookie cutter; place on a greased baking sheet.

3. Bake at 350° for 6 minutes or until golden brown; set aside. Fill each tortilla cup with 2 tablespoons meat mixture. Bake for 12-15 minutes longer or until tortillas are golden brown. Serve with toppings of your choice; garnish with toasted stars. **Yield:** 16 servings.

Sleepy-Time Shakes

~Dixie Terry, Marion, Illinois

1/2 gallon vanilla ice cream, softened

1 cup pineapple juice

1/2 cup milk

1/2 cup sweetened instant iced tea

1/2 cup sugar

2 star fruit, cut into 1/2-inch slices

In a mixing bowl, combine the ice cream, pineapple juice, milk, tea and sugar. Mix until smooth. Pour into chilled glasses; garnish with star fruit. Serve immediately. **Yield:** 7 servings.

Catch Some Z's

~Taste of Home Test Kitchen

1 tube (8 ounces) refrigerated
   crescent rolls

1 tablespoon butter, melted

2 tablespoons grated Parmesan
   cheese

1/4 teaspoon garlic salt

Pizza sauce, warmed, optional

1. Unroll crescent roll dough; press seams and perforations to seal. Cut dough with a 2-in. "Z" cookie cutter; place on ungreased baking sheets. Brush with butter. Combine Parmesan cheese and garlic salt; sprinkle over dough.

2. Bake at 375° for 5-6 minutes or until golden brown. Serve warm with pizza sauce if desired. **Yield:** 2 dozen.

Slumber Party Cookie Pizza

~Shirley Petryk, Redmond, Washington

1/2 cup butter, softened

1/2 cup peanut butter

1/2 cup sugar

1/2 cup packed brown sugar

1 egg

1/2 teaspoon vanilla extract

1-1/4 cups all-purpose flour

1/2 teaspoon baking soda

1/4 teaspoon salt

1/2 cup semisweet chocolate chips

1 can (16 ounces) vanilla frosting
   or 2 cups frosting of your choice

Red, black, white, green and yellow
   gumdrops

1/4 cup vanilla or white chips

1. In a mixing bowl, cream butter, peanut butter and sugars. Beat in egg and vanilla. Combine flour, baking soda and salt; gradually add to the creamed mixture. Stir in chocolate chips. Pat onto a greased 14-in. pizza pan. Bake at 350° for 20-25 minutes or until golden brown; cool.

2. Spread frosting to within 1 in. of edge. Using a sharp knife, cut red gumdrops into 1/4-in. slices. Cut black gumdrops into slices and cut a hole in the center. Cut white gumdrops lengthwise, then into mushroom shapes. Cut green gumdrops into slices and place a small piece of red gumdrop in the center. Dice yellow and more green gumdrops.

3. Arrange all gumdrop shapes over frosting. Melt white chips; place in a pastry or plastic bag. Cut a small hole in the corner; drizzle over pizza. **Yield:** 8-10 servings.

Confetti Caramel Corn

~Dorothy Smith, El Dorado, Arkansas

7 cups Trix cereal

2/3 cup butter

2/3 cup sugar

1/4 cup light corn syrup

2 teaspoons vanilla extract

1/2 teaspoon baking soda

1. Place cereal in a large bowl. In a saucepan, combine the butter, sugar and corn syrup. Bring to a boil over medium heat; cook and stir for 5 minutes. Remove from the heat. Stir in vanilla and baking soda. Pour over cereal and stir to coat.

2. Transfer to greased baking sheets. Bake at 300° for 25 minutes, stirring after 15 minutes. Break apart while warm. Cool completely. Store in an airtight container. **Yield:** 10 cups.

Sleeping Bag Brownies

~Sharon Wilson Bickett, Chester, South Carolina

1 cup butter, softened

1 cup sugar

1 cup packed brown sugar

2 eggs

2 teaspoons vanilla extract

2 cups self-rising flour

2 cups chopped pecans, optional

1-1/2 cups white frosting

Black, green, orange, pink and blue gel food coloring

16 mint parfait Andes candies

16 gumballs (1/2 inch)

1. Line a 13-in. x 9-in. x 2-in. baking pan with foil; grease the foil. In a mixing bowl, cream butter and sugars. Beat in eggs and vanilla until combined. Add flour; mix well. Fold in pecans if desired. Pour into prepared pan. Bake at 325° for 35-40 minutes or until a toothpick comes out clean. Cool on a wire rack.

2. Using foil, lift brownies out of pan. Remove foil. Trim 1/2 in. from all sides of brownies; set aside for another use. Cut the remaining large rectangle into 16 3-in. x 1-1/2-in. bars. Tint 2 tablespoons frosting black; set aside.

3. Divide the remaining frosting between four small bowls; tint with green, orange, pink and blue food coloring. Frost four brownies with each color. Place remaining tinted frosting in small resealable plastic bags. Cut a small hole in the corner of bag; pipe a contrasting color around the edge of each brownie. Pipe designs on top.

4. For pillow, place an Andes candy, imprinted side down, on one end of brownie. Pipe a dab of frosting on pillow to attach gumball. With reserved black frosting, pipe eyes and mouth on each gumball. **Yield:** 16 brownies.

Editor's Note: As a substitute for each cup of self-rising flour, place 1-1/2 teaspoons baking powder and 1/2 teaspoon salt in a measuring cup. Add all-purpose flour to measure 1 cup.

Slumber Party Pizza

~Taste of Home Test Kitchen

1 prebaked Italian bread shell crust (14 ounces)

3 cups shredded cooked chicken

1 cup barbecue sauce

1 cup (4 ounces) shredded mozzarella cheese

1/2 cup shredded cheddar cheese

Minced fresh parsley

Place the crust on a 14-in. pizza pan. Combine the chicken and barbecue sauce; spread over crust. Sprinkle with cheeses. Bake at 450° for 8-10 minutes or until cheese is melted. Sprinkle with parsley. **Yield:** 8 slices.

Latenight Breadsticks

~Taste of Home Test Kitchen

1/2 cup grated Parmesan cheese

1/4 cup finely shredded cheddar cheese

1/2 teaspoon Italian seasoning

1/2 teaspoon garlic powder

1/8 teaspoon onion powder

1 loaf (1 pound) frozen white bread dough, thawed

1/4 cup butter, melted

In a shallow bowl, combine the first five ingredients; set aside. Divide dough into 16 pieces; roll each into a 6-in. rope. Dip ropes in butter, then roll in cheese mixture. Place 2 in. apart on a greased baking sheet. Let rest for 10 minutes. Bake at 400° for 10-12 minutes or until golden brown. **Yield:** 16 breadsticks.

Farm

Holstein Brownies

~Jodie Rush, Perkins, Oklahoma

2/3 cup butter, softened

2 cups sugar

1/2 cup water

2 eggs

2 teaspoons vanilla extract

1-1/2 cups all-purpose flour

3/4 cup baking cocoa

1/2 teaspoon baking soda

1/4 teaspoon salt

2 cups (12 ounces) semisweet chocolate chips

1/2 cup chopped pecans

1 jar (7 ounces) marshmallow creme

GLAZE:

3/4 cup confectioners' sugar

2 tablespoons baking cocoa

2 tablespoons butter, melted

2 tablespoons milk

1. In a mixing bowl, cream butter and sugar. Add water, eggs and vanilla; mix well. Combine the dry ingredients; gradually add to creamed mixture. Stir in chocolate chips and pecans. Spread into a greased 13-in. x 9-in. x 2-in. baking pan.

2. Bake at 350° for 35-40 minutes or until a toothpick inserted near the center comes out clean. Cool on a wire rack for 5-10 minutes.

3. Place marshmallow creme in a microwave-safe bowl. Microwave on high for 20-30 seconds or until warm; spread over warm brownies. Cool completely on a wire rack.

4. For glaze, combine confectioners' sugar, cocoa and butter in a small bowl; stir in enough milk to achieve drizzling consistency. With the tip of a spoon, use glaze to form irregular shapes resembling Holstein spots. Cut into bars. **Yield:** 3 dozen.

Editor's Note: This recipe was tested in an 850-watt microwave.

Pigs in a Blanket

~Kay Curtis, Guthrie, Oklahoma

- 1 package (1/4 ounce) active dry yeast
- 1/3 cup plus 1 teaspoon sugar, *divided*
- 2/3 cup warm milk (110° to 115°)
- 1/3 cup warm water (110° to 115°)
- 1 egg, beaten
- 2 tablespoons plus 2 teaspoons shortening, melted
- 1 teaspoon salt
- 3-2/3 cups all-purpose flour
- 10 hot dogs
- 2 slices process American cheese

1. In a mixing bowl, dissolve yeast and 1 teaspoon sugar in milk and water; let stand for 5 minutes. Add egg, shortening, salt, remaining sugar and enough flour to form a soft dough. Turn onto a floured surface; knead until smooth and elastic, about 8-10 minutes. Place in a greased bowl, turning once to grease top. Cover and let rise in a warm place until doubled, about 1 hour.

2. Cut a 1/4-in.-deep lengthwise slit in each hot dog. Cut cheese slices into five strips; place one strip in the slit of each hot dog.

3. Punch dough down; divide into 10 portions. Roll each into a 5-in. x 2-1/2-in. rectangle and wrap around prepared hot dogs; pinch seam and ends to seal. Place seam side down on greased baking sheets; let rise for 30 minutes. Bake at 350° for 15-18 minutes or until golden brown. **Yield:** 10 servings.

Farm Mouse Cookies

~Kay Curtis, Guthrie, Oklahoma

- 1 cup creamy peanut butter
- 1/2 cup butter, softened
- 1/2 cup sugar
- 1/2 cup packed brown sugar
- 1 egg
- 1 teaspoon vanilla extract
- 1-1/2 cups all-purpose flour
- 1/2 teaspoon baking soda
- Peanut halves
- Black shoestring licorice, cut into 2-1/2-inch pieces

1. In a mixing bowl, cream peanut butter, butter and sugars. Beat in egg and vanilla. Combine flour and baking soda; gradually add to creamed mixture. Cover and chill dough for 1 hour or overnight.

2. Roll into 1-in. balls. Pinch one end, forming a teardrop shape. Place 2 in. apart on ungreased baking sheets; press to flatten. For ears, press two peanuts into each cookie near the pointed end. Using a toothpick, make a 1/2-in.-deep hole for the tail in the end opposite the ears. Bake at 350° for 8-10 minutes or until golden. While cookies are warm, insert licorice for tails. Cool on wire racks. **Yield:** 4 dozen.

Beach

Cool Waters Shakes

~*Taste of Home Test Kitchen*

4 cups cold milk

2 packages (3 ounces *each*) berry blue gelatin

1 quart vanilla ice cream

In a blender, combine 2 cups of milk, one package of gelatin and 2 cups of ice cream. Cover and process for 30 seconds or until smooth. Repeat. Pour into glasses and serve immediately. **Yield:** 6 servings.

Seashell Salad

~*Taste of Home Test Kitchen*

3 cups uncooked medium shell, spiral *and/or* wagon wheel pasta

1/3 cup vinegar

1/4 cup olive oil

1 teaspoon garlic salt

1 teaspoon sugar

1 teaspoon Italian seasoning

1/4 teaspoon pepper

1 medium sweet red pepper

1 medium sweet yellow pepper

2 tablespoons chopped green onions

1. Cook the pasta according to package directions until tender; drain and rinse in cold water. Place in a large bowl; set aside.

2. In a jar with tight-fitting lid, combine vinegar, oil and seasonings; shake well. Add peppers, onions and dressing to pasta; toss to coat. Cover and refrigerate until serving. **Yield:** 6-8 servings.

Edible Inner Tubes

~*Taste of Home Test Kitchen*

1 can (12 ounces) tuna, drained

1/3 cup seasoned bread crumbs

1/4 cup creamy Italian salad dressing

2 to 3 tablespoons Dijon mustard

2 tablespoons dill pickle relish

6 plain bagels

Lettuce leaves

In a bowl, combine the first five ingredients. Cut the bagels in half horizontally. Place lettuce on bottom halves; top with tuna mixture. Replace top halves. **Yield:** 6 servings.

Susie Sunshine Cake

~*Taste of Home Test Kitchen*

1 package (9 ounces) yellow cake mix

1 carton (8 ounces) frozen whipped topping, thawed

1 teaspoon grated lemon peel

1 teaspoon grated orange peel

Red and yellow liquid food coloring

2 medium lemons, sliced and halved

2 medium oranges, sliced and halved

2 blueberries

1 large strawberry

1. Prepare and bake the cake according to package directions, using a greased and floured 8-in. round baking pan. Cool for 10 minutes; remove from pan to a wire rack to cool completely.

2. Transfer to a 12- to 14-in. serving plate. Combine whipped topping and lemon and orange peels. Frost top and sides of cake. Place drops of red and yellow food coloring randomly over frosting (see photo 1 below). With a spatula, blend colors randomly (see photo 2).

3. Alternate lemon and orange slices around base of cake to form rays. Add two orange slices and blueberries for eyes. Slice the strawberry; use two center slices for the mouth, placing them on the cake with straight edges touching. Refrigerate until serving. **Yield:** 6 servings.

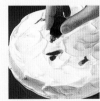
1. Place drops of red and yellow food coloring randomly over frosting.

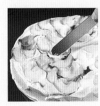
2. With a spatula, blend colors randomly over frosting.

Space

Flying Saucers

~*Taste of Home Test Kitchen*

1/2 cup mayonnaise

2 tablespoons Dijon mustard

4 large pita breads, halved

8 lettuce leaves

16 thin slices bologna

8 thin slices fully cooked ham

16 thin slices tomato

Combine the mayonnaise and mustard; spread about 1 tablespoon into each pita half. Stuff each with one lettuce leaf, two slices of bologna, one slice of ham and two slices of tomato. **Yield:** 4-6 servings.

Little Dippers

~*Taste of Home Test Kitchen*

1 cup (8 ounces) vanilla yogurt

3 tablespoons orange marmalade

1 tablespoon confectioners' sugar

1 large apple, sliced 1/4 inch thick

5 large strawberries, halved lengthwise

1 large kiwifruit, sliced 1/4 inch thick

In a small bowl, combine yogurt, marmalade and sugar. Cut the apple slices with a 2-1/2-in. star cookie cutter. Cut strawberries and kiwi with a 1-1/2-in. star cookie cutter. Serve with dip. **Yield:** about 6 servings (1 cup dip).

Moonbeam Munchies

~Taste of Home Test Kitchen

2 cups sugar

1 cup shortening

1 egg

2 teaspoons lemon extract

5-1/4 cups all-purpose flour

1 teaspoon baking soda

1/2 teaspoon salt

1 cup sour milk

1/2 cup water

5 drops yellow food coloring

1. In a mixing bowl, cream sugar and shortening. Add egg and extract. Combine flour, baking soda and salt; add to the creamed mixture alternately with sour milk. Mix well. Refrigerate for 2 hours or overnight.

2. On a lightly floured surface, roll dough to 1/4-in. thickness. Cut with a round cookie cutter. If desired, cut some circles in half and form into half moon shapes. Place on greased baking sheets.

3. Bake at 350° for 8-10 minutes or until the edges begin to brown. Remove to wire racks to cool. Combine water and food coloring; brush over cooled cookies. Allow to dry completely. Store in airtight containers. **Yield:** 6 dozen whole moons.

Editor's Note: To sour milk, place 1 tablespoon white vinegar in a measuring cup. Add milk to equal 1 cup. Prepared refrigerator sugar cookie dough can also be used.

Rocket Cake

~Taste of Home Test Kitchen

1 prepared ice cream cake roll (1-1/4 pounds)

1 can (16 ounces) or 2 cups vanilla frosting

Blue and red construction paper

1. Place ice cream roll vertically on a 10-in. plate. Frost top and sides. From blue construction paper, cut out four fins about 2-1/4 in. high and 1-1/2 in. deep. Insert fins along bottom edge of cake.

2. For the nose cone, draw an 8-in. circle on red construction paper. With a pencil, mark eight equal sections. Cut out a three-eighths section and discard; tape cut sides together to form a cone. Place on top of the cake. Serve immediately. **Yield:** 4-6 servings.

Cowboy

Chuck Wagon Burgers

~Sharon Thompson, Oskaloosa, Iowa

- 2 pounds ground beef
- 1 envelope onion soup mix
- 1/2 cup water
- 1 tube (16.3 ounces) large refrigerated biscuits
- 1/8 teaspoon seasoned salt

1. In a bowl, combine the beef, soup mix and water; mix well. Shape into eight 3/4-in.-thick patties. Grill, uncovered, or broil 4 in. from the heat for 5-6 minutes on each side or until meat is no longer pink.

2. Meanwhile, place biscuits on an ungreased baking sheet; sprinkle with seasoned salt. Bake at 375° for 12-14 minutes or until golden brown. Split; top each biscuit with a hamburger. **Yield:** 8 servings.

Bunkhouse Beans

~Sharon Thompson, Oskaloosa, Iowa

- 1 cup salsa
- 2/3 cup barbecue sauce
- 2/3 cup packed brown sugar
- 5 hot dogs, halved lengthwise and sliced
- 3 tablespoons dried minced onion
- 2 cans (16 ounces *each*) pork and beans, drained
- 1 can (15-1/2 ounces) chili beans, undrained
- 1 can (15 ounces) butter *or* lima beans, rinsed and drained

In a bowl, combine the first five ingredients; mix well. Stir in the beans; pour into an ungreased 2-qt. baking dish. Bake, uncovered, at 375° for 35-40 minutes or until bubbly. **Yield:** 6-8 servings.

Cowboy Boot Cake

~Sharon Thompson, Oskaloosa, Iowa

1 package (18-1/4 ounces) cake mix of your choice

1 package (8 ounces) cream cheese, softened

2 tablespoons butter, softened

1 tablespoon milk

1 teaspoon vanilla extract

5 cups confectioners' sugar

Food coloring of your choice

Skittles bite-size candies

1. Line a 13-in. x 9-in. x 2-in. baking pan with waxed paper; grease the paper. Prepare and bake cake according to package directions, using prepared pan. Cool for 10 minutes; remove from pan to a wire rack to cool completely. Wrap and freeze overnight.

2. Cover a 20-in. x 15-in. board with gift wrap or foil. Level cake top. To make boot, beginning from a short side, cut a 2-in.-wide strip. Cut strip into two pieces, one 5-1/2 in. x 2 in. and one 2-1/2 in. x 2 in. Cut a 10-in. x 2-1/2-in. strip from the large rectangle. To assemble base of boot, center the 10-in. x 2-1/2-in. piece widthwise on board 5 in. from bottom. Place remaining large rectangle on the right side, forming a backward L. Place the 2-1/2-in. x 2-in. piece under the long strip, forming the heel, and place remaining strip on the other side, forming the sole. Using a serrated knife, round corners of boot toe, sole, heel and top.

3. For frosting, in a mixing bowl, beat cream cheese, butter, milk and vanilla until smooth. Gradually beat in sugar. Set aside 1 cup. Spread remaining frosting over top and sides of cake. Tint reserved frosting desired color. Cut a small hole in the corner of a pastry or plastic bag; insert round tip. Fill bag with tinted frosting. Outline boot shape along bottom and top edges of cake. Fill in heel and toe on cake top, smoothing with a metal icing spatula. With remaining frosting and Skittles, decorate boot as desired. **Yield:** 16-20 servings.

Editor's Note: Measurements don't add up to 13 x 9 inches because cake may shrink slightly when it's baked.

Ice Cream Social

Cherry Crunch Ice Cream

~Dorothy Koshinski, Decatur, Illinois

6 eggs

2 cups sugar

2 cups milk

1 package (3.4 ounces) instant vanilla pudding mix

4 cups heavy whipping cream

1 teaspoon vanilla extract

Dash salt

1 cup old-fashioned oats

1/2 cup all-purpose flour

1/2 cup packed brown sugar

1/2 teaspoon ground cinnamon

1/3 cup cold butter

1 can (21 ounces) cherry pie filling

1. In a large saucepan, whisk eggs, sugar and milk until combined. Cook and stir over low heat until mixture reaches 160° and coats the back of a metal spoon. Remove from the heat; cool. Beat in the pudding mix, cream, vanilla and salt. Cover and refrigerate for 8 hours or overnight.

2. In a bowl, combine the oats, flour, brown sugar and cinnamon. Cut in butter until the mixture resembles coarse crumbs. Spread in an ungreased 15-in. x 10-in. x 1-in. baking pan. Bake at 350° for 10-15 minutes or until golden brown. Cool on a wire rack.

3. Stir pie filling into cream mixture. Fill cylinder of ice cream freezer two-thirds full; freeze according to manufacturer's directions. Refrigerate remaining mixture until ready to freeze.

4. After removing from ice cream freezer, stir a portion of oat mixture into each batch. Transfer to a freezer container. Cover and freeze for at least 4 hours before serving. **Yield:** 2-1/2 quarts.

Cinnamon Chocolate Chip Ice Cream

~Gloria Heidner, Elk River, Minnesota

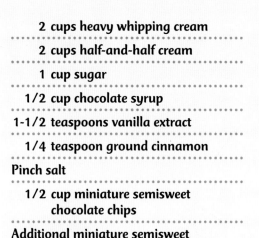

- **2 cups heavy whipping cream**
- **2 cups half-and-half cream**
- **1 cup sugar**
- **1/2 cup chocolate syrup**
- **1-1/2 teaspoons vanilla extract**
- **1/4 teaspoon ground cinnamon**

Pinch salt

- **1/2 cup miniature semisweet chocolate chips**

Additional miniature semisweet chocolate chips

1. In a bowl, combine the first seven ingredients; stir until the sugar is dissolved. Fill cylinder of ice cream freezer two-thirds full; freeze according to manufacturer's directions. Stir in chocolate chips.

2. Refrigerate remaining mixture until ready to freeze. Allow to ripen in ice cream freezer or firm up in your refrigerator freezer 2-4 hours before serving. Sprinkle with additional chocolate chips. **Yield:** about 2 quarts.

Fast Fudge Sundaes

~Sue Gronholz, Columbus, Wisconsin

- **1/2 cup semisweet chocolate chips**
- **1 square (1 ounce) unsweetened chocolate**
- **3 tablespoons butter**
- **1 cup confectioners' sugar**
- **1 can (5 ounces) evaporated milk**
- **1/2 teaspoon vanilla extract**

Ice cream of your choice

Place the chocolate and butter in a microwave-safe dish. Microwave, uncovered, on medium-high for 1 to 1-1/2 minutes. Stir in the sugar, milk and vanilla; beat until smooth. Microwave, uncovered, on medium for 5-6 minutes or until bubbly. Serve sauce over ice cream of your choice. **Yield:** 1-1/4 cups.

Editor's Note: This recipe was tested in a 700-watt microwave.

Homemade Ice Cream

~Teresa Stutzman, Adair, Oklahoma

8 cups milk, *divided*

6 eggs, *separated*

3 cups sugar, *divided*

3 tablespoons cornstarch

1/4 teaspoon salt

2 teaspoons vanilla extract

2 cups heavy whipping cream

Maraschino cherries, optional

1. In a large saucepan, bring 6 cups milk to a boil over medium heat. Remove from the heat and set aside.

2. In a mixing bowl, beat egg yolks; add remaining milk and mix well. Combine 2 cups sugar, cornstarch and salt; gradually add to egg mixture. Add to hot milk and bring to a boil. Cook and stir for 2 minutes or until slightly thickened. Pour into a clean mixing bowl; set aside.

3. Beat egg whites until soft peaks form; gradually add remaining sugar, beating well after each addition. Beat until stiff peaks form. Fold into warm milk mixture. Beat in vanilla and cream until well mixed. Refrigerate at least 5 hours or overnight. Freeze in an ice cream freezer according to manufacturer's directions. Garnish with cherries if desired. **Yield:** 3-1/2 quarts.

Ice Cream Sundae Dessert

~Kimberly McKeever, Shoreview, Minnesota

20 chocolate sandwich cookies, crushed

1/4 cup butter, softened

1/2 gallon vanilla *or* peppermint ice cream, softened

1 carton (8 ounces) frozen whipped topping, thawed

2 to 3 tablespoons chocolate syrup

1/4 cup chopped pecans

1. In a large bowl, combine cookie crumbs and butter. Press into the bottom of a 13-in. x 9-in. x 2-in. pan. Carefully spread ice cream over crust. Spread whipped topping over ice cream. Drizzle chocolate syrup on top; sprinkle with nuts.

2. Freeze until firm, about 2-4 hours. Remove from the freezer 15 minutes before serving. **Yield:** 16 servings.

Baseball

Dugout Hot Dogs

~Sue Gronholz, Columbus, Wisconsin

ZUCCHINI RELISH:
2-1/2 cups chopped zucchini
1 medium onion, chopped
1/2 cup chopped green pepper
1-1/4 teaspoons salt
1 cup sugar
1/2 cup plus 2 tablespoons vinegar
1-1/2 teaspoons celery seed
1/4 teaspoon ground mustard
1/8 teaspoon ground turmeric
1 teaspoon cornstarch
1 tablespoon water

HOT DOGS:
3/4 cup ketchup
2 to 4 tablespoons chopped onion
2 tablespoons brown sugar
2 tablespoons cider vinegar
10 hot dogs
10 hot dog buns, split

1. In a bowl, combine the zucchini, onion, green pepper and salt; cover and refrigerate overnight. Rinse and drain well; set aside.

2. In a saucepan, combine sugar, vinegar, celery seed, mustard and turmeric; bring to a boil. Add zucchini mixture; return to a boil. Reduce heat and simmer, uncovered, for 15 minutes, stirring occasionally.

3. Combine cornstarch and water until smooth; stir into saucepan. Simmer 6-8 minutes longer, stirring often. Cool; store in the refrigerator.

4. For hot dogs, combine ketchup, onion, sugar and vinegar in a saucepan; simmer 2-3 minutes. Add hot dogs; simmer 5-10 minutes longer or until heated through. Serve on buns topped with the relish. **Yield:** 10 servings (2 cups relish).

Ballpark Baked Beans

~Sue Gronholz, Columbus, Wisconsin

2 cans (16 ounces *each*) baked beans

1/4 cup packed brown sugar

2 tablespoons ketchup

2 teaspoons prepared mustard

1 can (20 ounces) pineapple tidbits, drained

In a large bowl, combine beans, brown sugar, ketchup and mustard. Transfer to a 2-qt. baking dish. Bake, uncovered, at 350° for 30 minutes. Stir in pineapple; bake 30 minutes longer. **Yield:** 10 servings.

Cap and Ball Cookies

~Taste of Home Test Kitchen

2 cups vanilla *or* white chips

1 tablespoon shortening

16 cream-filled chocolate sandwich cookies

1 tube red decorating frosting

1 package (12 ounces) chocolate and marshmallow cookies

12 chocolate wafer cookies

12 red M&M's

1. In a microwave or heavy saucepan, melt chips and shortening; stir until smooth. Dip sandwich cookies into mixture and allow excess to drip off; place on waxed paper to harden.

2. Meanwhile, spread red frosting over half of the bottom of each marshmallow cookie; press off-center onto a chocolate wafer, creating a cap.

3. Pipe a line of frosting where the cookies meet. Pipe stitching lines down sides of marshmallow cookies. Attach an M&M on top with a dab of frosting. On dipped sandwich cookies, pipe stitch marks to create baseballs. **Yield:** 12 caps and 16 baseballs.

Editor's Note: This recipe was tested with Nabisco Pinwheels.

Basketball

Slam Dunk Crab Dip

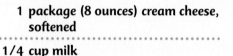

~Sharon Landeen, Tucson, Arizona

1 **package (8 ounces) cream cheese, softened**

1/4 **cup milk**

1 **package (8 ounces) imitation flaked crabmeat or 1 can (6 ounces) crabmeat, drained, flaked and cartilage removed**

1/4 **cup sliced green onions**

1/4 **cup chopped sweet red pepper**

1 **teaspoon curry powder**

1/2 **teaspoon garlic salt**

Assorted crackers

In a mixing bowl, beat cream cheese and milk until smooth. Stir in the crab, onions, red pepper, curry powder and garlic salt. Refrigerate until serving. Serve with crackers. **Yield:** 3 cups.

Courtside Caramel Corn

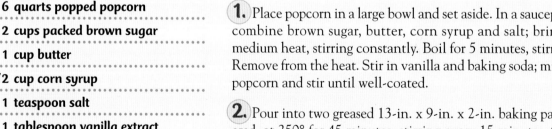

~Sharon Landeen, Tucson, Arizona

6 **quarts popped popcorn**

2 **cups packed brown sugar**

1 **cup butter**

1/2 **cup corn syrup**

1 **teaspoon salt**

1 **tablespoon vanilla extract**

1/2 **teaspoon baking soda**

1. Place popcorn in a large bowl and set aside. In a saucepan, combine brown sugar, butter, corn syrup and salt; bring to a boil over medium heat, stirring constantly. Boil for 5 minutes, stirring occasionally. Remove from the heat. Stir in vanilla and baking soda; mix well. Pour over popcorn and stir until well-coated.

2. Pour into two greased 13-in. x 9-in. x 2-in. baking pans. Bake, uncovered, at 250° for 45 minutes, stirring every 15 minutes. Cool completely. Store in air-tight containers or plastic bags. **Yield:** about 5-1/2 quarts.

Butterscotch Basketball Cookies

~Sharon Landeen, Tucson, Arizona

1 cup butterscotch chips

1 cup butter, softened

1/2 cup sugar

1/2 cup packed brown sugar

1 egg

2 tablespoons milk

2 teaspoons vanilla extract

3 cups all-purpose flour

FROSTING:

3/4 cup shortening

1/4 cup water

2 tablespoons all-purpose flour

1-1/2 teaspoons vanilla extract

4 cups confectioners' sugar

Paste food coloring

1. In a microwave, melt butterscotch chips; cool for 10 minutes. In a mixing bowl, cream butter and sugars. Add egg, milk and vanilla; mix well. Beat in melted chips. Gradually add flour; mix well. Cover and refrigerate for 1 hour.

2. On a floured surface, roll out dough to 1/4-in. thickness. Cut with a floured 4-1/2-in. gingerbread man cookie cutter and a 3-in. round cutter. Place 2 in. apart on greased baking sheets. Bake at 375° for 5-8 minutes or until edges are lightly browned. Cool for 1 minute; remove to wire racks to cool completely.

3. For frosting, combine shortening, water, flour and vanilla in a mixing bowl; mix well. Gradually beat in sugar. Place 1 cup frosting in a plastic bag; cut a small hole in corner of bag. Pipe shirt and shorts on players. Fill in outline and smooth with a metal spatula.

4. Tint 1/4 cup frosting black; place in a plastic bag. Pipe lines on round cookies to create basketballs; pipe hair, eyes and noses on players. Tint 1/4 cup frosting red; pipe a mouth on each player. Tint remaining frosting to match team colors of your choice; pipe around shirts and shorts and add a letter on shirts if desired. **Yield:** about 2 dozen.

Football

Pom-Pom Potato Salad

~Sister Judith LaBrozzi, Canton, Ohio

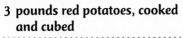

3 pounds red potatoes, cooked and cubed

1 cup sweet pickle *or* zucchini relish

1/4 cup chopped celery

3/4 teaspoon onion salt

1/2 teaspoon garlic salt

1/2 teaspoon celery seed

1/2 teaspoon pepper

4 hard-cooked eggs

1 cup (8 ounces) sour cream

1/2 cup mayonnaise

1 tablespoon cider vinegar

1 teaspoon prepared mustard

Additional hard-cooked eggs, cut into wedges

1. In a large bowl, combine the first seven ingredients. Cut eggs in half and remove yolks. Chop the whites; add to potato mixture.

2. In a small bowl, mash the yolks; stir in sour cream, mayonnaise, vinegar and mustard. Pour over potato mixture and gently toss to coat. Refrigerate until serving. Garnish with egg wedges. **Yield:** 18 servings.

Football Brownies

~Taste of Home Test Kitchen

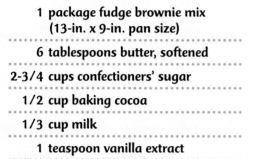

1 package fudge brownie mix
(13-in. x 9-in. pan size)

6 tablespoons butter, softened

2-3/4 cups confectioners' sugar

1/2 cup baking cocoa

1/3 cup milk

1 teaspoon vanilla extract

1/4 cup vanilla *or* white chips

1. Prepare the brownie batter according to package directions. Spread into a greased 15-in. x 10-in. x 1-in. baking pan. Bake at 350° for 13-15 minutes or until a toothpick comes out clean. Cool on a wire rack.

2. In a mixing bowl, cream butter, sugar, cocoa, milk and vanilla. Spread over cooled brownies. Loosely cover and chill for 1 hour or until frosting is set.

3. With a sharp knife, make lengthwise cuts 1-1/2 in. apart. Beginning in one corner, make 1-1/2-in. parallel cuts from a short side to a long side to form diamonds. In a microwave, melt chips at 50% power; stir until smooth. Place in a small heavy-duty resealable plastic bag; cut a small hole in a corner of bag. Pipe laces on brownies. **Yield:** about 3 dozen.

Touchdown Cookies

~Sister Judith LaBrozzi, Canton, Ohio

1 cup butter, softened

1 cup sugar

2 eggs

1 teaspoon vanilla extract

3 cups all-purpose flour

2 teaspoons cream of tartar

1 teaspoon baking soda

GLAZE:
2 cups confectioners' sugar

4 to 5 tablespoons hot water

3 to 4 teaspoons baking cocoa

1. In a mixing bowl, cream butter and sugar. Add eggs, one at a time, beating well after each addition. Beat in vanilla. Combine the flour, cream of tartar and baking soda; gradually add to creamed mixture. Cover and refrigerate for 3 hours or until easy to handle.

2. On a lightly floured surface, roll out dough to 1/8-in. thickness. Cut with a football-shaped cookie cutter. Place 2 in. apart on ungreased baking sheets. Bake at 350° for 8-10 minutes or until lightly browned. Remove to wire racks to cool.

3. In a mixing bowl, combine confectioners' sugar and enough hot water to achieve spreading consistency; beat until smooth. Place 3 tablespoons glaze in a small bowl; set aside. Add cocoa to remaining glaze; stir until smooth. Spread brown glaze over cookies. Pipe white glaze onto cookies to form football laces. **Yield:** 4-1/2 dozen.

Racing

Checkered Cookie Flags

~Taste of Home Test Kitchen

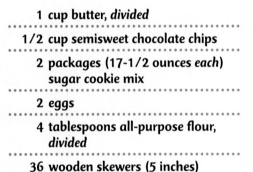

1 cup butter, *divided*

1/2 cup semisweet chocolate chips

2 packages (17-1/2 ounces *each*)
sugar cookie mix

2 eggs

4 tablespoons all-purpose flour,
divided

36 wooden skewers (5 inches)

1. In a large microwave-safe bowl, combine 1/2 cup butter and chocolate chips. Cover and microwave on high for 1-2 minutes or until melted; stir until blended. Add the contents of one cookie mix package, 1 egg and 2 tablespoons flour; stir until combined. Cover and refrigerate for 1-2 hours or until dough is firm.

2. Meanwhile, place the remaining butter in a microwave-safe bowl. Cover and heat on high for 1 minute or until melted. Add the remaining cookie mix, egg and flour; mix well. Cover and refrigerate for 1-2 hours or until dough is firm.

3. On waxed paper, roll out the plain and chocolate dough into separate 9-in. x 5-in. rectangles. Cut each rectangle into nine 1-in. strips. Stack the strips in groups of three, alternating plain and chocolate strips, and forming six separate stacks. Form two blocks by placing one plain-topped stack on each side of a chocolate-topped stack and one chocolate-topped stack on each side of a plain-topped stack; press together gently.

4. Cut both stacks into 1/4-in. slices. Place 3 in. apart on ungreased baking sheets. Bake at 375° for 10-12 minutes or until edges are golden brown. Immediately insert a skewer into each cookie. Remove from pans to wire racks to cool. **Yield:** about 3 dozen.

Hot Dog Race Cars

~*Taste of Home Test Kitchen*

8 green onions with roots

Mustard and ketchup

40 **toothpicks**

8 **hot dog buns**

32 **large pitted ripe olives, halved**

16 **slices process American cheese**

8 **hot dogs**

8 **radish slices**

1. Cut root end of onions into 2-1/2-in. lengths; dip roots in mustard. Insert a toothpick into opposite end; set aside. Place buns on plates. To fasten wheels, insert four toothpicks in each bun, two on each side. Place an olive half, cut side out, on each toothpick. Cut cheese slices into 3-1/4-in. triangles; set aside.

2. Cook hot dogs according to package directions; place in buns. Insert green onion, using the toothpick, into the center of hot dog for driver. Cut a small widthwise slit in hot dog in front of driver; insert a radish slice for the steering wheel.

3. Place one cheese triangle in front of steering wheel and one behind the driver. Cut a hole in the corner of a pastry or plastic bag; fill with ketchup. Pipe numbers on front cheese slices and sides of buns. Pipe eyes and mouth on driver. **Yield:** 8 servings.

Winner's Trophy Dessert

~*Taste of Home Test Kitchen*

1 **package (3 ounces) lemon gelatin**

2 **cups boiling water, *divided***

2 **cups vanilla ice cream, softened**

1 **package (3 ounces) orange gelatin**

1 **cup cold water**

1 **can (11 ounces) mandarin oranges, drained**

1. In a bowl, dissolve lemon gelatin in 1 cup boiling water. Whisk in ice cream until blended. Pour into 4-oz. stemmed glasses. Chill for 2 hours or until set.

2. Dissolve orange gelatin in remaining boiling water. Stir in cold water and oranges. Chill for 2 hours or until partially set. Pour over the lemon layer. Chill for 2 hours or until set. **Yield:** 8-10 servings.

Editor's Note: Reduced-fat ice cream or frozen yogurt may not be used in this recipe.

Fiesta

Chicken Tortilla Soup

~Laura Johnson, Largo, Florida

1 large onion, chopped

2 tablespoons olive oil

1 can (4 ounces) chopped green
   chilies

2 garlic cloves, minced

1 jalapeno pepper, seeded and
   chopped

1 teaspoon ground cumin

5 cups chicken broth

1 can (15 ounces) tomato sauce

1 can (14-1/2 ounces) diced
   tomatoes with garlic and onion,
   undrained

3 cans (5 ounces *each*) white
   chicken, drained

1/4 cup minced fresh cilantro

2 teaspoons lime juice

Salt and pepper to taste

Crushed tortilla chips

Shredded Monterey Jack or cheddar
   cheese

1. In a large saucepan, saute onion in oil; add the chilies, garlic, jalapeno and cumin. Stir in the broth, tomato sauce and tomatoes. Bring to a boil. Reduce heat; stir in chicken. Simmer, uncovered, for 10 minutes.

2. Add the cilantro, lime juice, salt and pepper. Top with tortilla chips and cheese. **Yield:** 7 servings.

Editor's Note: When cutting or seeding hot peppers, use rubber or plastic gloves to protect your hands. Avoid touching your face.

Black Bean Chicken Tacos

~Teresa Obsnuk, Berwyn, Illinois

2 cups all-purpose flour

1 teaspoon baking powder

1-1/2 teaspoons ground cumin, *divided*

2 tablespoons shortening

1/2 cup plus 1 tablespoon warm water

1 pound boneless skinless chicken breasts, cubed

2 cups salsa

1 can (15 ounces) black beans, rinsed and drained

1 teaspoon onion powder

1/2 teaspoon chili powder

Shredded lettuce, shredded cheddar cheese, chopped ripe olives, sour cream and additional salsa, optional

1. In a bowl, combine the flour, baking powder and 1/2 teaspoon cumin. Cut in shortening until crumbly. Stir in enough water for mixture to form a ball. Knead on a floured surface for 1 minute. Cover and let rest for 20 minutes.

2. Meanwhile, in a large skillet, combine the chicken, salsa, beans, onion powder, chili powder and remaining cumin. Cover and simmer for 15-20 minutes or until chicken juices run clear.

3. For tortillas, divide dough into eight balls; roll each ball into an 8-in. circle. In an ungreased skillet, cook tortillas, one at a time, until lightly browned, about 30 seconds on each side. Layer between pieces of waxed paper or paper towel; keep warm.

4. Spoon chicken mixture over half of each tortilla and fold over. Serve with lettuce, cheese, olives, sour cream and salsa if desired. **Yield:** 4-6 servings.

Party Salsa

~Toni Swanson, Gull Lake, Saskatchewan

16 medium ripe tomatoes, chopped

2 large onions, finely chopped

1 medium green pepper, finely chopped

1/2 cup minced fresh parsley

2 to 4 jalapeno peppers, seeded and
finely chopped, optional

2 cans (6 ounces *each*) tomato paste

3 garlic cloves, minced

1 can (4 ounces) chopped green chilies

3/4 cup vinegar

2 tablespoons lemon juice

2 teaspoons salt

1 teaspoon pepper

3 tablespoons cornstarch

1/3 cup cold water

In a large Dutch oven or soup kettle, combine the first 12 ingredients; bring to a boil. Reduce heat; simmer, uncovered, for 15 minutes. Combine cornstarch and water until smooth; stir into salsa. Bring to a boil. Cook and stir for 2 minutes; cool. **Yield:** about 2 quarts.

Editor's Note: When cutting or seeding hot peppers, use rubber or plastic gloves to protect your hands. Avoid touching your face.

Cheesy Green Chili Rice

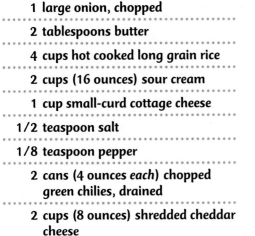

~Laurie Fisher, Greeley, Colorado

1 large onion, chopped

2 tablespoons butter

4 cups hot cooked long grain rice

2 cups (16 ounces) sour cream

1 cup small-curd cottage cheese

1/2 teaspoon salt

1/8 teaspoon pepper

2 cans (4 ounces *each*) chopped green chilies, drained

2 cups (8 ounces) shredded cheddar cheese

1. In a large skillet, cook onion in butter until tender. Remove from the heat. Stir in the rice, sour cream, cottage cheese, salt and pepper.

2. Spoon half of the mixture into a greased 11-in. x 7-in. x 2-in. baking dish. Top with half of the chilies and cheese. Repeat layers. Bake, uncovered, at 375° for 20-25 minutes or until heated through and bubbly. **Yield:** 6-8 servings.

Sopaipillas

~Glenda Jarboe, Oroville, California

1-3/4 cups all-purpose flour

2 teaspoons baking powder

1 teaspoon salt

2 tablespoons shortening

2/3 cup water

Oil for deep-fat frying

Honey

1. In a bowl, combine the dry ingredients; cut in shortening until crumbly. Gradually add water, tossing with a fork until mixture holds together. On a lightly floured surface, knead dough for 1-2 minutes or until smooth. Cover and let stand for 5 minutes. Roll out to 1/4-in. thickness. Cut with a 2-1/2-in. star cookie cutter or into 2-1/2-in. triangles.

2. In an electric skillet or deep-fat fryer, heat oil to 375°. Fry sopaipillas for 1-2 minutes on each side or until golden brown and puffed. Drain on paper towels. Serve immediately with honey. **Yield:** 1 dozen.

School

ABC Vegetable Soup

~*Taste of Home Test Kitchen*

1/2 cup uncooked alphabet pasta

3 cans (14-1/2 ounces *each*) beef broth

1 package (16 ounces) frozen mixed vegetables

1/2 teaspoon dried thyme

1/2 teaspoon dried basil

1/4 teaspoon pepper

Cook pasta according to package directions. In a large saucepan, combine the remaining ingredients. Bring to a boil. Reduce heat; cover and simmer for 5 minutes or until vegetables are tender. Drain pasta; stir into soup. **Yield:** 6-8 servings.

Ruler Stromboli

~*Taste of Home Test Kitchen*

1/2 cup chopped green pepper

1/2 cup chopped sweet red pepper

1 tablespoon butter

1 tube (10 ounces) refrigerated pizza dough

6 slices Swiss cheese, *divided*

8 ounces sliced deli turkey

5 sweet red pepper strips (2-inch pieces)

12 green pepper strips (1-inch pieces)

2 ounces cream cheese, softened

1/2 teaspoon milk

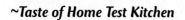

1. In a skillet, saute chopped peppers in butter until tender. On an ungreased baking sheet, pat dough into a 13-in. x 8-in. rectangle. Arrange four cheese slices lengthwise over half of the dough to within 1/2 in. of edge; top with turkey and sauteed peppers. Fold dough over filling; pinch edges to seal. Bake at 400° for 20-25 minutes or until golden brown.

2. Cut remaining cheese slices in half lengthwise; place along one long edge of the sandwich. Bake 1-2 minutes longer or until cheese is melted. Immediately press red pepper strips into the cheese to create inch marks and add green pepper strips for fractions. Let stand for 10 minutes.

3. In a small mixing bowl, beat cream cheese and milk until smooth. Spoon into a heavy-duty resealable plastic bag; cut a small hole in a corner of bag. Pipe numerals above red pepper strips. Slice and serve warm. **Yield:** 6-8 servings.

Schoolhouse Cake

(Pictured on page 283)

~Taste of Home Test Kitchen

- 1 package (18-1/4 ounces) yellow cake mix
- 1 can (16 ounces) vanilla frosting

Red gel food coloring

- 6 rectangular wafer sandwich cookies
- 2 graham cracker squares
- 2 milk chocolate M&M's
- 1 yellow Chuckles candy

1. Line a greased 13-in. x 9-in. x 2-in. baking pan with waxed paper; grease and flour the paper. Prepare cake batter; pour into prepared pan. Bake according to package directions. Cool on a wire rack. Invert cooled cake onto a large platter or covered board. Carefully remove waxed paper.

2. Cut two triangles off of cake to form roofline. For bell tower, cut a square out of one triangle and place above peak of roof. Place remaining triangle above square. (Discard remaining cut cake pieces or save for another use.)

3. Tint frosting red; frost entire cake. Place wafer cookies along top edge of schoolhouse roof and bell tower roof. For door, place one graham cracker square at bottom of schoolhouse. For the doorknobs, attach M&M's on door with frosting. Cut the remaining cracker square in half; place on cake for windows. Flatten Chuckles candy to 1/4-in. thickness; cut out bell shape and place in bell tower. **Yield:** 12-15 servings.

Straight-A Salad

(Pictured on page 283)

~Taste of Home Test Kitchen

- 1/2 cup plus 2 tablespoons olive oil
- 3 tablespoons red wine vinegar
- 2 tablespoons sugar
- 2 teaspoons spicy brown or horseradish mustard
- 1/4 teaspoon onion salt
- 1/8 teaspoon pepper
- 6 cups torn salad greens

Tomato wedges and cucumber slices

For dressing, combine the first six ingredients in a blender; cover and process until smooth. In a salad bowl, combine the greens, tomato and cucumber; add dressing and toss to coat. **Yield:** 6-8 servings (3/4 cup dressing).

School Bus Cake

~Leslie Miller, Butler, Pennsylvania

1 package (18-1/4 ounces) yellow cake mix

1 cup butter, softened

1 cup shortening

8 to 9 cups confectioners' sugar

1/4 cup milk

1 teaspoon vanilla extract

1/4 teaspoon salt

2 teaspoons black paste *or* gel food coloring

1/2 to 3/4 teaspoon yellow paste *or* liquid food coloring

2 cream-filled chocolate sandwich cookies, cut in half

2 yellow gumdrops

6 red gumdrops

1. Prepare cake mix according to package directions. Pour batter into two greased 8-in. x 4-in. x 2-in. loaf pans. Bake at 350° for 40-45 minutes or until a toothpick inserted near center comes out clean. Cool for 10 minutes; remove from pans to a wire rack to cool.

2. Place cakes end to end on a 22-in. x 8-in. covered board. Level if needed. From the top of one end, form the front of the bus by cutting out a section 1 in. deep and 3 in. long. (Save the removed piece for another use.)

3. For frosting, beat butter and shortening in a mixing bowl until fluffy. Beat in 6 cups sugar, milk, vanilla and salt. Beat in enough additional sugar until frosting reaches desired spreading consistency.

4. Remove 3/4 cup frosting; add black food coloring. Tint remaining frosting yellow. Frost entire cake yellow. Frost cut edge of cookies with yellow frosting to form wheel wells; place two cookie halves on each side of bus. Cut a hole in the corner of a plastic bag or insert a #5 round tip in a pastry bag; fill with black frosting.

5. Outline windows on both sides of bus; pipe stripes under windows. Pipe windshield and back window; fill in with black frosting. Pipe lines on front for grille. Place yellow gumdrops on front of bus for headlights; place red gumdrops on front and back for lights. **Yield:** 12-16 servings.

Fishing

Vegetable Bobbers

~Heidi Lloyd, Burlington, Wisconsin

8 cherry tomatoes, halved

8 cucumber slices (about 1/4 inch thick)

8 carrot sticks (4 inches x 1/4 inch)

Fresh dill or tarragon sprigs, optional

With a sharp knife, pierce a small hole in the center of tomatoes and cucumbers. Thread two tomato halves and one cucumber slice onto each carrot, forming bobbers. Place bobbers alongside fish; add dill or tarragon sprigs for seaweed if desired. **Yield:** 8 bobbers.

Hook, Line 'n' Sinker Mix

~Margo Francisco, Waukesha, Wisconsin

3 tablespoons butter, melted

1 tablespoon dried parsley flakes

3/4 teaspoon dried tarragon

1/2 teaspoon onion powder

1/4 to 1/2 teaspoon celery salt

1 cup goldfish crackers

1 cup pretzel sticks

1/2 cup Cheerios

1/2 cup dry roasted peanuts

In a 2-qt. microwave-safe bowl, combine the first five ingredients; mix well. Add crackers, pretzels, Cheerios and peanuts; toss to coat. Microwave, uncovered, on high for 1-1/2 minutes, stirring once. Cool completely. Store in an airtight container. **Yield:** 3 cups.

Editor's Note: This recipe was tested in a 700-watt microwave.

Catch-of-the-Day Fish

~Anne Willick, Waterford, Wisconsin

> 1 package (5 ounces) cheesy scalloped potatoes with skins
>
> 4 fresh or frozen fish fillets (about 1 pound), thawed
>
> 16 lime wedges
>
> 2 lemon slices, halved
>
> 4 ripe olive slices
>
> 8 pimiento pieces

1. Prepare scalloped potatoes, following the package directions for stovetop method. Place fish in an ungreased 13-in. x 9-in. x 2-in. baking dish. Using tongs, arrange potatoes on fish to look like scales.

2. Cover and bake at 450° for 8-10 minutes or until the fish flakes easily with a fork. Carefully transfer to serving plates. Garnish with lime for tails and fins, lemon for heads, olives for eyes, and pimientos for eyes and mouth. **Yield:** 4 servings.

Rod and Reel Breadsticks

~Lisa Reuter, Hilliard, Ohio

> 1 tube (11 ounces) refrigerated breadsticks
>
> 2 tablespoons butter, melted
>
> 1/2 teaspoon garlic salt
>
> 2 teaspoons grated Parmesan cheese
>
> 1 teaspoon sesame seeds

1. Separate dough into rolls; set four aside. Unroll remaining rolls; twist each to form a 14-in. rope. Place ropes 4 in. apart on ungreased baking sheets for rods.

2. For reels, place a coiled roll 1-1/2 in. from end of rod, with the coiled end touching the rod. Pinch rod and reel dough together to seal. Combine butter and garlic salt; brush over dough. Sprinkle with Parmesan cheese and sesame seeds. Bake at 375° for 12-14 minutes or until golden brown. Cool slightly; carefully remove from pans. **Yield:** 4 servings.

Zoo

Lazy Lion Melt

~Taste of Home Test Kitchen

1 to 2 tablespoons mayonnaise

1 to 2 tablespoons prepared mustard

2 carrot slices (1/8 inch thick)

3 hamburger buns, split

6 slices process Swiss cheese

12 ripe olive slices

12 pimiento slices

6 hot dog buns, split

6 thin slices cooked turkey *or other* deli meat

12 slices process American cheese

1 cup (4 ounces) shredded cheddar cheese

18 potato sticks

Shredded lettuce, optional

1. Combine mayonnaise and mustard; set aside. Cut each carrot slice into three triangles; set aside. For each lion, place half of a hamburger bun, cut side up, on an ungreased baking sheet (three lions per sheet). Spread with a small amount of the mayonnaise mixture. Top with a slice of Swiss cheese. Add two olives for eyes, a carrot triangle for nose and two pimientos for mouth. Position the top half of a hot dog bun, cut side up, below head for body. Spread with mayonnaise mixture. Top with turkey and American cheese, cutting to fit the bun. For the tail, slice 1/2 in. from one end of the hot dog bun bottom (see Fig. 1).

2. Cut remaining portion into four 2-1/4-in. strips for legs. Position the legs and tail with cut side up; spread with mayonnaise mixture. Cut one slice of American cheese into strips to fit over legs and tail. Place over the mayonnaise mixture, tucking under cheese on the body. Broil 6 in. from the heat until cheese is slightly melted and the lion holds its shape, about 2 minutes. Sprinkle shredded cheese on the end of the tail and around head. Broil 30 seconds longer or until cheese is melted. Transfer to a serving plate. Add potato sticks for whiskers. If desired, add lettuce under legs for grass. **Yield:** 6 servings.

FIG. 1
Cutting bun

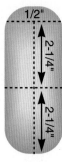

1/2"

2-1/4"

2-1/4"

Perky Olive Penguins

~Taste of Home Test Kitchen

1 can (5-3/4 ounces) jumbo pitted ripe olives, drained

1 package (3 ounces) cream cheese, softened

1/2 teaspoon dried minced onion

1/4 teaspoon prepared horseradish

1/8 teaspoon salt

Dash pepper

Dash garlic powder

1 medium carrot, cut into 1/4-inch slices

12 small pitted ripe olives

12 toothpicks with cellophane frilled tops

1 jar (2 ounces) sliced pimientos

1. Cut a slit from the top to bottom of 12 jumbo olives; set aside. In a mixing bowl, combine the next six ingredients; mix well. Fill a small heavy-duty plastic bag with cream cheese mixture. Cut a small hole in the corner of the bag; carefully pipe mixture into jumbo olives. Set aside.

2. Cut a small triangle out of each carrot slice; press triangles into small olives for a beak. On each notched carrot slice, position a jumbo olive so the white chest is lined up with the notch. Place the small olive, hole side down, over the jumbo olive so the beak, chest and feet are aligned. Carefully insert a toothpick through the top of head into body and carrot base. Wrap a pimiento around neck for a scarf. **Yield:** 1 dozen.

Zebra Sweets

~Taste of Home Test Kitchen

8 cups miniature marshmallows

6 tablespoons butter

12 cups crisp rice cereal

1 cup vanilla *or* white chips

1 teaspoon shortening, *divided*

1 cup semisweet chocolate chips

1. In a Dutch oven or large saucepan, heat marshmallows and butter until almost melted. Remove from the heat; stir in cereal and mix well. Press firmly into a greased 15-in. x 10-in. x 1-in. baking pan. Cut with a horse-shaped cookie cutter. Remove cutouts to waxed paper; set aside.

2. In a microwave or double boiler, melt vanilla chips and 1/2 teaspoon shortening. Spread over cutouts. Let dry on waxed paper. Melt chocolate chips and remaining shortening; place in a heavy-duty plastic bag. Cut a small hole in the corner of the bag; pipe mane, stripes, hooves, etc. on zebras. **Yield:** about 1 dozen.

Sun & Sand

Life Preserver Meat Loaves

~Taste of Home Test Kitchen

1 egg

1 can (5-1/2 ounces) spicy-hot *or* picante V8

1/4 cup milk

1 cup seasoned bread crumbs

1-1/2 teaspoons seasoned salt

1 teaspoon chili powder

1-1/2 pounds lean ground beef

Ketchup and mustard

1. In a large bowl, combine the first six ingredients. Crumble beef over mixture and mix well. Shape into six balls; flatten slightly. Make a hole in the center of each ball with the end of a wooden spoon handle.

2. Place in a greased 15-in. x 10-in. x 1-in. baking pan. Bake, uncovered, at 350° for 25-30 minutes or until meat is no longer pink and a meat thermometer reads 160°. Decorate with ketchup and mustard. **Yield:** 6 servings.

Rice Sand Castles

~Taste of Home Test Kitchen

3-3/4 cups cooked rice

3/4 cup frozen peas, thawed

3/4 cup frozen corn, thawed

4 ounces process cheese (Velveeta), cubed

1/4 teaspoon pepper

1. In a large microwave-safe bowl, combine all ingredients; mix well. Cover and microwave on high for 2-3 minutes or until heated through and cheese is melted, stirring twice.

2. To make sand castles, pack rice mixture into 1/2-cup and 1/4-cup measures; unmold and stack on dinner plates. **Yield:** 6 servings.

Editor's Note: This recipe was tested in an 850-watt microwave.

Seaside Gelatin Salad

~Taste of Home Test Kitchen

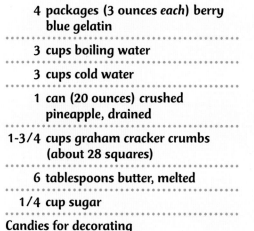

4 packages (3 ounces *each*) berry blue gelatin

3 cups boiling water

3 cups cold water

1 can (20 ounces) crushed pineapple, drained

1-3/4 cups graham cracker crumbs (about 28 squares)

6 tablespoons butter, melted

1/4 cup sugar

Candies for decorating

1. In a large bowl, dissolve gelatin in boiling water. Stir in cold water and pineapple. Pour into a 13-in. x 9-in. x 2-in. dish. Refrigerate until set.

2. In a bowl, combine the cracker crumbs, butter and sugar; cover and refrigerate. Just before serving, sprinkle cracker mixture over half of the gelatin to form a beach. Decorate as desired. **Yield:** 12-15 servings.

Beach Blanket Sugar Cookies

~Taste of Home Test Kitchen

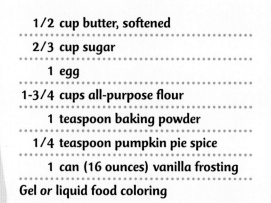

1/2 cup butter, softened

2/3 cup sugar

1 egg

1-3/4 cups all-purpose flour

1 teaspoon baking powder

1/4 teaspoon pumpkin pie spice

1 can (16 ounces) vanilla frosting

Gel *or* liquid food coloring

1. In a mixing bowl, cream the butter and sugar. Beat in egg. Combine the flour, baking powder and pumpkin pie spice; gradually add to creamed mixture. Cover and refrigerate for 1 hour or until easy to handle.

2. Divide dough in half. On a lightly floured surface, roll each portion into a 15-in. x 8-in. rectangle. Cut in half lengthwise; cut widthwise into thirds, forming six strips. Place 1 in. apart on ungreased baking sheets. Bend slightly if desired to form curves in cookies.

3. Bake at 350° for 10-13 minutes or until edges are lightly browned. Remove to wire racks to cool. Tint frosting with food coloring; decorate cookies as desired. **Yield:** 2 dozen.

Dinosaur

Padysaurus Pizza Pockets

~Robin Werner, Brush Prairie, Washington

- 3 to 3-1/4 cups all-purpose flour
- 1 package (1/4 ounce) active dry yeast
- 1 tablespoon sugar
- 1 teaspoon salt
- 1 cup warm water (120° to 130°)
- 1 tablespoon butter, melted
- 1 can (8 ounces) pizza sauce
- 12 slices pepperoni
- 1 package (2-1/2 ounces) thinly sliced fully cooked pastrami, chopped
- 1 package (2-1/2 ounces) thinly sliced fully cooked ham, chopped
- 3/4 cup shredded mozzarella cheese
- 1 egg, beaten

1. In a mixing bowl, combine 2-1/4 cups flour, yeast, sugar and salt. Add water and butter; mix well. Add enough remaining flour to form a soft dough. Turn onto a floured surface; knead for 4 minutes. Roll dough into a 14-in. x 10-in. rectangle. Cut with a 3-in. round cookie cutter. Reroll scraps to cut a total of 24 circles.

2. Place 1 teaspoon pizza sauce and a slice of pepperoni in center of 12 circles. Combine pastrami, ham and cheese; place equal amounts over pepperoni. Top with 1/2 teaspoon of pizza sauce if desired. (Save remaining sauce for another use or use for dipping.)

3. Cover with remaining dough circles; pinch edges or press with a fork to seal. Place on greased baking sheets. Brush with egg. Bake at 400° for 20-25 minutes or until browned. **Yield:** 12 servings.

Giant Dinosaur Cookies

~Robin Werner, Brush Prairie, Washington

1 cup butter, softened

1 cup sugar

1 egg

1 teaspoon vanilla extract

3 cups all-purpose flour

2 teaspoons baking powder

Food coloring, optional

1 can (16 ounces) vanilla frosting

Miniature *or* regular semisweet chocolate chips

Sliced gumdrops *or* small candies

1. In a mixing bowl, cream butter and sugar. Add egg and vanilla; mix well. Combine flour and baking powder; add to creamed mixture, 1 cup at a time, mixing well after each addition (dough will be very stiff). Divide into two balls; roll each ball directly on an ungreased baking sheet to 1/4-in. thickness. Cut cookies with a dinosaur cookie cutter, leaving at least 1 in. between cookies. Remove excess dough and reroll scraps if desired.

2. Bake at 400° for 7-9 minutes for small cookies and 10-12 minutes for large cookies or until lightly browned around the edges. Cool 1-2 minutes before removing to wire racks. Add food coloring to frosting if desired. Frost cookies. Decorate with chocolate chips for eyes and candies for spots. **Yield:** about 2 dozen 4-inch cookies or 1 dozen 8-inch cookies.

Dinosaur Eggs

~Robin Werner, Brush Prairie, Washington

2 packages (6 ounces *each*) lime gelatin

2-1/2 cups boiling water

1/2 teaspoon ground cinnamon

1 cup cold milk

1 package (3.4 ounces) instant vanilla pudding mix

Alfalfa sprouts, optional

In a large bowl, dissolve gelatin in boiling water; let stand at room temperature 30 minutes. Stir in cinnamon. In a large measuring cup with a spout, beat milk and pudding mix until blended, about 1 minute. Quickly whisk into gelatin until smooth. Pour into a 13-in. x 9-in. x 2-in. pan coated with nonstick cooking spray. Refrigerate 3 hours or until firm. Cut into ovals or use an egg-shaped cookie cutter. Serve over alfalfa sprouts if desired. **Yield:** 12-14 servings.

Editor's Note: For eggs shown in photo, use a Jell-O Jigglers egg mold. Coat inside and rim of each egg mold with nonstick cooking spray. Securely close each egg mold. Place mold, fill side up, on a tray. After whisking pudding mixture into gelatin, immediately pour it into the mold through fill holes just to the top of the egg shape. Refrigerate 3 hours or until firm. To unmold eggs, slide a dull flat knife between eggs. Gently pry between each egg. Turn mold over; shake gently to remove eggs. Makes 12 eggs.

Index

✓ Uses less fat, sugar or salt. Includes Nutritional Analysis and Diabetic Exchanges.

✓ Uses less fat, sugar or salt. Includes Nutritional Analysis and Diabetic Exchanges.

✓ Uses less fat, sugar or salt. Includes Nutritional Analysis and Diabetic Exchanges.

✓ Uses less fat, sugar or salt. Includes Nutritional Analysis and Diabetic Exchanges.

✓ Uses less fat, sugar or salt. Includes Nutritional Analysis and Diabetic Exchanges.

✓ Uses less fat, sugar or salt. Includes Nutritional Analysis and Diabetic Exchanges.

✓ Uses less fat, sugar or salt. Includes Nutritional Analysis and Diabetic Exchanges.

Deluxe Turkey Club Pizza, 249
Lazy Lion Melt, 288
Patriotic Picnic Club, 200
✓Raisin Bagel Stackers, 50
Ruler Stromboli, 282
Sandwich Bear, 30

✓Tender Turkey Meatballs, 109
Thick Turkey Bean Chili, 45
Turkey Divan Pizza, 54
Turkey Pita Tacos, 113
Turkey Ranch Wraps, 47

VEGETABLES *(also see specific kinds)*
ABC Vegetable Soup, 282
Firecracker Roll-Ups, 203
Vegetable Bobbers, 286
Veggie Cheese People, 63

Alphabetical Index

A

ABC Vegetable Soup, 282
Amy's Green Eggs and Ham, 17
Apple Brickle Dip, 84
Apple Peanut Salad, 59
Apple Pie Sandwiches, 66
Apple-Raisin Ladybug, 86
✓Apple Syrup, 9
Applesauce Sandwiches, 43

B

Bacon and Egg Bundles, 8
Bacon Biscuit Wreath, 35
Bacon Cheese Fries, 114
Bacon Cheese Strips, 7
Bacon Cheeseburger Pizza, 248
Bacon Cheeseburger Rice, 98
Baked Deli Sandwich, 55
Baked Potato Pizza, 248
✓Baked Potato Strips, 112
Ballpark Baked Beans, 271
✓Banana Chip Muffins, 10
Banana-Pear Caterpillar, 86
Banana Split Muffins, 12
Banana Split Shortcake, 127
Beach Blanket Sugar Cookies, 291
Beef 'n' Cheese Wraps, 48
Beehive Cake, 161
Beetle Juice, 244

Berry Cream Pancakes, 7
Berry-Stuffed French Toast, 29
Bewitching Ice Cream Cones, 206
Birthday Blocks, 150
Biscuit Tostadas, 42
Black Bean Chicken Tacos, 279
Black Cat Cookies, 209
Blarney Stone Bars, 192
BLT Pizza, 59
Boo Beverage, 209
Breakfast Bread Pudding, 26
Breakfast Pizza, 4
Brownie Pizza, 226
Brownie Turtles, 139
Brownies in a Cone, 232
Brunch Punch, 23
Buggy Birthday Cake, 160
Bunkhouse Beans, 264
Butterfly Cake, 245
Butterfly Pancakes, 2
Butterfly Sandwiches, 40
Butterscotch Basketball
  Cookies, 273
Butterscotch Popcorn Bars, 62

C

Candy Bar Pie, 132
Candy Cane Cookies, 184
Candy Christmas Tree, 171

Cap and Ball Cookies, 271
Caramel Apple Cupcakes, 213
Caramel Cashew Brownies, 239
Catch-of-the-Day Fish, 287
Catch Some Z's, 255
Caterpillar Cake, 242
Cauliflower Snowman, 173
Checkerboard Birthday Cake, 155
Checkered Cookie Flags, 276
Cheese Spread Dice, 252
Cheeseburger Mini Muffins, 58
Cheesy Green Chili Rice, 281
Cheesy Potato Beef Bake, 95
Cheesy Soft Pretzels, 74
Cherry Berry Smoothies, 4
Cherry Coke Salad, 46
Cherry Crunch Ice Cream, 266
Chewy Bread Pretzels, 85
Chewy Granola Bars, 76
Chicken Broccoli Shells, 90
Chicken in a Haystack, 104
Chicken Nugget Casserole, 88
Chicken Tortilla Soup, 278
Chili Bread, 33
Chilly Peanut Butter Pie, 146
Chocolate Banana Split
  Cupcakes, 231
Chocolate Caramel Apples, 218
Chocolate Chip Cookie Tart, 148
Chocolate Dominoes, 252

✓ Uses less fat, sugar or salt. Includes Nutritional Analysis and Diabetic Exchanges.

✓ Uses less fat, sugar or salt. Includes Nutritional Analysis and Diabetic Exchanges.

✓ Uses less fat, sugar or salt. Includes Nutritional Analysis and Diabetic Exchanges.

✓ Uses less fat, sugar or salt. Includes Nutritional Analysis and Diabetic Exchanges.